How Real Is Reality TV?

How Real Is Reality TV?

Essays on Representation and Truth

Edited by DAVID S. ESCOFFERY

McFarland & Company, Inc., Publishers
Jefferson, North Carolina, and London

Library of Congress Cataloguing-in-Publication Data

How real is reality TV? : essays on representation and truth /
   edited by David S. Escoffery.
      p.   cm.
   Includes bibliographical references and index.

   ISBN-13: 978-0-7864-2624-9
   (softcover : 50# alkaline paper) ∞

   1. Reality television programs.   2. Reality television
programs— Social aspects.   I. Escoffery, David S., 1972–
PN1992.8.R43H69   2006
791.45'6 — dc22   2006017326

British Library cataloguing data are available

Cover photograph ©2006 Comstock Images.

Manufactured in the United States of America

*McFarland & Company, Inc., Publishers
   Box 611, Jefferson, North Carolina 28640
      www.mcfarlandpub.com*

Table of Contents

v

Introduction: The Role
of Representation
in Reality Television

In the summer of 2000, following the enormous success of *Survivor* on CBS, many people in America assumed that reality television, in spite of its popularity, was destined to fade quickly from the cultural landscape. After all, just a few years previously, ABC had pinned its long-term hopes on the booming success of *Who Wants to Be a Millionaire*, expecting to ride the resurgent popularity of game shows to ratings dominance. Of course, audiences quickly grew tired of *Millionaire* and the many similar shows that sprang up on other networks (like FOX's *Greed: The Series* and NBC's *The Weakest Link*). The great revival of the prime time quiz show lasted only a season or two. In the recent history of American popular culture, we can see a number of other phenomena that went through similar cycles of enormous popularity followed by a quick decline. In the 1990s, boy bands like 'N Sync and The Backstreet Boys dominated the *Billboard* album charts before dropping off the radar just as quickly as they came. In movies, the success of *Scream* lead to a rash of ironic horror films (like *I Know What You Did Last Summer*), but that trend, too, faded quickly. It seemed logical, then, as all of the networks began to fill their slates with reality programs, that the fad would quickly run its course. People would soon grow tired of this trend, or Hollywood would beat it to death. Thus, there seemed to be no pressing need for a detailed scholarly analysis of reality television.

Cut to six years later. *Survivor* is still consistently one of the most popular shows in America. *American Idol* is another ratings phenomenon. And the top rated show in America for the summer of 2005 was *Dancing with the Stars*, a reality show based on the British hit *Strictly Come Dancing* in which celebrities are paired with professional ballroom dancers and then made to compete each week in different dance styles. The variety and continuing popularity of reality-based programming, both in America and around the world, cannot be denied, as evidenced by the number of different programs discussed in the essays collected here. Because this cultural phenomenon shows no signs of fading away, it is clearly important to study it carefully, to come to an understanding of its place in our cultural landscape.

If we want to examine the implications reality TV may have for contemporary society, it is essential to look into the notion of representation. Of course, representation — or the idea of something standing in for something else — has been a contested term at least since Plato declared that Poets would not be allowed into his ideal Republic because their artistic representations lead people several degrees away from the truth. Without going into the entire history of the complicated relationship between representation and truth — a project that would require several volumes — it should be clear that this very issue is central to any study of reality television. In the case of a reality show, we are given a representation (a TV program created for entertainment purposes) which purports to present "the truth" (the unscripted, real activities of real people). Understanding how audiences and producers negotiate the tricky middle ground between representation and truth in reality TV gives us insight into many issues important to society at large — political, economic, and personal.

The issue of representation in reality TV, however, operates on a number of levels. Beyond the larger question of how "real" the reality presented in these programs may (or may not) be, we must also look at more specific types of representation used in these shows. If, as Judith Butler argues, identity itself is a representation,* how are different identity categories depicted on reality shows, and what impact do these representations have on society? How are women depicted in these programs? What about African Americans and other minority ethnic groups, or homosexuals? Does the fact that the "character types" who appear in these shows are often real people saying unscripted things have an impact on the way these representations are read by society? Are people more likely to believe that women or African Americans or homosexuals are "like that" because it is a reality show and not a scripted drama or comedy? If so, how accurate are the representations of different identity categories on reality TV? Perhaps an even more important question is: how are they read by viewers?

Furthermore, reality TV does not just represent individuals and character types. It shows us social interaction, group dynamics, interpersonal

---

*Butler claims that identity is not inherent and natural, but rather constructed through acts of performance. It is, then, more representation than truth. For a more complete discussion of this idea, see her essay "Performative Acts and Gender Constitution: An Essay in Phenomenology and Feminist Theory," from Theatre Journal Vol. 40, Number 4 (1988): 519–31.

struggles, the process of voting, and even, perhaps, the workings of power itself. With these representations, again, we must ask how truthful reality TV really is, and what we learn about society from what is shown to us. Even though a program like *Survivor*, for example, is set in exotic locations (a deserted island, the jungles of Africa, etc.), there is an implied sense that the social interactions presented, the strategic game-playing and the alliance building, are simply exaggerated versions of things we all do at work, at home, on the playground, in any social setting. The extreme locale and the prize money magnify the interactions, making for compelling television, but we presumably learn some "truths" about human interaction. Thus, it is important to examine critically the representations of power and social interaction on these programs. How are they depicted, and how are they understood by audiences?

In the essays that follow, scholars from around the world take a closer look at the workings of representation in reality television. The essays in Part I examine the representation of "reality" itself, asking the question: how real *is* reality TV? Building on the questions examined in the first section, the essays in Part II look at audience reception of reality programs. How real do audiences think reality TV is, and what are the effects of reality TV on its audiences? Part III examines representations of gender roles on reality shows, delving into depictions of women and the possible effects of these representations on the larger society. In Part IV, the essays consider representations of otherness, examining issues of race, sexual orientation, and other forms of difference. Finally, Part V presents a discussion of power and politics, looking into the ways that reality shows depict politics, business, social interactions, and the workings of power.

Although not all reality programs are successful (notable failures include boxing bomb *The Next Great Champ*, *My Big Fat Obnoxious Boss*, and *Apprentice: Martha Stewart*), it is clear that unscripted shows will be a major part of television programming around the world for the foreseeable future. These shows are inexpensive to produce and carry with them the potential for huge profits. Given the fact that reality television is not going to go gentle into that good-night, it is important to understand its implications for contemporary society. The essays collected here ask important questions about the role of representation in reality television, providing a useful step toward a greater understanding of this phenomenon.

David S. Escoffery
Summer 2006

Part I
Representation and Reality
How "Real" Is Reality TV?

1

"When Will I Be Famous?" Reappraising the Debate About Fame in Reality TV

Su Holmes

> Every time a new ... reality TV event begins, we're deluged by broadsheet think-pieces railing against the C-list celebs infecting our culture [Hilton 21].

As this quote suggests, reality TV has undoubtedly emerged as one of the most visible cultural sites for debating the status of modern fame. Such debates have usually adopted a negative tone, but it is more appropriate to suggest that a number of critical positions have emerged. For example, in what is probably the most prevalent perspective in circulation, contestants have persistently been constructed as exemplifying, and in many ways accelerating, a fame culture in which an ethos of "famous for being famous" has regrettably triumphed over the concepts of talent and hard work (Holmes, "All You've Got"). It would be an understatement to suggest that public voices have expressed their disapproval for people who have achieved public (media) visibility and wealth, without utilizing the resources of entrepreneurial skills, education or obvious talent (Biressi and Nunn, *Reality* 145). Second, and related to the emphasis on undeserved fame above, has been a position which foregrounds the prominence of economics and manufacture. Here, contestants are seen as falling victim to the manipulative powers of a ruthless fame-making *machine*. Often yoked to an emphasis on the ephemeral nature of their celebrity, here we encounter cautionary tales about the price of public visibility and the lure of immediate wealth, a penalty when, as one program put it, "instant television fame is over in a dream."[1] This cautionary approach ranges more widely than the discourses of fame, and is part of a wider perspective which insists on "ordinary" people as ultimately vulnerable and exploited — at the mercy of ruthless, com-

7

mercial television producers and voyeuristic, uncaring audiences. Finally, and in contrast to the positions above, the "ordinary" person-turned-celebrity has been read in terms of democratisation, whether in relation to access to the airwaves, or the dynamics of public visibility itself. Regularly linked to Warholian clichés about everyone enjoying their 15 minutes of fame, the democratization thesis has largely been argued by broadcasters and producers (e.g. Bazalgette).

Reality TV now sits at the centre of television's economic structures, schedules and viewing cultures (Holmes and Jermyn, *Understanding* 1). Yet to imply acceptance, equilibrium and stability is to negate the highly *contested* nature of its cultural circulation. With a narrative peopled by broadcasters, journalists, public intellectuals, participants, viewers and academics, the debate around reality TV has been as visible as the emergence of the form itself — representing a contested field in which its cultural significance has been played out and worked through (e.g. Mathijs and Hessels). The role of "ordinary" people as performers and/or celebrities has been central to this process. It is possible to suggest that celebrity is less "a property of specific individuals, than it is constituted *discursively,* by the way in which the individual is represented" [emphasis added] (Turner et al., *Fame* 11). In this respect, then, the field of debate which has greeted reality TV is crucial: rather than simply providing a commentary on its relations with fame, it is actively *constitutive* of its social meanings. In short, in studying the phenomenon of celebrity and fame at any one moment, we are essentially studying traces of how it is *written about* (e.g. Gamson, *Claims*; Braudy), whether we are talking about celebrity producers, participants, journalists or academics.

In studying this discursive environment, this article is part of this process, but I approach the field with particular objectives in mind. While none of the positions above offer a very satisfying perspective on fame in reality TV, they are united in their suggestion that the relationship between television, "ordinary" people and celebrity is fundamentally *new.* Such claims are often made with very broad strokes, but they have made a rather successful bid for cultural legitimacy and acceptance. My suggestion here is that these arguments invite closer scrutiny on a number of different levels. The intention is not to *deny* change, nor to rehabilitate the cultural value of fame in reality TV (which would offer very little in the way of analytic purchase). Yet I do want to explore, interrogate, these claims to the new. Focusing first on the reality-pop shows (*Pop Idol/ Fame Academy*) and then on *Big Brother,* I look more closely at their discursive construction of fame, and what they suggest a celebrity is. This considers, for example, how the "anyone can be famous" argument — even when it is articulated with the most negative intentions—continues to function as part of the *mythic* construction of fame, of which we should be highly critical. Indeed, given that celebrity is, by nature, "hierarchical and exclusive," no matter how much it appears to expand (Turner, *Understanding* 83), it seems logical to study these shows less as a radical break with the past, than as part of our continuing cultural narrative of fame.

"I'm an academic — get me out of here?": *Reality TV, celebrity and cultural value*

Janet Jones and Ernest Mathijs have recently observed that *Big Brother* has become an academic as well as cultural phenomenon (2), attracting a remarkable amount of scholarly interest. While *Big Brother* has undoubtedly garnered the most attention, we might increasingly apply this conception to reality TV more widely (as this book and other publications attest). More so than a couple of years ago, it is now possible to step back and observe how the field has responded to the theoretical, critical and methodological challenges of reality TV and more specifically, its relations with fame.

Reality TV is clearly part of a wider context in which the sheer prevalence of celebrity culture in everyday life has never seemed so apparent. At the same time, we currently inhabit an age which is remarkably vocal about the phenomenon of celebrity. As Boyd Hilton, TV Editor of *heat* magazine aptly describes, "[P]ossibly the only thing ... more ubiquitous than celebrities are people complaining about them" (21). The current watchword in media commentary appears to be *change* — the prevalent sense that modern celebrity represents a qualitative break with the past (which is presented as a deeply regrettable shift). But what interests me here is that there has been a certain ambivalence about how academia has responded to these discourses.

Issues of taste and thus cultural value have long since shaped conceptions of celebrity (e.g. Turner et al., *Fame* 178), and it is thus no surprise that a degree of ambivalence has often structured academic approaches to celebrity. But given the contemporary status of modern fame, this issue now seems to demand more careful reflection than ever. As elaborated in more detail below, academic work (e.g. Gamson, *Claims*; Rojek; Marshall) — while it might agree that we have witnessed change — has provided far more complex accounts of the history of modern fame than is evident in the cultural dismissal of contemporary celebrity. In suggesting a distinction between these spheres when it comes to broader writing on fame (and in aiming to answer the question "what is celebrity?"), Turner explains:

First, commentary in the popular media ... tends to regard the modern celebrity as a symptom of a worrying cultural shift: towards a culture that privileges the momentary, the visual and the sensational over the enduring, the written, and the rational. Second, those who consume and invest in celebrity tend to describe it as an innate or "natural" quality.... [Here] the defining qualities of the celebrity are both natural and magical.... Third, and in striking contrast to this, the academic literature ... has tended to focus on celebrity as the product of a number of cultural and economic processes [*Understanding* 4].

While certainly useful in indicating the differing discursive investments in celebrity, such divisions are not as simple as they first appear. This is particularly so in relation to reality TV where the discursive environment has fostered roles which are in part interchangeable: academics and public intellectuals can become contestants/participants,[2] contestants can become media commentators, and producers can mingle with academics (e.g. Carter). Academic discourse is always part of the cacophony of voices commenting on fame in any one moment. For example, academic texts such as those by Daniel Boorstin (1961) and Leo Lowenthal (1961) are now read as elucidating aspects of the *history* of fame — the discourses and perspectives in operation during the time in which they were writing. In fifty years time, the same might be said of our contemporary work. Thus, while Turner acknowledges how discussion of celebrity is often shaped by notions of cultural value (*Understanding* 5), his own suggestion that the *Big Brother* housemates are "the epitome of the fabricated celebrity" (60), surely cannot exist outside this loop.[3] To be sure, existing academic work has complicated the sweeping sound-bite assertions made about celebrity in reality TV — foregrounding, for example, the notion of "ordinariness" as an ideological construct which cannot be taken at face value (e.g. Couldry, "Playing"; Bonner; Holmes, "All You've Got," and "Reality"; Biressi and Nunn, *Reality*).[4] Yet less has been challenged about its construction of fame. It is common, for example, to see the term "celebrity" suggesting a greater affinity with the press arguments than is explicitly acknowledged. In this respect, it is worth reminding ourselves of Leo Braudy's earlier comment in *The Frenzy of the Renown* that, when writing about fame, we should be wary of the "pose of objectivity that steals into language whenever one attempts to generalize" (11).[5] If academic work has increasingly conceived of celebrity as less a trait of a particular person than a discursive *mode of representation* (e.g. Turner et al., *Fame* 11), it is difficult to see how the contestants emerging from reality TV are *any less* celebrities than other names in the public sphere — they are, after all, subject to the same mode of "celebrification." As stated at the start of this article, it is not my aim here to somehow reclaim the cultural value of celebrity in reality TV. Rather, it is to call for a greater self-reflexivity about the discourses, value judgments and assumptions which structure our *own* discussion of this sphere, not least of all because they seem to constrain the questions we might ask of this field, and thus the conclusions we draw.

"The Will to Fame": From Unique Greatness to "Ordinary" Celebrity?

It is necessary to offer a very brief indication as to how the contemporary critiques of celebrity have emerged, while acknowledging that this narrative is neither objective nor exhaustive. Braudy's mammoth history of fame looks back to early Roman times, and argues that the will to fame has been part of western culture for centuries. In this respect, it relates to (and expresses) western ideals of achievement and individualism. Yet many critics agree that the growth and expansion of the mass media has had *the* determining effect on the processes and nature of fame (e.g. Turner, *Understanding* 10; Gamson, *Claims*; Rojek). Given its emphasis on the discursive construction of celebrity (particularly the popular explanations of fame which circulate in society at any one point), Joshua Gamson's work is particularly useful here.

Gamson essentially argues that certain positions on, or explanations of fame, have had a historical significance in vying for cultural visibility. In its early stages fame was largely limited to figures such as political and religious elites, with discourses constructing it as the province of "the top layer of a natural hierarchy" (Gamson, "Assembly" 260). Yet with the growth of arts and technologies with a wider range of public access, by the middle of the 19th century, celebrity was becoming established as a mass phenomenon. Public visibility became increasingly detached from aristocratic standing, with discourses of democracy — as epitomized by the American context — increasingly coming to the fore. This did not of course render the concept of uniqueness obsolete, but rather constructed a discursive framework which mediated between the concepts of an elitist meritocracy and an "egalitarian democracy" (261). With the Hollywood studio system representing celebrity's later period of industrialization, and with a controlled production system producing celebrities for a mass audience, the earlier theme of greatness became muted into questions of "star quality" and "talent" (264). While the focus may now have been predominantly on the culture of the personality, the primary narrative was still one of "natural" rise (264). However, the increasing visibility of the publicity machine itself gradually began to pose a threat to this myth. Shaped by industrial and cultural shifts such as the decline of the Hollywood studio system and the emergence of television, as well as the increasing growth of celebrity journalism, the second half of the 20th century witnessed the increasing prevalence of the manufacture discourse, where it henceforth becomes what Gamson describes as a "serious contender" in explaining celebrity (*Claims* 44). Chris Rojek offers a different yet related interpretation of this, where the shift is from achieved to attributed celebrity (fame is derived less from talent or skill than from repeated representation in the mass media and successful PR) (17) (see also Boorstin). However, with respect to Gamson's work, it is crucial to emphasize here that it is not that the older narratives of fame are rendered redundant, but rather that the two explanations jostle for cultural legitimacy in the same space. Indeed, Gamson suggests that by the late twentieth century it was possible to discern strategies intended to cope with the increasing disjuncture here. In particular, he points toward the twin devices of the exposure of the process and the construction of an ironic and mocking perspective on celebrity culture, both of which can be read as offering the audience a flattering position of power. I return to these discourses below in examining the construction of fame in reality TV.

Given that fame has often been traced in relation to western ideals of individualism (e.g. Dyer, *Stars*; Marshall), it has been perceived as intimately intertwined with the construction of social and cultural identity. In terms of the contemporary context, critics have pointed to not only the apparently more pervasive nature of celebrity, but its status as a means for self-validation. As Anita Biressi and Heather Nunn describe in relation to reality TV: "[It] ... arguably promotes and caters for the desire to be observed and to have one's existence validated through observation" (102). It is not difficult to see the plausibility of this when confronted with images of eager faces desperate to enter the mediated spaces of reality TV. As one participant pleaded while standing in the audition queue for *Big Brother 5*, "I promise I'll generate ratings and column inches. Please, give me the chance, this is all I have ever wanted."[6] But with celebrity offered as a means of symbolic validation, it is not so much fame in itself which is rendered "ordinary" (it would be a practical impossibility for us all to be famous, as then fame would not exist). Rather, played out again and again in reality TV, it is the *desire to be* famous which is naturalised and rendered "ordinary" here (Littler 12). I trace below why this discourse might be problematic.

Reality-Pop: From Packaging the *"Image"* to *"Lucky Breaks"*

In examining changing explanations of fame, the most useful aspect of Gamson's *Claims to Fame* is the suggestion that the cultural associations of celebrity are always contradictory and in process. It is my contention here that reality formats are less the epitome of a fame which has crept in, like a thief in the night, re-writing the script of modern fame, than they are paradigmatic of this continued negotiation of discourses in which meritocratic and democratic forces vie for cultural legitimacy. If, in the late 20th century, the increasing bid to go "behind-the-scenes" of the celebrity image, and an accelerated emphasis on the power of the audience, have in part worked to diffuse the threat posed to the authenticity of celebrity (e.g. Gamson, *Claims* and "Assembly"), the reality-pop programs are exemplary of this process.

Succeeding the international visibility of *Popstars* (2001, UK) which originated in New Zealand, *Pop Idol* was developed by 19TV/ Freemantle-Media in the UK in 2001. Following its lucrative success in both the British and American contexts (the first series of *American Idol* aired in 2002), the format has been launched in territories including Australia, Canada, Poland, Germany and Belgium. In 2002, the BBC launched *Fame Academy*, an Endemol program developed from an international format, and in 2004, ITV1 launched *The X-Factor*, in which judges Simon Cowell, Sharon Osbourne and Louis Walsh competed to produce the top act (managing either a group or a solo artist). Drawing on the generic precursor of the TV talent show, but extending this through a serialized form and appropriate reality aesthetic, the reality-pop shows are self-consciously organized around the search for a star, and the focus on a specific talent (singing). In this respect, their project is not to suggest that "anyone" can be famous at all. Indeed, the explicit aim is to move from a sea of hopefuls to an individualised winner. However, in public discourse, distinctions are rarely made between reality formats, and the same critiques of fame in reality TV have been directed at these shows as well.

First, it is immediately clear that the invitation to go "behind-the-scenes" of fame production, combined with an emphasis on the power of the audience, comprise the central narrative structure of these shows. Part of their claim to "reality" is that they are motored by a bid to display the cultural power of the behind-the-scenes impresarios who were once hidden from view (Stahl, 318). (In this sense, they have become as much about the celebrity of the judges as the contestants). These shows are undoubtedly produced for the scrutiny of a media-aware audience, a public conversant in the concept of image production and construction. Both *Pop Idol* and *Fame Academy* display these attitudes in typically blunt manner, during which instances concepts of talent or creativity are rendered irrelevant. On *Fame Academy* the judges persistently make reference to the wider context of television's commercial apparatus for record promotion with such comments as: "Can I imagine you selling millions of singles with that performance on *Top of the Pops*? Would that make me part with my money?" (28 September, 2003), and both programs place an emphasis on the commercial logic of the image. In *Pop Idol,* for example, judge and DJ, Neil Fox, openly rejects the idea that a contestant should go through on voice alone, by insisting: "But when the public vote they're buying into the image — it's part of the package" (1 November, 2003). In general, it is evident that in both programs, we openly see the strategies of styling the image, notably quite literally trying on elements of a new self week after week, as well occasions when the contestants are clearly dissatisfied with the artificial and enforced nature of this process. Indeed, it is worth noting here that, while articulating ideologies of individualism in many other respects, the programs do not trade upon the mythic ideology of fame as "an act of individual, personal transcendence" (McDonald 65). They resolutely display the *collective* nature of this process, the Taylorist division of labor inherent to the process of image production.

However, given that the manufacture discourse ultimately represents a threat to the commercial enterprise of celebrity, these programs provide exemplary evidence of how the two claims-to-fame stories continue to vie for legitimacy and cultural visibility. There is undoubtedly a clear emphasis on manufacture, but this is constantly chased by a parallel insistence on "specialness." Here, we are offered mythic constructions of the unique, authentic and gifted self. In terms of insisting upon an indefinable sense of specialness and charisma, the use of such phrases as "you've got the 'X factor'" or "star quality" have become something of a convention (as the title of *The X-Factor* clearly suggests), with the implication that, in viewing the show, *we* should look for these qualities too. The programs seem to suggest that manufacture is a necessary component in the process, but there must apparently be the indefinable magic of "star quality" upon which to build.

In stark contradiction to Gamson's emphasis on the strategy of irony in contemporary celebrity texts (see also Holmes, "Off Guard"), these shows are in many respects a site for re-peddling traditional myths of fame for contemporary consumption. *Fame Academy*'s singing coach and judge, Carrie Grant, earnestly explains in one edition, "The only place where success comes before work is in the dictionary" (14 December, 2002). In their emphasis on ordinariness, lucky breaks, specialness and hard work, they are literally paradigmatic of the success myth (Dyer, *Stars*), particularly when they constantly invoke older tropes of class mobility. Here, waitresses, train drivers and supermarket assistants are catapulted to a space which promises both symbolic and economic capital as the ultimate reward. As Biressi and Nunn note, although often submerged, fantasies of escape from class boundaries are a recurrent discourse in reality TV (*Reality*). Dyer adds that, although not the exclusive province of stardom, the success myth is central to ideologies of democracy in capitalist society (*Stars*): there may be power relations and hierarchical structures, but all individuals have the potential to "transcend social constraints and reach the top" (McDonald 65). As indicted, the programs do not aim to suggest that anyone can be famous, but they *do* suggest that with talent (itself a problematic construct) (e.g. Littler), hard work and luck, we all have the same chance (hence society, like stardom, is open).

There may appear to be a contradiction here, as the programs *do* dramatize constraints (or inequalities) in the opportunity for fame. In a highly self-conscious manner, much is made of how the "wrong" body shape, look or image may be a barrier to economic and symbolic success, and the judges freely acknowledge the industrial and ideological parameters within which they work. The programs, then, overtly acknowledge the popular perception of the music industry as an "over-rationalized, impersonal, alienating fame machine" (Stahl 327). But in this respect, they construct a triangulated struggle between, on the one hand, the demands of the industry, and on the other, the apparently close desires of the hopeful star and his/her audience. In this respect, the voting through of apparently unconventional or resistant choices (such as contestants who do not fit the ideal body image), generates only the impression that the rigid ideologies of the industry are being modified by this injection of ordinary power — whether we are referring to the presence of the contestants or the viewers (Holmes, "Reality").

If we return, then, to Gamson's warring explanations of fame here, the programs perform something of a clear ideological manoeuvre in their insistence that these narratives are not necessarily antagonistic, but can co-exist in relative harmony. Manufacture is a necessary component in the process, but it does not efface the importance of a unique, talented core. Equally, Gamson's suggestion that an increased emphasis on the power of the audience has functioned to smooth over the disjuncture between these polarities may highlight how the invocation of interactivity here *mediates* between the two narratives—further insisting on their complimentary relationship by reconciling elements of both. Indeed, with the public constructed as the ultimate discoverer of the star, the programs indicate the strength of Gamson's argument where contemporary discourses of fame are concerned: "*You* control the machine, it says. If *you* don't like me, *you* can grab the spotlight and throw it onto someone else more worthy" ("Assembly" 268).

This would position these programs less as sweeping away the value systems and hierarchies which may have characterized previous conceptions of fame, than as exemplary of a longer bid to juggle contradictory discourses on modern celebrity. But if part of this framework is the re-peddling of highly traditional, "anti-democratic, mystifying myths of meritocratic fame" (Gamson, "Assembly" 273), an objection might be that this is unsurprising — it is clearly in the interests of the commercial industries to perpetuate this perspective. But to argue that these are false discourses, or that we simply see through them, is also conceptually flawed. I argued at the start of this article that, in tapping into discourses on fame at any one time, we only have recourse to what is written about celebrity. When Gamson constructed his narrative of fame (including the mediation of Hollywood stars in the 1930s in terms of the deserving gifted self), he used popular cultural texts— magazines— in order to do this. For a phenomenon which only exists in representation, this *is* the reality of celebrity. It may well be the case that contemporary celebrity is played out for a more cynical and media-aware audience, not least of all because of changing emphases in discourses on fame. But this is a question about reading strategies rather than textual construction, and it is difficult in this respect to make an empirical comparison with the past.

Nevertheless, others may point to the often ephemeral nature of contestants' fame as further evidence of an active audience (that they are not investing in the mystifying myths of fame). It is certainly the case that the repeated exploitation, and thus conventionalization of these programs cannot be ignored here. Articulated through franchise after franchise on a global scale, any viewer might reasonably ask: how many truly "special" people can there be? The relative failure of many artists emerging from these shows, however, might actually be explained by the very commercial imperatives involved in their making. Turner has argued that reality TV, and the pop programs in particular, represent a bid by the media industries to centralize and rationalize the process of celebrity construction: "How might one make the production of celebrity a little more predictable? The most recent answer is to attempt to generate celebrity from scratch" (*Understanding* 52). While prefigured, for example, by the Classical Hollywood star system, Turner reads this strategy as minimizing potential conflicts between performer and industry, while also tying the performer to a specific text (on which they are particularly dependent) (54). But far from evidence of the excessively manufactured celebrity on these shows, this framework can again be seen to perpetuate more traditional myths of fame. For example, it clearly perpetuates the mystifying question as to why, with the same amount of exposure and PR, some acts fail (in the UK, Here'say, Gareth Gates, One True Voice, David Sneddon, Michelle

McManus) while and others succeed (Liberty X, Will Young, Lemarr or Girls Aloud). In fact, in imaging fame as a risky chance of opportunity, this structure seems more like a companion to the success myth than its cynical antagonist. The narrative path of these shows, as well as the circulation of the artists once the programs are over, functions to naturalize the belief, as Paul McDonald notes in a different context, "that life has its winners and losers and that is only natural" (65).

Famous *"For Being Yourself"*: Big Brother

This discussion of the reality-pop programs may be an argument for respecting differences between formats where the construction of fame in reality TV is concerned. *Big Brother* would certainly seem less traditional in this respect. It appears to be lacking some of the fundamental discourses of the success myth, largely the emphasis on work and traditional conceptions of talent. It is not organised around labor, but primarily around an excess of *leisured* time (Holmes, "All You've Got"), and overall, it is perhaps more honest about the fact that the acquisition of fame can simply be about being *media*ted. It is interesting, however, to note Biressi and Nunn's suggestion that, in *Big Brother*: "Their boredom becomes our diversion and our optional leisure time is filled with their enforced inactivity ... their 'labour' is actually our entertainment" (*Reality* 21). We might ask why labour is placed in inverted commas here. Like any other job, the contestants enter into a complex contract with the producers from the start, and while presented as only covering loss of earnings, contestants are in fact paid the minimum wage while in the house. In performing in the show, they are in part responsible for the production of what (in the UK), is Channel 4's most hyped and lucrative show of the year. As performers on which the show is economically dependent, they thus wield a certain amount of contractual power — something which is occasionally made explicit in the show. In the 2004 series in the UK, the contestants felt that Big Brother had unfairly deemed their most recent task to be a fail. Demoralized and angry, contestant Dan Bryan gestured toward the camera and warned: "Well, if they keep moving the goal posts, we can start swearing [in the live tasks] and using brand names. Either that or we refuse the next [live task].... They can't kick us all out — no live tasks, no program on Saturday night. No programme, no money" (12 June, 2004). Like angry workers about to revolt, there is an understanding here that their labor is sold (as is access to their personal lives) (see Andrejevic), in exchange for media visibility and (celebrity) status.

Simply because the show is not explicitly organised around the search for a particular talent, this does not mean that certain types of performance are not expected — modes which have much in common with light entertainment. This clearly taps into the wider discussion which has circulated around reality TV's claim to offer images of "ordinariness": its claim to edge closer to the everyday. Popular debate has largely questioned the claim to represent the ordinary here (important to television's construction of a shared space of community and participation) (e.g. Bonner; Couldry, "Playing"), given that reality TV often focuses on the extraordinary personality — the outrageous, the eccentric and the explicitly telegenic. As Jane Root's discussion of the history of "ordinary" people on television reminds us, producers do not want "ordinary people to behave like the amateurs they are" (97), but rather hope for the display of skills that professionals spend years perfecting. Winning contestants are often valued for their ability to offer what appear to be spontaneously amusing or comedic performances, containing everything from one-liners, impressions of celebrities, to catch-phrases. The fact that such contestants often then move into the field of light entertainment after the show — television presenting and appearances— again questions whether there is a radical break with modern celebrity. In this respect, *Big Brother* may still emphasize the virtues of a particular combination of "ordinariness" and specialness. Nevertheless, there are certainly apparent differences between the pop shows and *Big Brother* here, and on a surface level, the program appears unconcerned with the decline of meritocratic discourses of fame. In fact, however, I want to look again here at the possibility that there is much that is traditional in the program's mediation of celebrity.

First, a key link between the two formats is the relationship between discourses on an inner or core, self, and a concurrent emphasis on "ordinariness" — both during *and* after the achievement of celebrity status. The programs contain continual discussion of "who is being themselves?" and who is "performing for the camera?"[7] This is a crucial criterion in how the housemates judge and discuss one another, and as such, it functions to frame our own interpretive framework for the show. The spatial construction of the house, incorporating the localized privacy of the diary room where observations about fellow contestants can be expressed to the audience, fosters this discussion. Furthermore, the post-eviction interviews in *Big Brother* positively solicit this speculation, specifically asking contestants to judge the sincerity of the selves put on display in the house, and asking the evictee if they were ever able to forget the cameras were rolling (and thus present themselves "as they really are"). The answer is always yes. In terms of their celebrity construction in popular magazines, this discourse remains clear. For example, reality stars have featured prominently in the pages of celebrity magazines such as *heat* and *Now*. In an interview with Cameron Stout, winner of the fourth UK *Big Brother*, *heat* comments how:

> He certainly doesn't look like the £70,000 winner of Britain's biggest Reality TV show. But that's exactly what made viewers vote for him to win BB4. Cameron's down-to-earth attitude, friendly manner and — dare we say it — ordinariness were, for many, his most appealing qualities … [9–15 August, 2003: 4].

Equally, note the continued insistence on these qualities once released into the more extraordinary and privileged space of the media sphere. In an interview with Brian Dowling, winner of the second UK *Big Brother*, the magazine comments how: "In just over 12 months he may have gone from Ryan air steward to bona fide celebrity, but he's still the same warm, irreverent and bitchy character who won *Big Brother* last summer" (21–27 September, 2003: 76).

There are a number of points to bring out here in terms of this discursive negotiation of celebrity status. First, there is a claim to "ordinariness" (just like "you and me"). Star studies[8] has long since argued that stars are constructed through a paradox of the "ordinary" yet extraordinary (e.g. Dyer, *Stars*; Ellis). In the classical Hollywood period, for example, stars were recurrently constructed through a framework in which they inhabited the glamorous and extraordinary world of show business, but also enjoyed ordinary hobbies, domestic lives and harboured ordinary desires (e.g. Geraghty). Emerging in the 1930s, Gamson sees this discourse of "ordinarization" as one strategy offered as a response to the increasing visibility of the publicity machine:

> Early on, stars had been depicted as democratic royalty … popularly "elected" gods and goddesses. Lifestyle reports focused on "the good life," the lavish Hollywood homes, the expensive clothing, the glamour those watching could not touch…. [T]he presentation by the 1930s had become more mortal … a blown-up version of the typical [Gamson, "Assembly" 265].

In short, the textual exposure of real lives, particularly in their "more believable, 'ordinary' form" (265), aimed to foster a sense of intimacy between the famous and the fan, in part defusing the problems posed by the increasing visibility of the promotional apparatus. Evidently, decreasing the distance between celebrity and audience paradoxically offered a further threat given that, as Gamson observes: "if celebrities were so like the reader, why were they so elevated and watched?" ("Assembly" 266). This is where, as discussed, the discourse on the authentic gifted self kicks in. Stars are still "born" and not made (Ruby Keeler, for example, "was born with dancing feet") (266), but this sits alongside the claim to the "everyday" and the "ordinary." Gamson's argument significantly suggests that, even in this earlier period, the ideology of talent was rarely treated as sufficient to *explain* a rise to fame. Rather, it is the (deliberately) elusive terms such as "personality," "charisma," "star quality," or simply "It" which function as worthy evidence here. These are terms which — although more self-consciously used in the pop shows—continue to circle around the success of favourable characters from *Big Brother*.

Secondly, the textual and intertextual construction of reality stars also conforms to what has been identified as a core ideological function of stardom. Richard Dyer famously argued that stardom plays out discourses on identity and selfhood, and more specifically, notions of individualism in modern society (*Stars*; *Heavenly*). Working from a broadly Marxist perspective, he explained how the perpetual attempt to negotiate authenticity in the star image (the media emphasis on accessing the "real" person behind the image) works to promote a particular concept of personhood on which capitalist society depends. This is what he describes as "a separable, coherent quality, located 'inside' consciousness and variously termed 'the self,' 'the soul,' 'the subject...'" (*Stars* 9). Dyer emphasizes here that, while we may view celebrity as the province of performance, role-playing and image, the rhetoric of celebrity texts fosters a negotiation of authenticity (9), the possibility that a "real" lurks somewhere beneath.

In this respect, the very premise of reality TV, where "ordinary" people are valued and scrutinised for playing themselves, seems to push for a coincidence of public and private personae (we are privy to the revelation of intimate moments of selfhood). While now within the particular aesthetic and textual space of reality TV, this is a strategy which is far from new. In the classical Hollywood system, scholars have emphasized how celebrity was systematically built through publicity (and strove for an ideological coherence) that merged on- and off-screen personae (e.g. deCordova; Gamson, "Assembly"). In the example above, Brian Dowling is seen as being unchanged by fame, with the implication being that he is the same person on/off stage. This is what Dyer termed bearing "witness to the continuousness of [the self]" and, returning us to the ideology of the self, the appearance of sincerity and authenticity are two qualities which have historically been "greatly prized" in stars (*Stars* 11).

Certainly, under the influence of perceived shifts in celebrity culture, as well as the intervention of poststructuralist and postmodern strands of thought, Dyer's model of selfhood in stardom has been critiqued and challenged. Barry King's argument, for example, can be seen as an implicit challenge to Dyer's when he draws attention to the changed "existential parameters of stardom.... Today's stars ... epitomise the postmodern self, a decentred subject, deeply reflexive and disdainful of claims to identity" (45). Empirical work on audience reception also bears out highly playful modes of consumption in which the negotiation of authenticity may no longer be the organizing factor (see Gamson, *Claims*). Indeed, this may well speak to the ways in which, as established above, reality TV offers a highly *self-conscious* negotiation of the real.

The discussions about the performative nature of identity in the house —fostering a potential gap between reality and its production, as well as the "real" and the performed self— might well be viewed from this vantage point. The entire issue of *re*-presentation is explicitly put on the agenda by the program itself, in ways which may both assume, and flatter, the media literacy of the audience. But as Annette Hill's audience research has argued, capitalizing on the tension between performance and authenticity, reality TV nevertheless solicits us "to look for the 'moment of truth' in a highly constructed and controlled television environment" (324). Although it may adopt a self-reflexive approach to its representation of the real, neither the programs nor the audience have rejected "the *idea* of authenticity in factual entertainment" (336). Pivoting on what Hill describes as the process of "judging the integrity of the self" (336), the game of seeking out (what appears to be) the "real TV" moment is integral to the viewing pleasures offered by reality TV. In this respect we might note Justin Lewis' broader argument about the epistemological claim to the real in reality TV which, twinning fervent claims to authenticity alongside a circus of simulation, "television has become postmodern in form while remaining steadfastly modernist in its assumptions" (288).[9] What I am suggesting here is that not only has the emphasis on "being yourself" played a historically integral role in the ideological cultural construction of celebrity, but the extent to which reality TV has apparently *revived* this with a renewed vigour requires us to consider its mythic functions. In this respect, although writing prior to reality TV, Braudy's argument about fame since the Twentieth century seems particularly pertinent:

> The exemplary famous person here is especially the person famous for being himself or playing himself.... The frequent lack of actual accomplishment, which fame moralists find easy to mock ("famous for being famous") is *therefore totally functional*. It separates the famous less obviously but more absolutely from everyone else. The less you actually had to do in order to be famous, the more truly famous you are for *yourself, your spirit, your soul, your inner nature* [554; emphasis added].

This is further evidence that the media critique of reality TV as the province of "famous for being famous" should be taken to task: it again reproduces what I am suggesting here are *mythic discourses on fame*.

Conclusion: But When
Will I Be Famous?

We live in a society which insists that "we should be [famous] if we possibly can, because it is the best, perhaps the only, way *to be*" (Braudy 6). However, my aim here was to suggest that this really quite different from the possibility of everyone being famous. The fact remains that everyone is *not* famous. Jo Littler snaps this into focus when she argues that the increasing

> disparity between rich and poor, the risky lottery of social opportunity and the lack of cultural validation for many people in our society goes some good way to explaining the expansion of interesting in celebrity culture and the eagerness with which opportunities to become one are taken up and consumed [11].

Particularly from a class perspective (see Biressi and Nunn, *Reality*), this politicizes the idea that celebrity, and reality TV in particular, is perceived as a means of realizing one's identity in modern society. While fame may be increasingly constructed as accessible, democratic or "ordinary," unless we are all receiving the same symbolic and material reward, it is quite clearly "no such thing" (Littler 23). From this perspective, it remains crucial for us to question what has become an increasingly pervasive media narrative around contemporary fame, the most visible touchstone of which is reality TV. Whether intended to dismiss or validate its construction of celebrity, the democratization argument functions to support myths of fame. It unwittingly, but effectively, colludes with its ideological promise.

Related to this, I have taken to task the "famous for being famous" argument, which directs us more to *how or why* someone achieves celebrity. In this respect, reality TV appears less as the ambassador for, or instigator of, a new culture of fame, than it exemplifies how discourses on fame continue to work through a process of negotiation. These discourses have a history, and in order to redress the balance, I have deliberately focused on similarity at the expense of difference here — the links with constructions of celebrity from the past. Academia has always been excellently and thoughtfully critical of celebrity, and it remains one of the most fascinating spheres of film, television, cultural studies and beyond. But there is the sense in which these ever-pervasive cultural narratives of fame pose new challenges for this field, primarily in terms of how we position our own agenda, discourse and critique. In this respect, we might do well to recall Braudy's point that:

> Fame is metamorphic.... There can be no single perspective, no secret key by which we to unlock what it really is. Instead of seeking to determine its unchanging essence, we [should look] ... at how ... people tell stories about themselves and stories are told about them [591].

Reality TV, and its cultural circulation, is one such story. Contemporary fame is something we all appear to have an opinion on, so we (can) all contribute to this process. This is perhaps the most "democratic" aspect of the debate about fame in reality TV — let's enter it.

Works Cited

Andrejevic, Mark. *Reality TV: The Work of Being Watched*. Oxford: Rowman and Littlefield, 2004.

Austin, Thomas and Martin Barker, Eds. *Contemporary Hollywood Stardom*. London: Arnold, 2003.

Bazalgette, Peter. "*Big Brother* and Beyond." *Television*. October 2001: 20–23.

Biressi, Anita and Heather Nunn. "The Especially Remarkable: Celebrity and Social Mobility in Reality TV." *Mediactive*. 2 (2004): 44–58.

_____. *Reality TV: Realism and Revelation*. London: Wallflower, 2005.

Bonner, Frances. *Ordinary Television*. London: Sage, 2003.

Boorstin, Daniel. *The Image: A Guide to Pseudo-Events in America*. New York: Atheneum, 1971. Originally published as *The Image or What Happened to the American Dream?* (1961).

Braudy, Leo. *The Frenzy of the Renown; Fame and its History*. Oxford: Oxford University Press, 1986.

Carter, Gary. "Epilogue — In Front of Our Eyes: Notes on *Big Brother*." *Big Brother International: Formats, Critics and Publics*. Ed. Ernest Mathijs and Janet Jones, London: Wallflower, 2004. 250–257.

Couldry, Nick. *The Place of Media Power: Pilgrims and Witnesses of the Media Age*. London: Routledge, 2000.

_____. "Playing for Celebrity: *Big Brother* as Ritual Event." *Television and New Media*. 3.3 (2002): 283–293.

Cowell, Simon. "Michelle Vs Mark." *Now*. 24–31 December 2003: 22–3.

DeCordova, Richard. *Picture Personalities: The Emergence of the Star System in America*. Urbana and Chicago: University of Illinois Press, 1990.

Dyer, Richard. *Heavenly Bodies: Film Stars and Society*. London: BFI, 1986.

_____. *Light Entertainment*. London: BFI, 1973.

_____. *Stars*. London, BFI, 1979.

Ellis, John. *Visible Fictions: Cinema, Television, Video*. London: Routledge, 1982.

Gamson, Joshua. "The Assembly Line of Greatness: Celebrity in Twentieth-Century America." *Popular Culture: Production and Consumption*. Ed. C. Lee Harrington and Denise D. Bielby. Oxford: Blackwell, 2001. 259–282.

_____. *Claims to Fame: Celebrity in Contemporary America*. Berkely: University of California Press, 1994.

Geraghty, Christine. "Re-examining Stardom: questions of texts, bodies and performance." *Reinventing Film Studies*. Ed. Christine Gledhill and Linda Williams. London: Arnold, 2000. 183–201.

Hill, Annette. "Big Brother: The real audience." *Television and New Media* 3.3 (2002): 323–341.

Hilton, Boyd. "How I Learned To Stop Worrying and Love Celebrity Culture!" *Four Magazine*. 21 December, 2004: 21.

Holmes, Su. "'All you've got to worry about is having a cup of tea and doing a bit of sunbathing…': Approaching Celebrity in *Big Brother*." *Understanding to Reality TV*. Ed. Su Holmes and Deborah Jermyn, London: Routledge, 2004: 111–135.

_____. "'Off guard, Unkempt, Unready?': Deconstructing Contemporary Celebrity in *heat* Magazine." *Continuum: Journal of Media and Cultural Studies* 19.1 (2005): 21–38.

_____. "'Reality Goes Pop!': Reality TV, Popular Music and Narratives of Stardom in *Pop Idol.*" *Television and New Media* 5.2 (2004): 147–172.

Holmes, Su and Deborah Jermyn, eds. *Understanding to Reality Television.* London: Routledge: 2004.

King, Barry. "Embodying an Elastic Self: The Parametrics of Contemporary Stardom." *Contemporary Hollywood Stardom.* Ed. Thomas Austin and Martin Barker, London: Arnold: 2003: 29–44.

Lewis, Justin. "'The Meaning of Real Life.'" *Reality TV: Re-making Television Culture.* Ed. Susan Murray and Laurie Ouelette, New York: New York University Press: 2004. 288–302.

Littler, Jo. "Making Fame Ordinary: Intimacy, reflexivity, and 'keeping it real.'" *Mediactive* 2 (2004): 8–25.

Lowenthal, Leo. "The Triumph of Mass Idols." *Literature, Popular Culture and Society.* Ed. Lowenthal. California: Pacific Books, 1961. 109–140.

Marshall, P. David. *Celebrity and Power: Fame in Contemporary Culture.* Minnesota: University of Minnesota Press, 1997.

Mathijs, Ernest and Janet Jones, eds. *Big Brother International: Formats, Critics and Publics.* London: Wallflower, 2004.

Mathijs, Ernest and Woulter Hessels. "What Viewer?: Notions of "The Audience" in the Reception of *Big Brother* Belgium." *Big Brother International: Formats, Critics and Publics.* Ed. Ernest Mathijs and Janet Jones, London: Wallflower, 2004. 62–76.

McDonald, Paul. "I'm Winning on a Star: The extraordinary ordinary world of *Stars in their Eyes.*" *Critical Survey* 7.1 (1995): 59–66.

McGuigan, Jim. *Cultural Populism.* London: Routledge, 1992.

Moore, Allan. "Authenticity as authentication." *Popular Music* 21.2 (2002): 209–223.

Murray, Susan and Laurie Ouelette, eds. *Reality TV: Re-making Television Culture.* New York: New York University Press, 2004.

Turner, Graeme, Frances Bonner and P. David Marshall. *Fame Games: The Production of Celebrity in Australia.* Cambridge, Cambridge University Press, 2000.

Turner, Graeme. *Understanding Celebrity.* London: Sage, 2004.

Rojek, Chris. *Celebrity.* London: Reaktion Books, 2001.

Root, Jane. *Open the Box: About Television.* London: Comedia, 1986.

Stahl, Matthew. "Authentic boy bands on TV?: Performers and impressarios in *The Monkees* and *Making the Band.*" *Popular Music* 21.3 (2002): 307–329.

Notes

1. *Tonight with Trevor McDonald* (ITV1, 13 February, 2004)

2. I refer here to the example of Germaine Greer who entered the *Celebrity Big Brother* house in the UK in 2005. After leaving voluntarily, Greer returned to her role as intellectual critic of the format, foregrounding its exploitative and "degraded" nature.

3. This needs to be understood within a larger framework in which debates concerning cultural value — should they be on the agenda of television and cultural studies? Have they been suspended? — have a long academic history (see McGuigan).

4. Like other authors, it is for this reason I place the term "ordinary" in quotation marks in this article.

5. This element of ambivalence about how to discuss fame in reality TV perhaps in part

explains why — despite the proliferation of work on the form — the focus on celebrity has not been as prevalent as we might expect. It is often invoked as a side issue in relation to a broader focus, and two recent edited collections contain no explicit focus on the topic at all (Murray and Ouellette; Mathijs and Jones, *Big*).

6. *Big Brother's Little Brother* (C4, tx. 21 May 2004).

7. In the pop programs, this tends to take place in discussions of the contestants outside of the singing stage, where there are in part expected to be giving a performance. For example, in the 2004 series of *The X-Factor,* speculation surrounded the ultimate winner Steve Brookstein in the series itself and in popular media coverage. This suggested that he was arrogant, insincere and phony once the cameras stopped rolling. Equally, in relation to *Pop Idol,* we might note some of Cowell's "golden rules" for finding pop success, which include: "Don't imitate another performer," "Don't over-style yourself," "Believe in yourself," and "Be humble" (Cowell 22). These also privilege a core self.

8. This would also need to account for the specificity of the ways in which television fame has been discussed. John Ellis famously argued that television's textual structures and domestic identity produced not stars but "personalities," constructed through "ordinariness," familiarity and domesticity. While attention to media specificity remains important, it is also worth noting here that this in itself belies the extent to which discourses of cultural value have structured the academic discussion of television fame.

9. It is perhaps no surprise that these discourses retain their currency. After all, if celebrity *does* work through discourses surrounding individualism, the possibility that reality and artifice are indistinguishable threatens our own sense of self (Gamson, "Assembly" 276).

2

The Psycho-Economy of Reality Television in the "Tabloid Decade"

BETHANY OGDON

Among the rituals that serve as America's civic religion — sport, television, shopping — few are as genuinely shared as our collective belief in the saving graces of work. Work is literally the measure of our days. We speak of it as a virtue, originally imputed to Protestants, but we regularly round it out to a kind of ersatz patriotism when we invoke the "American work ethic." Even in our usually relativistic society, work remains sacrosanct. We demand it of our welfare mothers as well as our millionaires; politicians claim authenticity by saying they have worked for their living. We find those without jobs to be morally dissolute. To those whom we feel have shirked their responsibilities or need their character built we say, "Get a job" [Corbin].

Loss of Reality

In a March 2001 interview with the author of *White Collar Sweatshop: The Deterioration of Work and Its Rewards in Corporate America*, Katherine Mieszkowski dubbed the last two decades of the twentieth century "the age of overwork." Dawning in the early 1980s with the corporate "merger mania" unleashed by state and federal deregulatory policies and propelled through the 1990s by the "dot.com" boom, continuing deregulation, corporate mergers, buyouts, and successive waves of layoffs, "the age of overwork" saw Americans collectively entering the new millennium working the longest hours of any population in the industrialized world (Mieszkowski). Indeed, during the 1990s, in a single decade, the average American work year expanded by 184 hours (Phillips 113). On Labor Day 2001, the

International Labor Office released a report declaring that "after passing the Japanese as the world's most overworked population in the mid-1990s," Americans were now working "an average of 1,979 hours a year, about three-and-a-half weeks more than the Japanese, six-and-a-half weeks more than the British and about twelve-and-a-half weeks more than their German counterparts" (Reiss). At the same time that Americans devoted more and more of their waking life to wage earning, the wages they earned were in decline. According to Kevin Phillips, although "ordinary families gained [income] during the late 90s boom ... in 1999 analysts found that the average real after-tax income of the middle 60 percent of the population was lower than in 1977" (111) and that "the top 1 percent of the population had captured 70 percent of all earnings growth since the mid-seventies" (xiii).

In "Estranged Labour," Marx wrote that

> ... estrangement is manifested not only in the result but in the act of production — within the producing activity itself. How could the worker come to face the product of his activity as a stranger, were it not that in the very act of production he was estranging himself from himself? [...] If then the product of labor is alienation, production itself must be active alienation, the alienation of activity, the activity of alienation [qtd. in Tucker 59].

Marx's definition of production under capitalism as an activity of alienation is born out by a set of contemporary social phenomena that appear to relate directly to the economic phenomena outlined above. When interviewed about work trends, whether in publications devoted to issues of health, business, lifestyle, family, or current affairs, middle-class American wage earners frequently declare some variation of the statement, "I've got no life." A web search for information on the overwork phenomenon yields a vast array of articles with headlines that echo this predicament. Examples include "Long Hours of Work Leave No Time to Live" and "'Life Equals Work' is Americans' New Mantra." In a feature article for the *New Statesman* in 2003, British journalist David Nicholson-Lord noted the remarkable rise of the service sector during the 1990s. Referring specifically to the professional classes, he observed that "...we are increasingly remote from reality, in the sense that we want jobs done — but do not wish to do them ourselves." By "jobs" he did not mean "work," but rather shopping and gardening, taking care of children, planning holidays, giving dinner parties and walking the dog, jobs that when hired out looked to Nicholson-Lord "suspiciously like paying someone to live your life for you" (Nicholson-Lord).

Recent studies in the U.S. document the fact that over the past twenty years work has increasingly encroached upon family dinners, time spent with friends, time spent with children, sex, illness and injury, and perhaps even remaining alive. Not surprisingly, US employees take the least vacation time of any national population in the industrialized world, an average of 13 days per year (IWantMyVacation.com).[1] In fact, one in five Americans decline to take any vacation time at all. According to John de Graaf, thirty-three percent fewer American families eat dinner together now than they did in the early 1980s, and parents spend forty percent less time with their children than they did in the 1960s (Hwang). In the U.S., one in five workers does not even take the "sick time" owed them by their employers, instead showing up to work "whether they're ill, injured, or have a medical appointment" (Reiss). A 1999 article entitled "World-class Workaholics" noted that, "while American's aren't necessarily boasting about their new-found status as the foremost workaholics of the Western world, they aren't clamoring for a 35-hour workweek either" (Lardner). American employees are instead honing their time-management and "multitasking" skills and continuing to increase their work hours even while one in three claim to experience feeling overworked as a "chronic condition" (Families and Work Institute 1).

The chronic condition of the subject in "the age of overwork" is the body's registration of stress, fatigue, and, at bottom, estrangement from what is commonly referred to as "*real* life." Marx might call this condition "a loss of reality," a loss that increases in direct proportion to an increase of time spent at waged labor. Marx's "loss of reality" is a loss of "enjoyment of self in man," or more simply, a loss of "human life." For Marx, private property and "human life" are in direct opposition to one another: under a system of private property (capitalism), the subject is alienated while the "positive transcendence" of private property is "the sensuous appropriation for and by man of the human essence and human life." This "sensuous appropriation" is, according Marx, "human efficaciousness and human suffering, for suffering, apprehended humanly, is an enjoyment of self in man." (Tucker 73). The idea that "...suffering, apprehended humanly, is an enjoyment of self in man" suggests the psychoanalytic concept of *jouissance*. In one sense, *jouissance* can be defined as "being" in and for itself. Inaccessible to reason, *jouissance* can be experienced as either painful or pleasurable, but it is *enjoyed* in either case. In his *Dictionary of Lacanian Psychoanalysis*, Dylan Evans describes *jouissance* as beyond the limits of the Freudian pleasure principle and the symbolic field within which that principle functions: "Beyond this limit, pleasure becomes pain, and this 'painful pleasure' is what Lacan calls *jouissance*; '*jouissance is suffering*'" (Evans 92). Marx's "loss of reality" (reality as "enjoyment of self in man," "suffering," the "human essence") is commensurate with a loss of *jouissance*, that ungraspable part of the subject that escapes all symbolization — its suffering, its *enjoyment,* its *life* in and for itself.[2]

If "the age of overwork" can be characterized by a loss of reality for those who toil under its regime, then it might seem somewhat striking that one of the most prominent of the popular cultural phenomena to emerge and flourish during this "age" is something called *reality* television. The near simultaneous emergence of these two phenomena (the "age of over-work" and reality television) is especially striking if one becomes convinced that the reality produced by reality television's various programming formats during the late '80s and throughout the '90s was, in fact, the very same reality that is lost to wage earners in ever increasing amounts under capitalism's current regime. This paper argues that what reality television programs produced, throughout the 1990s and across all sub-genres, was a never-ending stream of sounds and images marking their "real people" participants' "enjoyment of self," *jouissance*, or, what Lacan has also called "the human factor" (Lacan 124) and Juliet Flower MacCannell "the human soul" (MacCannell).[3] In producing these images, 1990s reality television fueled the engine of a psycho-economy dependent upon a labor relation of inter-passivity fitted to the contours of a society in the midst of working itself to death.

Reality Found

In hindsight one can identify the exact moment that what would come to be, by the early 1990s, commonly referred to as "reality TV" emerged onto the popular cultural landscape. That moment was the evening that *A Current Affair* made its debut on New York City's WNYW/channel 5 in 1986. The program, a televisual version of Rupert Murdoch's tabloid publications *The Star* and *The New York Post*, was nationally networked through Murdoch's FOX-owned and affiliated television stations in 1987 and over the next few years was joined in the nightly television line-up by other tabloid news shows (*Hard Copy, Inside Edition*), "police reality" shows (*COPS, America's Most Wanted, Rescue 911*), home video/"found footage" shows (*Totally Hidden Video, America's Funniest Home Videos*) and "shock-umentaries" (*World's Scariest Police Chases VIII, When Animals Attack 4*). Initially "Reality TV" was a term mostly used to describe police *video verite* (*COPS*) and re-enactment programs (*America's Most Wanted*). However, as the daytime talk show underwent a distinct transformation in the early 1990s (*Richard Bey, Ricki Lake, Jenny Jones, Sally Jesse Raphael*), the term was increasingly used to refer to a diverse group of reality-based sub-genres that all shared a quite singular, if difficult to articulate, essence.

In his wide ranging analysis of reality television, *Tabloid Culture: Trash Taste, Popular Power and the Transformation of American Television*, Kevin Glynn remarks that reality TV is "a genre (or more accurately a collection of genres) that is not susceptible to easy definition or summary characterization because of both its internal diversity and its many overlaps with other sets of television genres" (2). It might seem obvious that reality television's common generic denominator is reality itself. After all, reality television shows all feature real people doing and/or talking about things that actually happened or are happening in reality. Although "real people" frequently appear on non-reality television programs, they are, in fact, the genre's most obvious common denominator. Two aspects in particular stand out with regard to the "real" or "ordinary" people of 1990s reality television, however, aspects that themselves were core defining features of the genre. First, if the ordinary American could be described as increasingly overworked during the '80s and '90s (and into the present), then I would suggest that reality TV's "real people" were consistently offered up as extraordinary, as a kind of televisual *lumpenproletariat*, a non-productive underclass, distinctly at odds with notions of the average, (exceptionally) hard-working American. Secondly, all reality television programming formats worked to expose these "real" people that populated their environments in ways that produced a constant stream of images of passive enjoyment ("enjoyment of self in man") for use by reality TV's overworked national viewing audience.

Reality and the Real

In their 1966 study, *The Social Construction of Reality*, sociologists Peter Berger and Thomas Luckmann argue that among all of the multiple realities available to human experience, the one which presents itself as most real, as "paramount," is "the reality of everyday life" in the "here and now" (Berger and Luckmann 21). For Berger and Luckmann, "paramount reality" manifests most reliably through what they refer to as "symptoms of subjectivity." They designate the reality shared by subjects who are "face to face in the here and now" as the one we take most for granted as real because it is the only reality in which the other's subjectivity continuously impinges upon our own through a maximum of symptoms: "No other form of social relating can reproduce the plenitude of symptoms of subjectivity present in the face-to-face situation. Only here is the other's subjectivity emphatically close. All other forms of relating to the other are, in varying degrees, remote. In the face-to-face situation the other is fully real" (28–9).

The language Berger and Luckmann use to describe what supports the realness of the most real form that reality takes is uncanny in its potential for psychoanalytic inflection. What Berger and Luckmann are calling the "symptoms of subjectivity" (facial expressions, body language, vocal intonation, and so forth) are, psychoanalytically speaking, symptoms of the inaccessible, traumatic core of the real which constitutes the subject's being in its absolute alterity and, as such, what introduces traces of the real into every intersubjective encounter in the "here and now." In other words, they are symptomatic of what is "fully real," and thus absolutely obscure, in the subject. To quote Lacan: "However much he groans, explodes, curses, he still does not understand; nothing is articulated here even in the form of metaphor. He produces symptoms, so to speak, and these symptoms are at the origin of the symptoms of defense" (73).

Although Berger and Luckmann's pragmatic analysis of the social construction of reality is hardly psychoanalytic in its understanding of "emphatically close" social interactions as rationally positive, enabling, and even psychologically *soothing*,[4] it *is* in perfect accordance with psychoanalysis when it claims that it is through the other that "realness" manifests in its most palpable form. And, perhaps the other through which realness is felt *most* palpably is that "point of the Real in the very heart of the subject" itself (Zizek, *Sublime* 180).

This "point of the real," however, is discomfiting, anxiety-producing. This is because the subject, according to Lacanian psychoanalysis, is subject of the signifier. The signifier quite literally *subjects* the subject, and it is a subjection that the subject does not suffer lightly. Paradoxically, however, it is precisely this subjection that liberates the subject to go about its business in the reality of everyday life: "The subject is always fastened, pinned, to a signifier which represents him for the other and through this pinning he is loaded with a symbolic mandate, he is given a place in the intersubjective network of symbolic relations" (Zizek, *Sublime* 113). The truth of signification is that, while it is only through the signifying process that the subject gains positive identity, nonetheless something always seems to be "missed," no matter how many signifiers are called upon to take up their representational duties. This "missed" *something* has been described by Copjec as "that object which is the excess of the subject, which causes the subject to be excentric to, or other than itself" (155). The irreducible gap in meaning produced by the symbolic register "resides" within the subject as an alien and alienating object where it is perceived as a foreign body disturbing self-identity. It is, says Lacan, "the absolute Other of the subject."

Picking up on Freud's observation that to obey the New Testament's commandment to "love thy neighbor as thyself" is next to impossible, Lacan asks: "And what is more of a neighbor to me than this heart within which is that of my *jouissance* and which I don't dare go near? For as soon as I go near it ... there rises up the unfathomable aggressivity from which I flee..." (186). If what is unapproachable within the subject can be conceived of as one's internal "neighbor," then it is definitely a neighbor who, like "Father-Enjoyment" (Zizek, *Enjoy* 171) himself, *enjoys*. And if one's own *jouissance* makes its estrangement felt as an impossibly proximate "neighbor," then what about that neighbor whom one meets face-to-face in the here-and-now? The conflicted orientation towards "the other" that begins in the self as the subject's relationship to his Thing quickly externalizes in the form of the fantasy that one's neighbor, that guy down the street, must surely be harboring within himself his own outrageous "dirty little secret," which is to say, some particularly obscene species of enjoyment. And, moreover, behind the closed doors and drawn curtains of his deceptively normal looking little house, he is in there actually *enjoying* his enjoyment. It is a fantasy that is at the root of all ideologies concerning cultural "others," of course. "The ultimate paradigm of the unknowable Thing," writes Zizek, "is man himself, our neighbor — the other as person" (Zizek, *For They* 199).

Fantasies of the other's obscene enjoyment are not only instances of disavowal ("I myself know nothing of enjoyment" or "I work hard and mind my own business") and displacement ("It is not I who enjoys, it is *You!*"), they are also the subject's attempt to have its cake and eat it too. Such fantasies are a method by which the subject attempts to *enjoy* at a safe distance from its own Thing and, in the very same move, locate an acceptable target upon which to unleash the aggression that rises up in immediate reaction to the impossibility of that Thing. Moreover, these fantasies might also be understood as a way to "mask" or "sew up" the void of impossible enjoyment; one way to convince oneself that, in fact, enjoyment is *not* impossible because right over there the other plainly *is* enjoying, even if we will have to make him suffer for it later.

Factory of the Real, or Manufacturing Passivity

At the very least, reality television formats function as straightforward documentation of the "reality" such fantasies insist upon. Viewers of reality TV *themselves* plainly know nothing of the enjoyment it documents, for the vast majority of Americans will never see themselves, or any conceivable proximation of themselves, there illuminated by what Carpignano et al. have referred to as "a democracy of lighting" (qtd. in Robbins 110). It is equally plain that these formats document the "fact" that since it cannot possibly be "I" who enjoys, then it must be "*You*" because quite clearly *someone* is "in there" enjoying. Indeed, reality television reiterates this "fact" over and over again, whether that "You" is one of Jerry Springer's impossibly "obscene" guests who suddenly bolts from her chair to lift her skirt and shake her ample hindquarters in delirious abandon, or the impossibly obese fellow whose obscene crapulence is "caught on tape" by the tabloid

news cameras as he is forklifted out of the side of his house and into a waiting truck for a trip to the hospital. Reality TV's "real people" are *always*
one's neighbors, *never* oneself.

According to Kevin Glynn's thesis, this "image-*repertoire* of deviance"
represents the "everyday struggles" of "subordinated or disempowered
people" against "the culture of the power bloc" ("Tabloid Television" 27).
As documentation of "the people's" ability "to taste in defiance" of bour-
geois norms and values, this *repertoire* of images should, he argues, be
understood to function as a direct "aesthetico-political" assault on the
unequal power relations which the universalization of those norms and
values has so long helped to sustain. But while it is indisputable that the
reality television participants described above are indeed "tasting in
defiance of" (27) what is commonly referred to as socially acceptable
behavior, it is equally indisputable that these people are "tasting" for the
general enjoyment of a nation of television viewers who would not be
caught dead enjoying like *that* in front of *their* neighbors. This is not at
all surprising, for to draw near to what is "in excess" of oneself is to find
oneself dispossessed, to be relieved of one's self-possession, to be rendered *passive*.

Zizek describes the fundamental state of passivity as that state experienced by the subject held in thrall of its Thing:

> The object which gives body to the surplus-enjoyment fascinates the subject, it
> reduces him to a passive gaze impotently gaping at the object; this relationship,
> of course, is experienced by the subject as something shameful, unworthy. Being
> directly transfixed by the object, passively submitting to the power of fascina-
> tion, is ultimately unbearable: the open display of the passive attitude of "enjoy-
> ing it" somehow deprives the subject of his dignity [Zizek, *Plauge* 115].

What Zizek describes as "the open display of the passive attitude of 'enjoying it'" is experienced by the subject as the uncontrollable protrusion of its
non-symbolizable "substance," which is to say its *being*, into the "rationality" of everyday reality where its "monstrosity" manifests upon exposure.
Take, for instance, that common "face-to-face situation" in which you are
standing around joking with a group of friends. One of them tells a particularly good joke and everyone begins to laugh; you yourself are laughing and laughing, beside yourself with glee, your voice taking on a life of
its own, becoming louder and louder, increasingly "out of control," when
suddenly, even as you are still enjoying yourself, an unfathomable and
"monstrous" snort erupts into the pleasant scene from god-knows-where.
You stop laughing, look around, and to your absolute chagrin, you see
everyone just sitting there, staring and silent. One need only stop for a
moment and contemplate one's personal experience of this not uncommon
scenario to understand why the relationship of the subject to its enjoyment

is fundamentally passive, and, moreover, why the open display of "enjoy-ing it somehow deprives the subject of his dignity."

One must take care not to let the preceding description of someone transfixed by "what is in them more than themselves" encourage a too-ready association of enjoyment with "having a good time," however. To be transfixed by *jouissance* is, ultimately, to *endure*, to *suffer* a paralysis of sen-sibility, to become *estranged* from oneself, to transgress the active world of sense altogether. And, while this paralysis of sensibility may be most spec-tacularly and excessively "marked" by a wildly gyrating body, a frenzied chorus of cacophonous shrieks, or even a particularly loud guffaw, it is per-haps more *intensely* marked by the slow flush that stealthily creeps across a face, the glaze of embarrassment that settles over a pair of eyes, a sudden exhalation of breath, or simply the inability to move a muscle or utter any sound whatsoever. Strangely, the open display of the subject's substantive passivity is somehow even more repulsively compelling when it manifests through these "quiet" symptoms than when it manifests through the loudly declaratory ones.

Although its producers go through the motions of declaring it a nar-rative medium through which stories of the human condition may be told and life lessons might be learned, reality television is essentially an immense video-factory which ceaselessly produces a never-ending "image-*repertoire*" of passivity.[5] And even if it is the spectacularly excessive image which gar-ners the most fanfare, it is the image which literalizes the passivity of the subject in its "gaping impotence," the close-up of the human face frozen in silent mortification, which is the most disturbing. Indeed, it is this lat-ter image which forms the core of most reality formats, from the daytime talk show, with its penchant for springing horrifying surprises on its "bliss-fully ignorant" guests, to police *video verité*, with its civic-minded zeal for tracking down people it can expose "caught in the act," to the tabloid news program, with its populist commitment to providing viewers with up-to-the-minute stories of life's little, and not so little, "embarrassing moments," to what is commonly referred to as the "shockumentary," or "disastertain-ment" program, with its willingness to broadcast any piece of amateur videotape that manages to document living beings, human or animal, transfixed by nature's "cruel and awesome force."

One exemplary reality program stands out against the rest with regard to the genre's general taste for the "open display" of passivity, specifically passivity as it manifests in the image of silent mortification. A derivation of the daytime talk show, *Forgive or Forget* conceives of itself as a "healing space" in which guests may confess their commission of a particularly ter-rible "sin" against a loved one and in return be offered the opportunity to "begin again" through the "gift of forgiveness." The program's compelling lure, however, is that whether or not forgiveness will be granted remains an open question until the "final moment of truth" arrives. After a guest has divulged every detail of some horrible behavior (for instance, abusing a best friend's child or selling a girlfriend's possessions to the local pawn shop), undergone a thorough chastising by a self-righteously indignant studio audience, and been reduced to a mass of stuttering explanations and tearfully incoherent apologies, each one must stand alone before a towering door that has been erected in the middle of the stage there to await, in full view of everyone, his or her very own moment of truth. Will the door swing open to emit a forgiving and loving "enemy?" Or will it swing open to reveal "only" a horrifying, gaping void? While the structurally inescapable moment of waiting for the answer in anxious non-knowledge ensures an image of each and every guest paralyzed in silent mortification, it is that moment when a guest is confronted with a negative response in the form of *absolutely nothing* which provokes the most crystalline image of the subject reduced "to a passive gaze impotently gaping at the object" (Zizek, *Sublime* 155). What sets *Forgive or Forget* apart from other reality television programming is the fact that it reveals its *raison d'être* so explicitly. The show's obsessive repetition of the exact same carefully scripted scene, a scene which thrusts participants before "the abyss" in the most remarkably literal fashion, virtually guarantees the "open display" of the subject transfixed in passive suffering before enjoyment's obscure power of fascination.

Again, it is not that spectacularly carnivalesque instances of tabloid excessivity are less symptomatic of the subject's substantive passivity — they are not; rather, it is that these other (critically and analytically ignored) "quiet images" make this passivity visible in a particularly direct and obvious way. In point of fact, these two orders of symptomatic image, the "quiet" image and the "loud" image, often appear in immediate succession: tabloid television's wild outbursts of inarticulate mayhem are nearly always preceded by a few moments in which participants are caught frozen into identical *tableaux vivants* of dumbstruck incomprehension. Upon being apprehended by the law, for example, the drug dealers and wife-beaters of FOX Television's *COPS* all react differently — some flying into foul-mouthed rages, others helplessly struggling as their limbs abandon all rational relationship to each other — yet, they may all be observed experiencing the same *preceding moment* of transfixion before the object. Here something obscure and moving, something imperceptible just behind the eyes, seems to pull in opposite directions; some Thing arresting any movement or thought.

This moment of stupefaction is intimately related to the too-close approach of the subject's unfathomable "internal other," which is to say, that non-signifying, non-signifiable being which is, according to Lacan, the subject's very life substance. Take, for example, the circumstances of Tony, who appeared on a June, 1998, *Sally Jesse Raphael* show, entitled "*Why Did You Leave US?!,*" in the hopes of being reunited with a father who steadfastly refused to acknowledge his son's existence. His self-possession visibly and incrementally disintegrating, Tony tearfully waded through detail after detail of his tormenting predicament for Sally and her audience before finally stopping to look out into a sea of strangers' faces and ask his conspicuously absent father, one last time, to come out and greet him. As the show cut to a commercial break, a huge, and ominously portentous, graphic washed across the screen: "And When We Come Back.... WATCH TONY BREAK DOWN!" And he did, with a vengeance. Upon hearing that there would be no happy reunion, he fell apart; shrieking and bawling, face crumpled in agony. This theatrical manifestation of Tony's pain immediately raises, of course, the problematic specter of the possibility of "fakery" that is daytime talk television's constant shadow. However, whether Tony is a shameless dramatist or a person dis-arranged in heartbreak is a matter of little consequence because, in either case, the *reality* is a spectacular image of enjoyment's horrifying passivity. Moreover, in the seconds preceding his outburst, Tony too underwent that requisite and unfakable moment of transfixion, his paralyzed inability to react in any way at all to the horrible news, the appearance of pure nothingness on his gaping face, a repulsive and fascinating image of the real's approach.

If reality television's generic commonality is the variously inflected image of the subject reduced to "the open display of passively 'enjoying it,'" which is itself always an image of "symbolic death," the "shockumentary" might suggest itself as the pure, unmediated distillation of the genre's collective aim. Eschewing the mediating influences of hosts, anchors, studio audiences, backstage producers, cooperative law enforcement officers, in-house camera operators, and any pretense whatsoever of contributing to the "common good," shows with titles such as *Disaster Strikes!* and *Close-Call 2: Cheating Death* are composed solely of amateur video out-takes (often less than a minute long and "looped" to repeat multiple times) that document moments in which the subject appears to receive its "final letter," to meet, in the words of Lacan, "that other death, the death that simply involves kicking the bucket" (303): a shrieking woman hanging by one leg from the top of a Ferris wheel; a mud-covered, naked baby's lifeless form dropping from the arms of his rescuer; a petrified hostage sitting next to a gunman in the back of a car; or an actor hanging by the neck in front of a football stadium full of spectators. Indeed, this last "shockumented" image may well be unsurpassable in its blatant exposure of the subject in its fundamental passivity. Broadcast on NBC's "shockumentary" series, *The World's Most Amazing Videos* (June 1999), this piece of videotape, shot during a shabbily "down market" outdoor performance of *Jesus Christ Superstar* in Peru, showed "Judas" dramatically running to the scaffolding "tree" from which he would presently "hang" himself in abject remorse for his betrayal of Jesus. He climbs onto a platform, drops the noose around his neck, and flings himself into mid-air. For a second his body hangs, quiet and elongated, at the end of the rope, then his hands begin to weakly claw at his neck, and, finally, as the narration informs viewers that he is suffocating before an audience misrecognizing his silent suffering for a fine performance, his arms fall slack to his sides and his head falls forward onto his chest. *Amazing Videos* replayed the clip five times: over and over the actor jumps, the hands claw, the rope tightens, the body hangs still.

In his essay on the Lacanian "letter," Zizek writes:

> [W]hen the subject's presence is exposed outside the symbolic support, he "dies" as a member of the symbolic community, his being is no longer determined by the symbolic network, it materializes the pure Nothingness of the hole, the void in the Other (the symbolic order), the void designated, in Lacan, by the German word *das Ding*, the Thing, the pure substance of enjoyment resisting symbolization [Zizek, *Enjoy* 8].

The image of the Peruvian, hanging dumb and still, is no more than the distilled image of Tony in his spectacularly mobile dis-arrangement, of course.[6] In *both* images the subject's presence is exposed outside the symbolic support: unhinged from the signifier, no longer "free" to explain, protest or lie, the weeping and shrieking talk show guest and the unconscioius "shockumentary" victim are televised in the equally open display of their submission to something that lies beyond all reason. But it is in the image of the Peruvian that the void assumes, in a kind of reverse transubstantiation, the unmistakable proportions of an object as such. Here the radical negativity that haunts the subject, that is perceived as something alien and living within the self, that is imagined in the heart of the other as his secret monstrosity, that obscenely protrudes into the symbolic network of everyday reality as "the pure substance of enjoyment resisting symbolization," may be observed in the form of its object-correlate: a hard, "miserable little piece of the real," utterly senseless in its brute materiality, dangling at the end of a rope.[7] And even if the subject's being, its life substance, its one true Thing, finds a theoretically astute image in that of the human body rendered as cold and lifeless and real as the scaffolding upon which it hangs, the open display of such an image also suggests an inexorably unforgiving attitude toward that Thing which Lacan also called, quite simply, "the human factor."

The "Psycho-economics" of Passivity

"The necessary minimum of subjectivity," writes Zizek, is "to get rid of — transpose to the other — the inert passivity which contains the density of [one's] substantial being" (Zizek, *Sublime* 116). To describe the manner by which the subject "off-loads" onto the other the "density of its substantial being," which is to say its fundamental passivity, Zizek introduces the concept of *interpassivity*. Though he uses the example of his own habit of recording televised movies so that he can continue working in the evenings (movies he never gets around to watching) to illustrate the way in which an "other" (in this case the VCR) can be made to assume the burden of one's enjoyment, Zizek is careful to point out that interpassivity describes the most basic structure of subjectivation itself. As the "primordial defense against *jouissance*," interpassivity consists of the subject's constitutive externalization of its "inert Being" in the object: "[T]he signifier is interactive for me, it is active on my behalf, in my place, while the object is interpassive, it suffers for me" (115–116). If reality television can be described as a video-factory which industriously produces a never-ending "image-*repertoire*" of passivity, as demonstrating a steadfast commitment to the staging of photo opportunities which work to reduce "real people" to desubjectified states of "gaping impotence" before the object, then might not its massive production of such images suggest an interpassive function for reality television? And perhaps reality television's interpassive function finds special resonance within a culture that has become increasingly active in this "age of overwork" under global capitalism. According to Zizek, the need for interpassivity increases along with an increase in one's activity: "The more I am active, the more I must be passive in another's place — that is to say, the more there must be another object which is passive in my place, on my behalf" (Zizek, *Plague* 117).

Which subjects find themselves in a position to "benefit" from such an interpassive relation? Structurally speaking, it would have to be those subjects who do not appear transfixed on the televisual reality screen. It cannot escape notice that of the multitude of "domestic disputes" documented by FOX Television's long-running reality program, *COPS*, not one of them has ever involved a doctor, lawyer, professor, computer analyst, corporate middle-manager, or, for that matter, anyone who lives in a "nice" neighborhood. This "video apartheid" also characterizes the daytime talk television show. During the late '80s and throughout the '90s, every time one switched on the TV set, it was made abundantly clear that the "properly productive citizen" was nowhere to be found within reality television's "real world." According to academic popular culture critics Vicki Abt and Leonard Mustazza, reality television's daytime talk shows "showcase the hideously personal, the trivial, the ludicrous, and socially insignificant ideas that are the hallmarks of what is sometimes referred to as low-class behavior — not to mention cognitive and linguistic errors that so tellingly distinguish certain people" (22). These writers characterize the talk genre as a "kind of social index of America's cultural malaise," a malaise which "involves the inauthentic feelings, lack of citizenship skills, family disorganization, increasingly violent youths, and stubbornly resistant social ills of minorities and the poor" (23). A 1998 article in *Rolling Stone* magazine, entitled "Strippers who Kill! Killers who Strip! We've Seen the Enemy and He's on 'Jerry Springer,'" made a point similar to that of Abt and Mustazza without losing sight of the attracting qualities of the reality spectacle:

> When one lady topples sideways, her dress rides up, revealing a knot of thick red veins and chubby, cottage-cheese thighs. That part of it is disgusting. But the display of fighting and its aftermath is pretty cool. The security guys step up ... and lay on.... The guests, in their ripped shirts, with their crapped up hair, look at Jerry as though they don't have a care in the world, as though they never did. Jerry allows this. He does not call them "asshole," "f—k-up," "trailer trash," "scum," or "freak." Jerry does not judge [Hedegaard 43].

I am not suggesting that the 1990s reality television species of "real people" all belonged, in fact, to a non-productive underclass; most of them probably had jobs. What I am suggesting is that these "real people" were emphatically embodied through the conventions of the genre and, furthermore, were put into situations guaranteed to produce images of "inert passivity." The television audience was denied the possibility of meaningful identification with those it watched precisely because of this method of objectification. Moreover, television audience members, by virtue of being constituted as a public (the nation), were temporarily disembodied themselves. Thus, whether one actually worked or not, when functioning as a member of the television viewing public, one could imagine oneself as a member of a hard-working nation of productive American citizens.

Zizek's observation that "the object is interpassive, it suffers for me" takes on politically significant proportions when one imagines the object as one of reality television's "real people." The "tabloid other" is not just any marginalized member of society, but the other who falls through every crack of the economic order, both the economic order of the social field and the (psycho)economic order of subjectivity itself. Robbed of its own subjectivity, reality TV's "*lumpenproletariat*" other becomes the *doppelganger* of the properly active subject of late-capitalist America, the "obscene little man" who follows this subject around like a shadow, giving body to its lost enjoyment. 1990s reality television instituted a paradoxical labor relation in which the most alienated members of society worked (for free) to produce the "lost reality" of the productive (overworked) classes and thereby bear the burden their subjective alienation for them.

Works Cited

Abt, Vicki and Leonard Mustazza. *Coming After Oprah: Cultural Fallout in the Age of the TV Talk Show.* Bowling Green: Bowling Green State University Popular Press, 1997.

Berger, Peter and Thomas Luckmann. *The Social Construction of Reality.* New York: Anchor Books, 1966.

Corbin, Michael. Rev. of *White Collar Sweatshop: the Deterioration of Work and its Rewards in Corporate America* by Jill Andresky Fraser. *Baltimore City Paper.* 14 March 2001. <http://www.citypaper.com/arts/print_review.asp?id=1715>

Copjec, Joan. *Read My Desire: Lacan Against the Historicists.* Cambridge: MIT Press, 1994.

Evans, Dylan. *An Introductory Dictionary of Lacanian Psychoanalysis.* London: Routledge, 1996.

Families and Work Institute. *Overwork in America: When the Way We Work Becomes Too Much.* Executive Summary. 1–11. <http://www.familiesandwork.org/press/Overworkinamericarelease.html#overwork>

Glynn, Kevin. "Tabloid Television's Transgressive Aesthetic: *A Current Affair* and the 'Shows that Taste Forgot.'" *Wide Angle.* 12.2 (1990): 22–45.

_____. *Tabloid Culture: Trash Taste, Popular Power, and the Transformation of American Television.* Durham: Duke University Press, 2000.

Hedegaard, Erik. "Strippers Who Kill! Killers Who Strip! We Have Seen the Enemy And He's on 'Jerry Springer.'" *Rolling Stone.* 14 May 1998. 43–47.

Hwang, Sonja. "North Americans Desperately Overworked and Craving a Healthier Quality of Life." Press release. <http://www.emediawire.com/printer.php?prid=172280>

IWantMyVacation.com. (For international labor statistics, click on "You Need a Vacation") <http://www.iwantmyvacation.com>

Lacan, Jacques. *Seminar VII, The Ethics of Psychoanalysis, 1959–1960.* Trans. Dennis Porter. Ed. Jacques-Alain Miller. New York: W.W. Norton and Company, 1986.

Lardner, James. "World-Class Workaholics." *US News & World Report.* 20 Dec. 1999.

MacCannell, Juliet Flower. "Perversion in Public Places." University of Michigan: Advanced Study Center, Working Paper Series, 1998. <http://www.usnews.com/usnews/issue/991220/overwork.htm>

Mieszkowski, Katherine. "The Age of Overwork." *Salon.* 1 March 2001. <http://archive.Salon.com/tech/feature/2001/03/01/white_collar_sweatshop/>

Nicholson-Lord, David. "The New Feudalism." *New Statesman.* 3 Feb. 2003. [http://www.newstatesman.com/200302030017>

Phillips, Kevin. *Wealth and Democracy: A Political History of the American Rich.* New York: Broadway Books, 2002.

Reiss, Matthew. "American Karoshi." *The New Internationalist.* V343 March 2002. <http://www.newint.org/issue343/karoshi.htm>

Robbins, Bruce, ed. *The Phantom Public Sphere.* Minneapolis: University of Minnesota Press, 1993.

Simon, Harvey B. "Can Work Kill?" *Scientific American.* April 2002. 44–46.

Third World Traveler. "A Better Kind of Wealth Tax" by Leon Friedman. (from *The*

American Prospect Magazine. 16 Nov. 2000. <http://www.thirdworldtraveler.com/Economics/BetterWealthTax.html>

Tucker, Robert C., ed. *The Marx-Engels Reader.* New York: W.W. Norton and Company, 1972.

Zizek, Slavoj. *Enjoy Your Symptom! Jacques Lacan in Hollywood and Out.* New York: Routledge, 1992.

_____. *For They Know Not What They Do: Enjoyment as a Political Factor.* Eds. Chantal Mouffe and Ernesto Laclau. London: Verso, 1991.

_____. *The Plague of Fantasies.* New York: Verso, 1997.

_____. *The Sublime Object of Ideology.* Eds. Chantal Mouffe and Ernesto Laclau. London: Verso, 1989.

3

Training Camps of the Modular: Reality TV as a Form of Life

Barry King

Critical interest in reality TV programming has tended to focus on problems of form and genre definition. One particular concern, voiced in an influential article by John Corner, and echoed by Brian Winston, centres on the negative impact of reality TV on the documentary tradition. Corner observes that we live in a Post Documentary era, meaning by this that there been a proliferation of television programmes and series that claim to "show reality." This proliferation — creating hybrid forms such as docu-soaps, reality game shows, love shows, mockumentaries, etc. — calls into question the exclusive purchase over the real that once was unquestionably nested in the Griersonian documentary tradition. If reality TV participants are manifestly perceived as performing for the camera, does this not serve to underscore that documentary, as in Grierson's famously ambiguous definition — the creative use of actuality — has always created the performances it records and observes?

For those concerned with the civic role of documentary, the debunking thrust of the new hybrids and, above all, their popularity pose a threat. If objectivity is exposed as an alibi for interpretation, the authority of the documentary tradition will be lost (see Palmer). For some writers, this loss would not be a bad thing. Those who, like Corner, lament the decline of the documentary are insisting on outmoded binaries such as the real and the fictive, essence and performativity (see Holmes and Jermyn). In the categorical promiscuity of reality TV, lurks a progressive utopian potential that arises from the nimble poaching of the audience.[1]

The proclamation of "utopian" elements in reality TV shows, of course, does not dispose of issues of the "real." If documentary has a "fictional" quality, there is still the matter of some examples being more or less fictional than others or, for that matter, more or less utopian. As Brian Winston has astutely observed, reality TV genres do not so much depart from objectivity, but, like cynics made out of former idealists, demand an absolute standard of realism that rules out any formative process on the part of the documentarist.

For all that, reality TV advances its own reality principle which is based on notions of authenticity and the value of exposing the "false" faces that the participants present to the camera (see Benton and Cohen 51–2). This "reality principle" has many aspects, but one is obviously paramount — truth is to be found in the subjective and personal, which provides the key to understanding social life (see Palmer).

In this paper, although sharing concerns about current trends, I chart a different path, one that entertains some connections with the other key focus of research into reality TV — what the popularity of reality TV tells us about the condition of audiences. What follows is more concerned with the ontology of reality TV as a form of governance (see Elmer). In essence, I mean to ask what aspects of everyday experience pre-dispose people to seek truth inside manifest fabrication.

There is no single answer to this question, of course, but I will argue that reality TV is part of a general cultural condition which I term modularity. Stemming from the organization of work and imposing an imperative to perform, modular settings are colleges for affective moulding — the learning of dispositions, habits and interests that reproduce a larger cultural formation. Reality TV does not simply reflect such trends; it plays its part, under the disarming bracket of entertainment and perhaps *schadenfreude*, of codifying them as a form of life.

To shed light on these issues, I have selected a little known Australian/New Zealand program, *The Resort*. In part, this is because *Big Brother* has been well analysed, but also *The Resort* represents an attempt to reconcile two different modes of interpersonal control — one externally imposed and typical of *Big Brother*, and the other the fun-oriented, yet more invasive mode typified by *Survivor*. I will return to the ideological work of *The Resort* at the end of this paper.

The Resort

The Resort was televised in an actual place, rather than on a set location. It first aired in Australia (Network Ten) and New Zealand (TV3) during January 2004. The concept behind the show was that a dozen or so people would take on the challenge of running an exclusive island resort for their peer group of 18 to 35 year olds. The Resort was located on Malolo Island in the Mamanucas group of islands in Fiji. It was a failed timeshare investment opportunity which went under because an Australian businessman, Frank Yeates, had flouted environmental regulations by failing to provide adequate sewage and water systems. After a successful court battle with the time share investors, Touchdown Productions took over the lease and developed the concept for the show. Announcing its airing on New Zealand television, the leading national paper, the New Zealand *Herald*, called *The Resort*, an extended advertisement for its own product, offering participation at a price:

> ... for $1490 you, too, could party in this Fiji island paradise, being renovated and run by bitchy blondes, carping brunettes and a mixed bag of stud muffins. If there's one thing we've learned from the reality telly phenomenon, it's impossible to overestimate the appeal of being on TV ["*The Resort*"].

The Resort also contained a challenge reminiscent of the *Survivor* series. The contestants were not told that, soon after their arrival on the island, 120 guests would be arriving. They thus had to get the resort into shape as quickly as possible.

In its general features, *The Resort* conforms to Kilbourne's definition of reality TV as the recording of unscripted events in the lives of individuals and the group, with an attempt to simulate real life through dramatic reconstruction. The incorporation of material suitably edited into an attractively packaged program permits the promotion of the show on the strength of its reality credentials.

In promotional literature, *The Resort* was billed as the "ultimate" docusoap because, unlike other reality shows— such as *Temptation Island* with its mixture of infidelity and the promise of gratuitous sex — viewers were offered the opportunity to stay at the titular Resort. About 120 guests were expected each week, though this target turned out to be rather ambitious. After a week's stay, guests were asked to rank the performance of individual cast members. Any member of the cast getting a negative vote two weeks in a row was "let go" and lost the opportunity to participate in the profits derived from the business .

The cast as finally assembled contained 8 females and 7 males, in the age range 19 to 28, including a woman who has competed in the Miss World Bikini Competition and a former DJ who claims to know every drinking game. What is similar about all the participants is their background in what could be generally termed personal service occupations— this is particularly true of the women and follows obvious gender stereotypes. The characteristic labor experience for the cast is *emotional labor*— the provision of a pleasing self in a situation in which provider-client relationships are paramount.

In such shows, there are, generally, two kinds of client, the producers who require from the contestants emotionally charged footage and the audience who "vote" through the ratings and more directly through telephone or e-mail polls for the retention or removal of contestants. An usual feature of *The Resort* was that a significant "client segment" was present as paying guests, voting for the expulsion or retention of contestants on the basis of their appraisal of the quality of the service they had received during their stay. The link between a prize and pleasing the guests meant that the fusion between personality projection and economic gain was strong. Working *The Resort* was similar to selling on commission or providing personal services for cash. This alignment of the interpersonal and commercial indicates a degree of commodification that is unusual even for reality TV.

The "Sales Pitch" is a pervasive feature of the program, with the "host" Jon Stevens—late of Noiseworks and INXS—shilling to the camera to encourage viewers to come to "the biggest party island in the Pacific" and offering the cast as models of what island living is all about. *The Resort* is presented as a "sex on holiday" soap, highlighting the problems, successes and disappointments of turning physical attractiveness into sexual conquest and doing so in a public space. Mixed-sex proximity and the pressure for intimacy within the peer group are the driving dramatic forces, evoking the dating culture of High School. On many occasions, Stevens verbalises this central interpretative framework of managing the resort and the "ever fragile relationships with each other that makes life here so colourful."

Stevens is not merely the framer, but also the framed—a hunky celebrity sex interest caught in the web of desire presented. Two of the girls, the rivals Tabs and Eva, compete for Stevens' interest—despite, or, perhaps, because of the fact Eva is "embroiled" with another contestant, Beau. "Bikini model" Tabs is the arch-enemy of "show girl" Eva, who is the object of desire of "love-sick" Beau. "Footballer" Aaron has a thing going with "singer" Beck and yet is still best friends with "beauty queen" Amanda. The action goes on and on, the desire for desire spinning on screen and, hopefully, off. Finally, the pervasiveness of the pitch is also re-enforced by captions that play over captivating visuals of paradise, inviting viewers to stay at The Resort and, in one case, showing a job advertisement for a cook capable of making good "tucker" and skilled at handling interpersonal conflicts.

The Resort *as Format*

In discussions about reality TV, the term format is both vague and insistent. For the Format Registration and Protection Association (FRAPA), a commercial outfit dedicated to protecting intellectual property in franchises, such as *Big Brother* and *Survivor*, the debate is entirely pragmatic. A format that has proved itself commercially in the global television market place, like *Big Brother*, is a valuable market asset somewhat akin to a personal creative expression.

Form is an elementary and complex aesthetic concept, and format appears as a compact or abbreviated version of that concept. In other words, the commercial supervention of format has aesthetic consequences for the traditional concepts of form and content. If format regulates the relationship between form and content in the pursuit of economic advantage, what does this mean for theorizing reality TV as a (blurred) genre? We need a bit of theory to identify the semantic shift and re-centring involved.

In Hjelmslevian glossematics, a fourfold distinction is made between form and substance — meaning by the latter something approximating to the stuff of signification. Louis Hjelmslev distinguishes a plane of content and a plane of expression, both of which have a substance and a form (see Eco). Although Hjelmslev's model has been developed in relation to language, it can be applied to television discourse :

Hjelmslevian Planes:

Plane of Content	Substance — Images the TV apparatus can produce	Form — Minimal visual units (e.g. shot, scale)
Plane of Expression	Substance — All sensory events and data within human range	Form — Intelligible human behaviour in a given culture

Reality TV strongly foregrounds the organisation of substance through a double and fused articulation of form on the two planes. For example, on the plane of content "visual substance" is packed into a hybrid shooting style that combines a stylized "follow the subject" shooting format derived from Direct Cinema, with reaction shots to camera (see Winston). On the plane of expression, the form of the signifying material is not limited to aesthetic devices, but works as a pattern of interaction defined by the rules of the game — for example, plot lines always end in the contestants voting each other on or off the show, with or without audience participation. As Charlie Parsons, the originator of *Survivor*, put it, reality TV is: "Producer created environments that control contestant behaviour" (qtd. in Brenton and Cohen 54).

It is not that the content of reality TV is unique — indeed, most definitions indicate that it is an opportunistic blending of genres such as the game show, the talk-show, the docu-soap, etc. It is the control of behavior behind and in front of the camera in the service of the format that is unusual. A format is the semantic equivalent of a *chiasma*— a fusing of two separate planes of meaning through a dual manipulation of form. In less technical language, a format is a template which ensures that the stream of real events that make up a particular show follow a predictable and rule-governed pattern of interaction, regardless of variations in local or specific content.

In its disciplinary workings, defining the kinds of on-screen interactions that are shown and the kinds of participants that are selected, a format is the equivalent of a Foucauldian diagram. In fitting themselves to the format, all participants, in front or behind the camera and in the editing suite, conform to a dramatic diagram — the iteratively reproduced map of positions between the forces that constitute a disciplinary process. The diagram, in turn, is the medium through which the format is preserved and constructed as a modular text that will fit with minor variations into a global distribution chain.

Consistent with its visualisation of space as charged with the uncertainties of desire, *The Resort* avoids the more clinical gaze of a continuous on-line feed of closed-circuit television (CCTV) found in *Big Brother*. Although footage of the cast quarters are shown, these, like the recurrent references by the cast to camera set ups, are only made available in an edited and highly editorialised form that feeds the plot of romantic intrigue.

The denizens of *The Resort* are free to cavort in hidden spaces, and it is those hidden, molecular spaces that are identified as the armature of viewer involvement and guest participation. For example, cast asides to the camera about being selected in an auction for an intimate one-on one dinner date with a guest are suffused with sexual promise. One member of the cast, Pete, observes that his date is a lucky girl because he has endured four weeks of sexual abstinence. This promise of a Viagra-like enthusiasm manages to combine the notion of close attention to client satisfaction with an unequivocal claim of unabated male potency. The viewer is, alas, never to learn if the bargain is delivered. Perhaps becoming a guest is the only way to certainty?

The Resort does share some features with *Big Brother* — it is an example of Erving Goffman's notion of the total institution. The cast live where they work, and the relationships they have with their fellow workers are 24/7. Being a cast member is a total role. There is no segmentation between work and leisure, or a division between public and private. Cast members confront a near irreconcilable set of role demands. They are required to be supervisors and supervised at different times, to be a team player and a performance evaluator, a companion and counsellor, a potential romantic partner, concierge, recruiter for the resort, guest activity co-ordinator, kitchen and cleaning staff, and crisis manager. How the individuals respond to these challenges as well as the periodic vote determining who stays and who goes is the mainstay of the drama.

But unlike *Big Brother*, the cast members of *The Resort* have significant roles in the management of their work setting and get to judge and evaluate their peers. If *Big Brother* evaluates its casts, in *The Resort* the control structure is not bureaucratic and remote, but present and embodied. So, despite its more "relaxed" setting, *The Resort* is an example of a more invasive system of *concertive* control — team process begins from a set of beliefs, moves through to norms and finally sets rules that are as much if not more finely grained and oppressive than panoptic surveillance (see Barker).

If everyone plays a Big Brother role, watching, in a spirit of rivalry, everyone else's performance, the separation between the cast and those who control their environment remains advantageously uncertain. There can be many changes in relationships, reversals of status and losses of face. Sexual rejection by other cast members and by the guests remains an ever present possibility. Doing a good job is no guarantee of appreciation, and vice versa. Finally, the team culture of self-monitoring and fretful rivalry is redoubled by the presence of on-site managers and by the guests, who serve as surrogates for the viewers at home.

Role ambiguity and uncertainty is aggravated by the centrality of sexual attraction as a plot device, and this is compounded by media visibility. One cast member, Christie, has ongoing problems because her boyfriend becomes jealous on viewing scenes of apparent sexual intrigue, re-enforcing the already blurred boundary between mediated and non-mediated behaviour. For the cast, the interpenetration between work roles and personality is pronounced — they are meant to serve as the sex interest for other participants as well as for the guests. Their selection — all have trim, well-sculpted and well groomed bodies — indicates a physiognomic standard and a particular beauty qualification.

Cast members operated in the full glare of publicity under repeated exhortations to candour. Where the cast were reluctant to "tell all," the media was happy to oblige. The *Sydney Sun-Herald*, seeking to generate exciting copy, invited its readers to share shady secrets about the cast. In this manner, Reba's history as a stripper came to light. This extra intensity of scrutiny meant that cast members were forced to protect their "authenticity" by conforming as closely as possible to the stereotypical expectation set up by casting on the basis of looks. Needing to be become less truthful in order to seem authentic, the cast were driven to become what the format required in the way of "valid" local content.

Repeatedly, *The Resort* evoked the logic of *defensive physiognomics* — if one looks right on camera then one *is* right — only to press the cast to reveal (on camera) the strain of maintaining that look on camera and the ever present possibility of a breakdown. The inescapable cameras (and what they represent, the capacity to edit) encouraged viewers to fashion themselves as insiders on the basis of remote observation. As a result of these processes, and certain artlessness in construction, *The Resort* provided an unusually stark projection of a Hobbesian war of each against all set in an ironically beautiful island paradise.

Logics of Display

As will be recalled, Foucault in *Discipline and Punish* identified an emergent discipline of the gaze: *panopticism*. In its literal embodiment, prisoners are placed in cells that are constantly open to surveillance from a central vantage point. Confined to individual cells, prisoners face the ever-present, but finally unverifiable, possibility that they are being watched at all times. Bentham's design of the panopiticon is, Foucault argues, a concrete expression of a more diffuse societal practice in which an older optical ratio, typical of feudal power relationships, of *the many watching the few*, was replaced by *the few watching the many*. As Mathiesen has pointed out, the transformation that Foucault described is overdrawn. Conspicuously, the emergence of the mass media has created a synoptic regime. In such a regime, it is still the case that the many watch the few, but the few can theoretically include anyone, regardless of social rank or function. The Internet, for example, contains both possibilities: corporate or Governmental surveillance of user activities, and private citizens (if they have Internet access) watching the powerful, the rich and the famous, for trivial and sometimes not so trivial purposes. Reality TV shows that incorporate audiences voting to remove contestants, such as *Big Brother* or *Survivor*, may be said to empower audiences through reduction of cultural differences to the exercise of a vote. As an expression of the audience's will, voting does not constitute an internally coherent representation of audience involvement, but it does cast the audience in the role of the observer and judge of participant behavior.

Yet the contrast Mathiesen draws between the carceral and the viewer society is too dichotomous. Synopticism can be thought of as a qualification of the pervasiveness of the panoptic gaze. But just as plausibly, it might be said to be masking the logic of surveillance with a patina of empowerment.[2] Donating attention and judging another's on-screen performance accepts the logic of a condition of on-going detailed scrutiny.

As for the subjects of reality TV whose condition resembles a state of incarceration, they seem to have embraced the same counter-logic of affirmative self-display found in the contemporary penitentiary. It is sufficiently commonplace to attain the status of a motion picture cliché that prisoners are drawn to a cult of body building. (Much the same might be said of efforts at self-education and qualification as a way of valoriza-tion doing time.) Whatever else might be said about body-building as a means of enhancing physical power and homoerotic allure, the cult of the well-defined body is an affirmative appropriation of the panoptic gaze. That gaze is thereby deprived of the opportunity to demean its objects and is con-fronted with a subject that is good to look at. Perhaps we find here that the disciplinary rule that the soul is the prison of the body is reversed. The body is selected to be the prison of the soul, the physical manifestation, and the resource to be deployed in the affirmation of a personal agency that cannot be touched by the "system." The very concept of internalizing the disciplinary gaze implies a level of skill and determination that is poten-tially admirable (Watson 13–14). So it can come about that the purpose of the panopticon, to discipline the felon, is re-articulated into a discourse of empowerment, one that is confined, but empowerment nonetheless. Here we encounter on the micro-level the tactics of individuals who, through the deployment of performance techniques and self-fashioning, claim the right to define the terms on which they become objects of the carceral gaze.[3]

In relation to reality TV, and those who are legally free, it seems nec-essary to emphasize that the synoptic gaze — the regime in which the many watch the few — must encompass the fact that the many who watch the few do so in order to learn the successful (or unsuccessful) elements of being "fit to be seen as one of the few" — of being *worth* being looked at and not being demeaned.[4] Audience fascination with the exposure of the "real" face of the contestants is now better phrased as a fascination with the outcome of a contest of self-definition under conditions of surveillance.

The Ur-formats of *Big Brother* and *Survivor*— the first modeling the closed panopticon, the second a less bounded space that permits contest-ants to perform synoptically — represent the two sides of a dialectic of dis-play in which teamwork and work process are rendered as drama.

Modularity as a Worldview

As Foucault argued, what is born in the confined space of the prison or clinic is a concentrated expression of widespread system of regulation that characterizes society as a whole. This is especially true in the work-place in the advanced economies where concertive control manages aes-thetic labor. Models, salespeople and service workers in this workplace must engage in strategic impression management. The fact that such practices are widespread offers a real-world example of the more fictive practices of reality television (Mann 347–69).[5]

Today's self is primarily conceptualized as a narcissistic project, a condition of imagining that one is constantly scrutinized. Once a condition only foisted upon females, many young and not so young men and women now view themselves in private as if they were before a permanent audience that is evaluating their behavior. This imaginary audience has its gaze codified and expressed in concrete detail by the mass media, and are carefully scanned for what are the currently prominent "styles of the flesh" (see Abercrombie and Longhurst).

In this context, figures in the media, whether as relatively ordinary "stars" of reality TV or as the carefully crafted personae of more traditional celebrities, become examples of potentially viable public images for the business of writing on the self. This is less a matter of idolization, though it can be, than a strategic and opportunistic scavenging for self-images that have the primary characteristics of being pre-tested, efficacious brands, organized in order to compete with peers. The logic of physiognomic validation — the notion that how one looks is what one is— is central to advertising and media celebrity. Not surprisingly, it infuses the scenarios of reality TV, and energizes the plot dynamics of sexual attraction. Indeed, given that these are ordinary people performing in the spotlight, without the benefit of the cosmetic protection and training afforded mainstream stars and celebrities— there is here a kind of heroism of the ordinary that is admirable.

But to model oneself on that which has already been intensively modeled for mass approval is to be *a model of a model*. The process of fitting into a predefined mode of appearance and behavior that can be transferred to anyone is the condition of modularity.[6] Such a condition has the following features:

a. Totalities are *nothing more* than an aggregation of components. These components can be combined in various ways because they are conceived to be functional equivalents permitting substitution, addition and recombination. Totalities in this sense are "only" empirical. They have no underlying essence. If they had an essence, they would not be transferable.

b. Since no specific configurations are deemed necessary or essential, any given content has no more than a present validity, as new configurations are certain to emerge. But nonetheless, in the compressed space of the present, all configurations are treated as essential.

c. All cultural practices are equally valid, so long as they work in a given situation.

d. Because of the speed of turn over in fashion, the central principle of any present configuration is to maintain coherence for as long as possible (see Blair).

It might be expected that a modular worldview should lead to the endorsement of change and plasticity. However, as a grounded practice, modularity transpires as a paradoxical search for, if not the perfect, then the *best* rendition. What follows from all this is a procedural version of the sublime, which intimately celebrates and valorizes the essential rendition or performance (see Nye 283, 291).

From the perspective of contemporary work organization in advanced economies, modularity is an axiomatic principle of current management practice. The new model worker is a performer, and the new organisation a kind of theatre. Correspondingly, for employees the path to employment and retention of a job depends on presenting and representing the self in order to fit in with a changing work environment, much like an actor auditioning and playing different roles. Since personality is less easy to adjust than appearance, the look or the physiognomic coding of the worker assumes a profound functional importance. The simulation of commitment must not be revealed in itself to be a simulation and requires the self to treat each moment as a process of "deep" acting. Workers are expected to be seamlessly identified with the current project and yet ready to change as required.[7]

A Modular Practicum

The Resort is an example of a modular text. Such texts, pervasive in the media, present examples of the alteration, by various techniques, of the self and its identity. The audio-visual media also act as motors for the diffusion of modular dispositions, offering an ever expanding repertoire for self-fashioning. Media imagery is peopled with individuals who bear witness to the power of the media to develop, enhance and preserve a successful self-image, reflexively permitting viewers to work on their own bodies in real time.

What is projected in modular texts is a synthetically engineered utopia. Such a utopia insists, paradoxically, that the self is not constrained by its by biological and social constitution (as a member of a specific race, ethnicity, gender, sexual orientation, nationality and so forth) and can be out-contextualized or transported to other contexts without losing the identity and capacity of a viable agent (Lury 3). The paradox arises because out-contextualization is dependent on technologies— and, by extension, those who control access to and use of them. These technologies act as "smoothing" machines for eliminating difference in favor of singularity. The collectively determined individual becomes a portfolio self, dependent but seeing dependency as a barrier to self-development. The monadic view of the self that emerges is *experimental individualism*— the self as an entity that does not say: I am what I am, but I am what I can become (Lury 19).

Modularity as a way of life imposes its own conservative ethical standards. If the "look" is optional, then how you look is how you chose to look, a freely expressed revelation of your desired identity. People who do not choose to be what they could be are, rightly, condemned to the obloquy of their ill-fitting appearances. In the modular text, the viewer/spectator is addressed as one who is ready to play the codes of appearance to his or her advantage. In a world in which the importance of place and locality no longer prevails over the flow of global information and power, the viewer can find in modular imagery a small place, which is simultaneously local and global.

The living space of the cast is visualized as a struggle to fit the singularity of their own feelings to the format as personified in the camera or the guests. They are required to commune with an absent audience whose only commonality is that they understand, and perhaps share, the formula of tabloid romance. In other words, the cast is required to be modules in a scheme of action, or the format that is given by the very medium in which they have chosen to be confined.

The Real Context and the Context of the Real

> It is through the promotion of "life style" by the mass media, by advertising and by experts, through the obligation to shape a life through choices in a world of self-reflexive objects and images, that the modern self is governed [Niklas 256–8].

Considering the format of *The Resort* and similar shows, it is striking how closely they fit into a managerial interpretation of the new work order as theatrical performance. In this rendition, what is important for the individual is control over the impression that others form of the self. Impression management will lead to interactive advantages and personal esteem (see Goffman). Demands on the individual cascade down from the corporate level which seeks to control the impression external stakeholders, such as customers and shareholders, form of its activities. Employees are expected to skilfully project the image that they are the customer's friend or confidante, and they are expected to engage in long term relationship marketing. Nor does the market exist solely outside the firm, which is likely to be a dispersed system of divisions and, within divisions, of project teams. Although interdependent, each work team is expected to treat all the other work teams on a market basis, and within the team, each employee seeks to out-perform every other.

The popularity of the performance metaphor has led some authors to suggest that the theatre or the movies provide the exemplars of the modern organisation (e.g. Pine and Gilmore). Such suggestions are not purely fanciful. The rise of global communication networks and the Internet prioritise the notion of interaction and communication that lies at the centre of the theatrical idea of performance. Being a node in a distributed network requires sustaining a continuous relationship of connection with a range of interactants or *an audience of others*. Skill in interaction is as much a precondition for producing a specific commodity or service as it is for communicating.

In many jobs, technical skills are much less important than the physiognomic qualities of the workers themselves— the aesthetics of appearance, speech and demeanour (Warhurst, et al.).[8] As personality becomes a key variable in the realisation of profits and the effective delivery of services, employees at the high and low end of service work are expected to engage in "deep acting," intensively and iteratively manipulating their appearance and behaviour before others (Sennett 112).

Under these new expectations, playing a part in the team generates its own form of stardom. Stars network to gain information, take joint ownership, whether as leader or follower, of group tasks in order to realise team goals, persuade others to accept the cogency and urgency of the task at hand, exercise the multi-dimensional skill of seeing the project in the larger context and through the eyes of critical others such as co-workers, customers, competitors and bosses (Kelley 31). Star workers, in short, adapt themselves to a team project, in a limited time frame, as though it were their central life purpose. In other words, the star worker responds to the same demands as those required by the format of reality TV.

Get with the Format!

These background trends can be taken to pre-dispose audiences to take an interest the emotional dynamics of reality TV. The *Big Brother* format, with its more closed and surveillance-saturated mise-en-scene, is an expression of the culture of low skill end service work, so called *MacJobs* where the performance is highly scripted and subjected to constant scrutiny. The *Survivor* format, with its looser mise-en-scene and more synoptically grounded pattern of interaction, addresses the upper end of service teamwork, or the high skill, high wage *IMacJobs* implicated in the maintenance and support of management systems. Here, the typical mode of relationship is networking with real and virtual teams. In such jobs, individual "creativity" and self-expression are required to fit into the team culture, and the self must be adjusted to interactive demands (du Gay 182). In sum, there are some hard facts behind reality TV. A network society is marked by a structural split between a core labor force of service employees and managers and a larger "peripheral" disposable labor force.

At the core there is affluence, relative security of employment and a cosmopolitan life style based on networking with peers in a global cultural environment. The disposable labor force, shuttled in and out of employment as market conditions suggest, by contrast is poorly paid and shut out from the networks of information upon which corporate decision making is based. This distinction between those who are programming and those who are programmed is replicated — imaginatively — in the world of reality TV.

Empowered by following the ever-changing demands of emoting, the casts of reality TV hope to win visibility and marketability as much as cash. In so doing, they rehearse the survival skills of those in an insecure job market. Such a rehearsal performs ideological work for the world of the dispersed workplace and the total demands of short term projects. Reality TV teaches the highs and lows of performance to those who must perform or else. There is, however, a variability in how this ideological work is done. *Big Brother* draws the concept of work as performance back into the context of the prison, the closed, endlessly scanned, panoptic space and endlessly repeated meaningless tasks. Each cast member, then, has a kind of *MacJob* that they cannot leave, which fascinates because it is worse than everyday experience.

The Resort with its open vistas and looser modes of surveillance, its celebration of partying and looking good, its belief in open communication of feelings and the ultimate value of surviving in the team plays with an *IMacJob* rhetoric of good work and interpersonal satisfaction. In spite of its light hearted and positive key, though, *The Resort* offers a space in which individuals might find a measure of consolation in the spectacle of each other's insecurity. Although the island appears to be a caring and care-free environment, then, the regime of *The Resort* insinuates a closer form of control than was ever possible in Bentham's panopticon. In *The Resort*, the affirmative quality of synoptic display evolves into a more finely grained concertive control, in which the body becomes the prison of the soul.

A poor clone of *Survivor*, *The Resort* was cancelled after a mere six weeks because of poor ratings. But the structures of feeling constructed by it, and its artless drive to ratify subordination through the positivities of fun, sex and spectacle, resonate on in other more successful specimens. For a short time and with a kind of revealing rawness, *The Resort* made a modest contribution to the project of disciplining the self to its full subsumption as a service commodity (see Murray).

Works Cited

Abercrombie, Nicholas and Brian Longhurst. *Audiences: A Sociological Theory of Performance and Imagination.* London: Sage, 1998.

Barker, J. R. "Tightening the Iron Cage: Concertive Control in Self-Managing Teams." *Administrative Science Quarterly* 38.3 (1993): 408.

Benton, Sam and Reuben Cohen. *Shooting People: Adventures in Reality TV.* London: Verso, 2003.

Blair, John. Modular *America: Cross-Cultural Perspectives on the Emergence of the American Way.* New York: Greenwood Press, 1988.

Corner, J. "Performing the Real: Documentary Diversions." *Television and New Media* 3.3 (1992): 255–69.

Deleuze, Gilles. "Postscript on Societies of Control." *OCTOBER* 59 (1992): 3–7.

du Gay, Paul. *Consumption and Identity at Work.* London: Sage, 1996.

Eco, Umberto. *Theory of Semiotics.* Bloomington, IN: Indiana UP, 1976.

Elmer, Greg. "A Diagram of Panoptic Surveillance." *New Media and Society* 5.2 (2003): 231–47.

Foucault, Michel. *Discipline and Punish: The Birth of the Prison.* Trans. Alan Sheridan. Harmondsworth: Penguin, 1987.

Goffman, Erving. *The Presentation of Self in Everyday Life.* Woodstock, NY: Overwood Press, 1973. Originally published 1959.

Holmes, Su and Deborah Jermyn. "Introduction." *Understanding Reality Television.* Ed. Su Holmes and Deborah Jermyn. London: Routledge, 2004.

Kelly, Robert E. *Star Performer: Nine Breakthrough Strategies You Need to Succeed.* London: Orion Business Books, 1998.

Kilborn, Richard. "'How Real Can You Get?': Recent Developments in 'Reality' Television." *European Journal of Communication* 9.4 (1994): 421–39.

Kroes, Rob. *If You've Seen One, You've Seen the Mall: Europeans and American Mass Culture.* Urbana: University of Illinois Press, 1996.

Lury, Celia. *Prosthetic Culture: Photography, Memory and Identity.* London: Routledge, 1998.

Mann, S. "Emotion at Work: To What Extent Are We Expressing, Suppressing and Faking It." *European Journal of Work and Organisational Psychology* 3 (1998): 347–69.

Mathiesen, Thomas. "The Viewer Society: Michel Foucault's 'Panopticon' Revisited." *Theoretical Criminology* 1.2 (1997): 215–234.

Murray, Patrick. "Marx's 'Truly Social' Labour Theory of Value." *Historical Materialism.* 7 (2000): 99–136.

Niklas, Rose. *Governing the Soul.* London: Routledge, 1990.

Nye, David E. *American Technological Sublime.* Cambridge, MA: MIT Press, 1994.

Palmer, G. "Big Brother: An Experiment in Governance." *Television and New Media* 3.3 (2002): 295–310.

Pine, B. Joseph II and James H. Gilmore. *The Experience Economy: Work Is Theatre and Every Business a Stage.* Boston: Harvard Business School Press, 1999.

"The Resort Offers Participation at a Price." *New Zealand Herald* 19 Feb. 2004. 1 June 2004 <http://www.nzherald.co.nz/entertainment/entertainmentstorydisdisplay.cfm?storyID=355>

Sennett, Richard. *The Corrosion of Character: The Personal Consequences of Work in the New Capitalism.* New York: W. W. Norton, 1998.

Warhurst, C., et al. "Aesthetic Labour in Interactive Service Work: Some Case Study Evidence from the 'New' Glasgow." The *Service Industries Journal* 20.3 (2000): 1–18.

Watson, Sean. "The New Bergsonism." *Radical Philosophy* 92 (1998): 13–14.

Winston, Brian. "The Primrose Path: Faking UK Television Documentary, 'Docuglitz' and Docusoap." *Screening the Past* 8 (1999). 6 Jan. 2003 <screeningthepast.media.lat robe.edu.au/archives/FMPro>

Notes

1. Producers and audiences alike comment on the fact that reality programs tend to blur the line between truth and fiction, as noted several times by Jan De Mol, creator and part owner of the *Big Brother* franchise. I doubt John Corner or Brian Winston would disagree, but for them that is exactly the problem.

2. For further discussion of the implications of reality programming on panoptic and synoptic systems of surveillance, see Daniel Trottier's essay, "Watching Yourself, Watching Others: Popular Representations of Panoptic Surveillance in Reality TV Programs," Ch. 16 in this collection.

3. The larger framing of this contrast is the debate between Deleuze and Foucault on disciplinarity and the society of control. See Gilles Deleuze's "Postscript on the Societies of Control," from *OCTOBER* 59 (1992): 3–7.

4. The example of postfeminism and power-dressing comes to mind here.

5. See especially pp349–350. See also Ashley Mears and William Mears, "Not Just a Paper Doll: How Models Manage Bodily Capital and Why They Perform Emotional Labour," *Journal of Contemporary Ethnography*, 34.3 (2005): 317–343, and Randy Hooson, *Dignity at Work*, Cambridge University press, 2001.

6. Erving Goffman's work is the clear precedent for much recent work in this area.

7. Once again, being protean in appearance seems to evoke notions of the post-modern self, as an a-centric and groundless performance of identity. But this would miss the central feature of the new scene, the requirement for a show of persuasive commitment to what are essentially transitory projects.

8. In post-industrial rejuvenated cities such as Glasgow, they claim, "it is clear that employers are utilising labour and seek markets that do not, in the first instance, require technical skills, but, instead, rely to a large extent upon the physical appearance or more specifically, the embodied capacities and attributes of those employed" (2).

Part II

Representation and Audiences

How Do Audiences Decode/ Understand Reality TV?

4

Viewer Interpretations of Reality Television: How Real Is Survivor *for Its Viewers?*

RICHARD E. CREW

As the 2003 television series *The Reality of Reality* observed, the "reality" television genre has traditionally been associated with "real life — unwritten, unrehearsed and uncertain." John Lee Jellicorse locates historical antecedents for reality television in an "actuality"[1] genre, a category that includes Matthew Brady's still photographs of the Civil War and the early film documentaries of John Grierson and Robert Flaherty. However, as evidenced during recent television seasons, the popular "reality" television shows do not fit neatly into these classic "actuality" or "reality" categories. This is at least in part due to "entertainment criteria" displacing "knowledge criteria," resulting in the "formation of hybrid styles of factual programming" (Corner, *Critical* 96).

Genre distinctions in television programming are important to media industries, academics, and journalistic critics, but viewing audiences in particular use genre to direct their choices and influence their expectations (Mittell 1). Scholars and critics have been prolific in decrying the breakdown of traditional generic boundaries evidenced by today's forms of reality television. Bluntly stated, they claim the current reality programming "dupes" its audience regarding what is "real" and what actually occurred (Corner, "Framing" 293). Despite these hybrid reality programs being around for more than a decade, and increasing in popularity since the 2000–2001 television season, there is minimal scholarship that investigates this type of reality television from the specific perspective of the viewing audience.

In this case study, the television series *Survivor*[2] was chosen as a representative of the current breed of hybrid reality programs, and examined using the framework of audience reception theory. The study sought to discover how *Survivor* is interpreted by its viewers: What are this program's appeals? How "real" is the content for the audience? Do regular viewers expect it to be spontaneous, accurate, or fair?

Survivor, like many contemporary television offerings, is termed a "reality program" by the industry, by the media that publish program listings, and by viewers themselves. However, a summarizing content analysis (Flick 191) of the series reveals it contains the following programmatic elements:

carefully-selected cast members;

manufactured story lines;

staged reality;[3]

competitions (both sports-like events and mental games);

serial drama (each *Survivor* series of approximately 13 episodes constitutes an extended, on-going drama);

a highly-produced soundtrack;

an exotic location (frequently in a "Robinson Crusoe setting")

a one million dollar incentive to be the sole *Survivor*.

All these elements help blur the traditional concept of reality in the program. This study examined the attitudes of *Survivor* viewers to determine the consequences for viewer meaning when actuality is mixed with other genres in a television program.

Theoretical Underpinnings of the Survivor *Study*

This case study emulated the ethnographic approaches used by Janice Radway and David Morley. Radway's use of focus group methodology in *Reading the Romance* was collective, similar to the *Survivor* research. For *Survivor*, however, the goal was pure discovery with no social agenda, which, therefore, differs from the taxonomic nature of Morley's focus group study for *The Nationwide Audience* that correlated meaning with social status.

This study builds on the work of Ien Ang, and Tamar Liebes and Elihu Katz, regarding how the nature of a text can impact audience interpretation. The study was framed by Stanley Fish's concept of interpretive communities, and the primary data were derived from tertiary texts as described by John Fiske.

Glenn Geiser-Getz's "COPS and the Comic Frame: Humor and Meaning-

Making in Reality-Based Television" used a similar approach to this study — which today is commonly referred to as "audience reception theory." Specifically, Geiser-Getz used ethnographic methods— primarily focus groups (201)— to study how a college fan audience of the reality-based television program *COPS* experiences the text, receives pleasure from that experience, and interprets messages about the police, the public, and the city.

Audience reception analysis as a perspective operates on the border between social sciences and the humanities. This theoretical framework views media use as itself a significant aspect of everyday life, and not merely a diversion or utility. It rejects both the stimulus-response model of media effects and the idea of an all-powerful text or message. Audience reception analysis focuses on the ways in which individuals make meanings from media messages, with the view that audiences are active receivers and interpreters.

The study of *Survivor* used this theoretical framework of audience reception analysis as the beginning of a quest to fill the gap in our knowledge about how viewers respond to the growing number of hybridized reality television programs.

Method

A qualitative method along with a concurrent "nested" quantitative method (Creswell 218) was employed. This choice of methodology followed the recommendation of Anders Hansen et al. to use a combination of research methods to "light up the most angles" of the multidimensional and complex processes of mass communication (1).

Focus groups were the primary method of data collection. Heeding a warning by Earl Babbie that "as you develop a theoretical understanding of what you're observing, there's a constant risk that you'll observe only those things that support your theoretical conclusions" (299), a five-step Likert like scale ("*Survivor* Attitude Scale") was administered to research participants immediately following their focus groups. This "concurrent nested" mixed methods strategy was also used in separate studies by David L. Morgan and JoEllen Shively. Such studies use the broad but "thin" data from a quantitative tool to guide the interpretive analysis of the wealth of detail from focus group material. This methodology satisfies Babbie's recommendation that, "[i]n conducting field research, even rough quantifications ... might provide a safeguard against selective perception and misinterpretation" (298–299).

Data collected from both methods were then mixed, or triangulated, during the analysis phase. The purpose was to gain broader perspective, enrich description, and, as Sharan Merriam recommends, enhance internal validity (207).

Design

The data gathered were individual and group opinions on the "categories" of content most important for viewers to enjoy *Survivor.* The study's strategic assumption was that the most important content categories identified by the research subjects would, after analysis, identify the meanings viewers have for the mixed genre of *Survivor.* The investigator suggested a range of content categories during the focus groups and on the *Survivor* Attitude Scale. (Criteria for determining content and categories appear in Appendix A.) Additional content categories and meanings, not posed by the investigator, were collected from the tertiary texts of the focus group conversations. These provided additional findings that, in some cases, proved to be surprising.

Sampling

Field research was conducted in the Seattle, Washington area, with four focus groups held during November and December of 2003. *Survivor* is more heavily watched in this city than in others: for example, on May 1, 2003, *Survivor* received a 20 rating in the Seattle market compared to an 11.6 rating nationwide (McFadden 45).[4] The viewing audience in Seattle provided a comparatively large pool of regular viewers from which to recruit the sample.

Recruiting took place during a six-week period in the fall of 2003, a period when new *Survivor* episodes were being telecast. Criteria for inclusion in the sample were that (a) participants be 18 years or older and (b) they be regular viewers of *Survivor.* (The latter criterion was defined as "having watched several seasons of the program.") Potential participants were screened by telephone to determine: desire to participate in a group discussion, availability for the scheduled evenings and locations, age, and *Survivor* viewing history. The number of participants for each focus group was set between 6 and 10, following recommendations by Peter Lunt and Sonia Livingstone (3). A total of 36 participants attended the four sessions.

The nationwide *Survivor* audience during the study period according to Nielsen Media Research was comprised of approximately 55 percent women and 45 percent men. The participants in this study were 60 percent women and 40 percent men, providing a rough approximation of the women-to-men ratio among *Survivor* viewers.

It is difficult to assume that the full range of responses to a study can ever be captured through such a qualitative method. However, given the redundancy in the *Survivor* responses collected, the researcher was satisfied with the patterns that emerged over the four groups and with the consistency of the data.

Analysis

The focus group transcripts were initially analyzed using the steps recommended by John Creswell (192). The first step was "open coding" of the transcripts. This analysis produced themes, and then initial categories were developed from recurring patterns in the data. In the second step, data were "selectively coded," merging the initial categories into a reduced number of core categories.

Next, the quantitative data from the *Survivor* Attitude Scale were grouped into categories and mean scores determined for each category. (Each mean score was a number between 1 and 5. The higher numbers indicated a category was "very important" to enjoying *Survivor*.) For additional analysis, the percentage of 4's and 5's ratings (signifying high importance) and the percentage of 1's and 2's ratings (signifying low importance) were calculated. These statistics are displayed in table form in Appendix B.

The results of both methods were then triangulated by developing linkages between the core concepts from the focus groups and the highest and lowest ranked categories from the *Survivor* Attitude Scale results. Norman Denzin (244) described this procedure as "between-method" triangulation.

Finally, following Strauss and Corbin (147), a central category was identified that pulled the other categories together, forming an explanatory whole. As the theoretical drive of this study was inductive, this triangulation of data took place within the core methodology — the focus group — as recommended by Janice Morse (203).

Findings and Discussion

The triangulation procedure involved identifying categories in focus group discussions and linking them to the amount of interest and importance indicated by similar *Survivor* Attitude Scale categories. The findings from this process are outlined in Figure 2.

CENTRAL CATEGORY: Real people in challenging situations.

MAJOR CATEGORIES & THEIR COMPONENTS:

GROUP & INTERPERSONAL DYNAMICS

- Real people interacting with each other
- Interpersonal relationships between "tribes" (teams)

NON-REALITY GENRE ELEMENTS

- Team and individual competitions in the show's "challenges" (similar to a sporting event)
- The different strategies to playing the "game" of outlasting the others (like a game show)
- The continuing story from week-to-week (the serial nature of the program)

REAL PEOPLE

- Not actors
- Revealing personal ethics
- Honest emotions

SPONTANEOUS, UNPREDICTABLE, SURPRISING

- Unscripted
- Accurate and honest depiction of people and events
  - Producer manipulation is expected, with necessary editing and the need to create narrative — but viewers expect fairness

THE "REALITY" OF SURVIVOR

- Editing is necessary or show would be boring
- Show has "enough" reality

Fig. 2. Triangulation results

A discussion of these findings follows as they relate to the research questions posed for this study.

HOW IS A HYBRID REALITY PROGRAM LIKE SURVIVOR INTERPRETED BY ITS VIEWERS, AND WHAT ARE ITS APPEALS?

From the categories identified by the two research methods, a central category was abstracted that pulls the others together into an explanatory whole. The categories all relate to the statement that: *Regular viewers watched Survivor to see real people in challenging situations.* More specifically, from the group discourse and *Survivor* Attitude Scale, the investigator concluded that: *the Survivor reality show is about non-actors — real people — in stressful and competitive situations.*

Focus group members believed that the game show element, in which the winner (the "sole Survivor") receives a one-million-dollar prize, gave many of the cast members permission to exhibit certain behaviors. Some on the show demonstrated questionable ethical actions (lying and cheating), some manipulated the loyalty of others, and some ostracized teammates. This unscripted behavior was one of the primary attractions of the program, and the investigator's notion is that viewers compare what they are seeing to their own ethical codes.

Cast members were faced with the interpersonal challenges of being strangers living together in a harsh environment. According to the sample, *Survivor*'s regularly scheduled sport and mental competitions, conducted while living on very little food and with primitive shelter, resulted in a range of credible (honest) emotional reactions from the cast. With the serial narrative of each *Survivor* series running for approximately 13 weeks, regular viewers of *Survivor* found the series compelling, whether they liked or disliked the actions of cast members or the choice of the ultimate winner.

The investigator checked the strength of the main theme —*real people in challenging situations*— by posing the following question during all the focus groups. Here is the response from one of the sessions.

MODERATOR: Let me ask you, if they took the show *Survivor*, and they hired actors and they scripted the show ...

1ST WOMAN: No.

2ND WOMAN: No way.

MODERATOR: ... would the show appeal to you?

1ST WOMAN: No. I think you would know too much about who you would be rooting for from day one and how they'd be, you know, type cast. You'd have like the Meg Ryan character and then you'd have the Sylvester Stallone character and you'd have the this and that.

MAN: And my experience is, the show is way more interesting than a committee of writers, trying to write a show that would keep me entertained for the same amount of time.

MODERATOR: Because?

MAN: Well, for one, if somebody wrote that a woman Boy Scout leader would decide a guy is so annoying, she's not only going to deprive him of $100,000, but is willing to take a $900,000 hit in order to keep him from having that, it would be hard to believe that as a motivation in a sitcom or drama. *[NOTE: This was one event on Survivor.]*

2ND WOMAN: Or it would be ultra-predictable.

MAN: But when you know that there is a *real* outcome for that, then you sort of say, "Wow, that was a big decision."

2ND WOMAN: Yeah.

3RD WOMAN: It wouldn't have the same credibility. It just wouldn't. I mean, the only good analogy, is *CSI* versus like *Forensic Files*. *CSI* is all scripted. It doesn't have the believability factor that a real video interview with, you know, someone who actually was at a crime scene. It just doesn't — it lacks something.

Clearly the *real people* and the *unpredictability* of a television program without a script were what these viewers enjoyed about *Survivor*. *One surprising finding* came from learning *why* this hybrid format is appealing. When participants were asked, "What do you like about *Survivor*?" the answers frequently included references to being tired of traditional scripted shows with actors.

HOW REAL IS THE CONTENT OF *SURVIVOR* FOR THE AUDIENCE?

The findings revealed the show was real (authentic) for the audience for these reasons: *the lack of a formal script, the cast of non-actors, the honest emotions displayed,* and *the elements of surprise and unpredictability.*

Most research subjects understood there was a structure to *Survivor* that, while not a script, mapped out the activities of the cast. As one woman related, this did not take away from the authentic elements of the show:

> [The producers] created a structure and they said within this we're going to put real people that feel their real emotions. [The cast chose] their own actions. The interactions are real between each other.

Such viewers believed they were witnessing insights into personalities and group behavior — an important and "real" ingredient of the show for them.

Surprisingly, the mix of different genre elements in *Survivor* actually contributed to the show's reality format. Since the games and competitions determined which cast members were temporarily exempt from being expelled, this added unpredictability to the series and heightened the group and interpersonal dynamics. Additionally, the serial component of *Survivor* was an antidote for what these viewers believed was unappealing about many television programs: scripted, predictable plots that are conveniently resolved at the end of 30 or 60 minutes. Therefore, the investigator concluded that these non-reality elements served to heighten the authentic aspects of *Survivor*.

Members of the sample group know that *Survivor* producers control what they see through the manipulation of activities, editing, and casting decisions. Viewers accepted the manipulation of the narrative as necessary to make *Survivor* an entertaining one hour program. Some stated that a "true reality show" would be boring without intensive editing. This confirms Richard Kilborn's observation about reality television, "Viewers are ... aware that what is seen on the screen is in every sense a constructed reality" (422).

Among some sample group members there was also a sophisticated understanding of the "degree" of reality in television programs. The *Joe Schmo* series was brought up in the focus group discourse. In this show the cast was all actors *except* for the lead character. Specifically, the lead character (Matt) *thought* he was in a reality show competing for a large cash prize, while everyone else, including the viewers, knew it was a ruse. To this focus group member, real vs. fake reality was detectable:

> They [*Joe Schmo*] kind of had a script, a loose script, that they had to work around, because [unpredictable] things were happening all the time, because of Matt [the non-actor]. But it wasn't the same [as *Survivor*], because — it wasn't just that we knew it was fake, a fake reality show, but because it *was* [fake]. Like the conversations didn't seem quite as believable.

One focus group member summed up the consensus of the groups regarding the "realness" issue on *Survivor* by exclaiming, "It's real enough for me!"

DOES THE AUDIENCE EXPECT THE PEOPLE AND EVENTS ON SURVIVOR TO BE PRESENTED WITH ACCURACY AND FAIRNESS?

Survivor is scheduled in primetime with other entertainment programming and does not look like any of the news, public affairs, or documentary television forms. Since the focus groups perceived it as "entertainment," *Survivor* seems to have license to roam beyond truth, accuracy, and fairness in the presentation of people and events. "It [*Survivor*] is what it is," several research subjects stated.

However, while *Survivor* was entertainment to everyone in the sample, they split regarding any requirement that a reality show be fair, accurate or truthful. The "fair/accurate/true" category ranked lower on the *Survivor* Attitude Scale than the investigator expected, with only 62% giving these statements items 5's and 4's. However, in the focus groups strong reactions came from some when the moderator asked, "What if you found out portions of the show were rigged?" or, "Do you think the producers are fair to all the characters?" Some members indicated they would "stop watching" if the show was rigged. Others were at least "bothered" that the editing might only be highlighting certain cast members' characteristics, possibly creating stereotypes. But several participants pointed out *Survivor* does not claim to be a documentary, and they believed the entertainment value was more important than fair/accurate/true issues. The findings for this question were consistent with Stuart Hall's notion that individuals bring contradictory and conflicting discourse into their readings of media texts (136–137).

Of more concern to some in the sample was the possibility that the physical and mental competitions might be structured to favor specific cast members, similar to rigging a sporting event or a game show. Most did not believe this was happening ("We would know if they were rigging it..."). The majority also felt that if producers shared strategy or personal information about some cast members with others, that would clearly be cheating — and it would factor into their viewing decisions about the show. The investigator hypothesized that if the credibility of *Survivor* were impinged through such actions, it could be analogous to the television quiz show scandals of the 1950s.[5] However, only three focus group members (out of 36) felt strongly that this would be a problem for *Survivor*.

Therefore, as a hybrid form — a reality/game/sport combination — this study's participants did not hold *Survivor* to the strict standards associated with any of these individual genres.

Other Findings

SURVIVOR AS EXPERIMENT; SURVIVOR AS A DEMONSTRATION OF INTERPERSONAL/GROUP DYNAMICS

In the initial group, the investigator was surprised to hear one of the first participants refer to *Survivor* as "a sociological experiment." In fact, in all groups the show was appreciated for the authentic interpersonal and group dynamics on display. These findings confirm concepts put forth in two non-empirical writings that discussed *Survivor*. In "The Culture of Surveillance," Vincent Pecora observed that, "Reality television is simply making exoteric [*sic*] (if also trivializing) ... the filmed inquiry into group dynamics that social psychologists have carried out esoterically for decades" (355). In her consideration of the show's psychological appeal, Barbara Schapiro concluded that, "Survivor creates a reality of physical and social stress and then allows us to witness the exposure of human character through the contestants' interpersonal responses and interactions" (280).

Although this study was not specifically investigating the *Survivor*-as-social-experiment thesis, the findings confirmed the Pecora and Schapiro notions that this was an important appeal of the program.

CATEGORIES THAT WERE THE LEAST IMPORTANT

The categorical aspects of *Survivor* having *the least importance* for viewer enjoyment were the "fantasy," "million dollar prize," and "shame/humiliation" elements. The fantasy of the exotic locations, the cast appearing in swimsuits, and the one million dollar prize did not register as important with the sample groups. Research participants were asked in several ways about the prize money. They responded that the million dollars was the reason the cast wanted to be on the show, but it was not a reason to watch the show. Who won the prize was not important (although viewers always favored specific cast members), but it was *the process* of winning the prize that made *Survivor* appealing.

The "shame/humiliation" factor was unimportant, and this was a significant finding in the study. One non-empirical writing about *Survivor* (Shapiro 274) has advanced the notion that viewers watch to see cast members humiliated or rejected. While some focus group members in this study indicated they use *Survivor* as a vicarious experience, none found appeal in watching cast members being socially ostracized or voted off the show. In fact, reactions frequently ran counter to this concept, as voiced by this group member: "Some of the times that seem to trouble me the most is [*sic*] when someone's being humiliated. I don't really like that."

VOYEURISM AND SURVEILLANCE

The uses and gratifications model of mass communication (Blumler and Katz) identifies "surveillance of the environment" as an important reason why people use media. Vincent Pecora (350) suggested that audience "voyeurism" is another appeal of programs like *Survivor.* The *Survivor* study concluded that voyeurism, both as "peeking" into others' lives and a prurient interest, *was not* an appeal. While the sample *did* acknowledge the surveillance concept, the appeal of being "voyeurs" was rejected, as exemplified by these discussion excerpts.

> It's sort of become normal to have the very inner personal experiences portrayed on television for everyone to be able to listen to and see. It's part of television in general that I think we like and has become normal.
>
> I don't think of it so much as voyeuristic ... I think the people who do this are basically attention seekers who have chosen to be on there.... If you choose to be on national TV, you're fair game, as far as I'm concerned.

In a recent empirical study published after the *Survivor* study began, Robin Nabi, et al. evaluated the hypothesis that reality-based TV is popular because it appeals to the voyeuristic nature of the population. Their results concurred with this study's findings that voyeurism is questionable as an appeal.

Summary and Conclusions

This case study of the *Survivor* reality series provided insight and understanding about the phenomenon of reality television. In particular, it demonstrated how viewers perceive a hybrid reality show and interpret it as "real enough," but also as an entertainment vehicle.

Survivor viewers in this case study enjoyed seeing what happens to real people (vs. actors) put in unusual situations: i.e., they enjoyed the spontaneity (vs. a scripted show), the interaction and competition between individuals and groups, and the personal ethical decisions made by cast members. The authentic actions and reactions of the show's participants, as well as their honest emotions, were important to viewers. Sample members knew that the program was heavily edited and that producers emphasized the physical and behavioral stereotypes of cast members. Viewers, however, generally trusted that the "truth" of what they saw had not been significantly altered. Although they watched the series for entertainment, viewers found the program useful for self-reflection, for observation of society and human behavior, for release, and for education.

The study's participants could not imagine the *Survivor* show produced with actors and a script, indicating the importance of real people as cast members and their unpredictable actions. Surprising to the investigator, the physical and mental competitions (known as "challenges") on the show and the continuing "game" being played contributed to the "reality" of the show. Some viewers thought the "game" and the living conditions brought out the true character of the participants. The majority of the research participants did not condone the ethics and activities cast members used to play the "game," and they saw these as object lessons against which to compare their own behavior and beliefs.

Most of the study's viewers accepted a certain amount of manipulation by producers to keep the show interesting and entertaining; however, some said they would be disillusioned to learn that the show was "fixed" for certain people to succeed or for others to fail. Viewers were quite forgiving of *Survivor's* reality construction, provided they felt they were seeing honest emotions, spontaneous and unpredictable stories, and authentic actions by participants (vs. "acted" behavior).

The conclusions discussed above do not indicate that "fact" and "fiction" have less meaning for viewers. Rather, following on the work of Stuart Hall and others previously discussed, this study confirmed that these terms are always under negotiation between the media and the viewers. It suggests that media scholars will need to adjust their definitions of the relationship between television and realism, between fact and fiction, and between the factual and the entertaining.

A significant understanding evolved from the study: that viewers believed a reality show hybrid like *Survivor*, despite having elements of other genres, presented the real (authentic) emotions, interpersonal actions, and individual ethical choices of its "real" participants. And viewers actively looked for the "reality" contained within the artifice of this program.

Another significant — and unexpected —finding was that the *Survivor* audience enjoyed the unpredictable, unscripted nature of the program *primarily because* they had tired of the predictable 30 and 60 minutes comedies and dramas that conveniently resolve at the end of each television show.

Negative findings were also significant. Audiences *do not* watch *Survivor* as voyeurs, for the fantasy elements, or to witness the shame or humiliation of the show's participants. Some of these negative findings are counter to lay writings in the popular press and those hypothesized in non-empirical writings.

Opportunities for Future Study

The *Survivor* study has merely scratched the surface of how audiences negotiate between fact/realism and fiction/construction in one of television's mixed format reality shows. Additional case studies using similar methodologies will hopefully now be conducted for other hybrid reality shows in order to provide enough data to formulate theory regarding the nature and impact of these non-fiction television formats.

This study suggests that television programming has become highly predictable, and reality television hybrids provide a more unpredictable and therefore more enjoyable viewing option. Future study should also explore the possibility that reality drama is replacing fictional drama for a significant number of viewers.

Other audience groups need to be included as subjects of study to continue the examination of the negotiation process between audiences and media texts. The sample of regular *Survivor* viewers in Seattle was largely white and middle class. As low-income, low-education, and non-white viewers are also a large component of many reality-based programs (Geiser-Getz 212), future studies should examine different groups ethnographically. This approach will contribute additional knowledge to how the different subcultures that comprise television's audience make meaning from hybrid reality programs.

Appendix A

Content for the focus groups and *Survivor* Attitude Scale was determined through (a) a summarizing content analysis (Flick 191) of the typical *Survivor* program, (b) a review of the critical literature on reality television programs, and (c) the researcher's findings during a pilot study. In the pilot stage conducted in April 2003, a list of open-ended questions related to the "ingredients" of reality shows in general, and *Survivor* in particular, was devised and administered in telephone interviews to 10 regular *Survivor* viewers. These participants were identified using opportunistic and snowball sampling techniques. The content areas generating the most discussion and in which interviewees had the strongest opinions were incorporated into the final focus group script and *Survivor* Attitude Scale.

Figure 1 lists the specific origin of each content category used in this study.

Category	*Source*
Real people (vs. actors)	Content analysis
Authentic emotions and actions	Pilot interviews
Spontaneous (not scripted)	Pilot interviews
Group and Interpersonal dynamics (like a sociological experiment)	Content analysis
Non-reality elements (games, serial nature)	Content analysis
Fair, accurate, truthful	Richard Kilborn, Max Frankel, Ib Bondebjerb
Voyeurism, surveillance	Vincent P. Pecora, Steven Reiss & James Wiltz, Barbara A. Schapiro
Shame, humiliation	Barbara A. Schapiro
Personal power, control	Content analysis
Scheming, lying	Pilot interviews
Fantasy elements (million dollar prize, attractive bodies, exotic location)	Content analysis
Winning one million dollars	Content analysis

Fig. 1. Content categories for research question design

Appendix B

TABLE 1: "*SURVIVOR* ATTITUDE SCALE" RESULTS

Question posed: "What elements of *Survivor* are important to your enjoyment of the program?"
Sample Number = 36

Categories	Mean Score (5 = very important 1 = not important)	Frequency (%) of #5 & #4 Choices	Frequency (%) of #2 & #1 Choices
Group & interpersonal dynamics	4.42	89%	1%
Non-reality genre elements	4.37	91%	3%
Real people (vs. actors)	4.32	90%	2%
Spontaneous/unscripted/unpredictable	4.07	77%	5%
Honest emotions	4.06	73%	4%
Voyeurism & surveillance	3.91	72%	7%
Fair/accurate/true	3.85	62%	12%
Personal power & control	3.59	58%	17%
Scheming/lying/deceiving	3.15	36%	28%
Fantasy (money, participants in swimsuits, exotic locations)	2.76	31%	44%
Shame & humiliation	2.59	12%	46%
The one-million dollar prize	2.44	16%	52%

Works Cited

Anderson, Kent. *Television Fraud: The History and Implications of the Quiz Show Scandal.* Westport: Greenwood, 1978.

Ang, Ien. *Watching 'Dallas': Soap Opera and the Melodramatic Imagination.* New York: Methuen, 1985.

Babbie, Earl. *The Practice of Social Research.* Boston: Wadsworth, 1998.

Bondebjerb, Ib. "Public Discourse/Private Fascination: Hybridization in 'True-Life-Story' Genres." *Television: The Critical View.* Ed. Horace Newcomb. London: Oxford University Press, 2000. 383–400.

Blumler, Jay G., and Elihu Katz, eds. *The Uses of Mass Communications.* Beverly Hills: SagePublications, 1974.

Corner, John. *Critical Ideas in Television Studies.* Oxford: Clarendon Press, 1999.

_____. "Framing the New." *Understanding Reality Television.* Eds. Sut Holmes and Deborah Jermyn. London: Routledge, 2004. 290–299.

Creswell, John W. *Research Design: Qualitative, Quantitative, and Mixed Methods Approaches.* Thousand Oaks: Sage Publishing, 2003.

Denzin, Norman K. *The Research Art.* New York: McGraw Hill, 1989.

"Everything Old is New." *The Reality of Reality.* By Lee Olson. Bravo Television. 9 Aug. 2003.

Fish, Stanley. *Is There a Text in This Class?* Cambridge: Harvard University Press, 1980.

Fiske, John. *Television Culture.* London: Routledge, 1987.

Flick, Uwe. *An Introduction to Qualitative Research.* Thousand Oaks: Sage Publishing, 2002.

Frankel, Max. "Seeing is Always Believing." *The New York Times* 9 November 2003: 36.

Geiser-Getz, Glenn C. "COPS and the Comic Frame: Humor and Meaning-Making in Reality-Based Television." *Critical Approaches to Television.* Eds. Leah R. Vande Berg, Lawrence A. Wenner, and Bruce E. Gronbeck. Boston: Houghton Mifflin Company, 1998. 200–213

Hall, Stuart. "Encoding/Decoding." *Culture, Media, Language.* Eds. Stuart Hall, Dorothy Hobson, Andrew Lowe, and Paul Willis. London: Hutchinson, 1980. 128–138.

Hansen, Anders, Simon Cottle, Ralph Negrine, and Chris Newbold. *Mass Communication Research Methods.* New York: New York University Press, 1998.

Holmes, Su, and Deborah Jermyn. *Understanding Reality Television.* London: Routledge, 2004.

Jellicorse, John Lee. *Actuality Genres Study Guide.* Greensboro: UNC Greensboro, 2001.

Kilborn, Richard. "'How Real Can You Get?': Recent Developments in 'Reality' Television." *European Journal of Communication* 9 (1994): 421–439.

Liebes, Tamar and Elihu Katz. *The Export of Meaning: Cross-Cultural Readings of Dallas.* New York: Oxford University Press, 1990.

McFadden, Kay. "'Survivor,' 'West Wing' and Sci-Fi Float Quirky Seattle's Boat." *The Seattle Times* 5 May 2003: 45.

Merriam, Sharan B. *Qualitative Research and Case Study Applications in Education.* San Francisco: Jossey-Bass, 1998.

Mittell, Jason. "A Cultural Approach to Television Genre Theory." *Cinema Journal,* 40.3 (2001):3–25.

Morgan. D.L. "Seeking Diagnosis for a Family Member with Alzheimer's Disease." Presented at Annual Meeting, American Sociological Association, Los Angeles, 1994.

Morley, David. *The 'Nationwide' Audience: Structure and Decoding.* London: British Film Institute, 1980.

Morse, Janice M. "Principles of Mixed Methods and Multimethod Research Design." *Handbook of Mixed Methods in Social Behavioral Research.* Eds. Abbas Tashakkori and Charles Teddlie. Thousand Oaks: Sage Publishing, 2003. 189–208.

Nabi, Robin L., Erica N. Biely, Sara J. Morgan, and Carmen R. Stitt. "Reality-Based Television Programming and the Psychology of its Appeal." *Media Psychology* 5 (2003): 303–329.

Nielsen Media Research. *Report on Television.* New York: Author, 2003.

Pecora, Vincent P. "The Culture of Surveillance." *Qualitative Sociology,* 25.3 (2002): 345–358.

Radway, Janice. *Reading the Romance: Women, Patriarchy and Popular Literature.* 1987. Chapel Hill: University of North Carolina Press, 1991.

Reiss, Steven, & James Wiltz. "Why America Loves Reality TV." *Psychology Today* 34 (2001): 52–54.

Schapiro, Barbara A. "Who's Afraid of Being Kicked Off the Island? The Psychological Appeal of 'Survivor.'" *Journal for the Psychoanalysis of Culture & Society,* 7.2 (2002): 274–280.

Shively JoEllen (1992). "Cowboys and Indians: Perceptions of Western Films Among American Indians and Anglos." *American Sociological Review* 57 (1992): 725–34.

Strauss, Anselm L., and Juliet M. Corbin. *Basics of Qualitative Research.* Thousand Oaks: Sage Publishing, 1998.

Notes

1. "Actuality" is defined by Jellicorse as "a work (film, audio, televisual) that captures a setting or event that would have occurred naturally regardless of the presence of the camera" (269).

2. At the time of this study, the television program *Survivor* had achieved considerable ratings success during its three-year run.

3. According to Jellicorse, in a staged reality show, "subjects are placed in a contrived, structured situation so that the audience can observe how they interact with the environment and among themselves" (316).

4. A ratings point represents one percent of total television households in any given market.

5. At that time, as related by Kent Anderson, the exposure of cheating behind the scenes of a game show called *Twenty-One* shook audience trust, leading to lower ratings and the near-death of the genre.

5

Marketing "Reality" to the World: Survivor, Post-Fordism, and Reality Television

CHRIS JORDAN

> I hear some producers say they really don't want the advertising community involved in their precious creative work. What's more creative than telling 30-second stories and seeing billions of dollars of products fly off the shelves? [Mark Burnett, executive producer of *Survivor*, qtd. in Littleton].

Three events occurred in China in 2001 that suggest that reality TV serves as a vehicle for global advertisers interested in cultivating new markets: state-owned television network CCTV produced a show entitled *Survival Challenge* based on the CBS prime time hit *Survivor*; China joined the World Trade Organization (WTO); and spending on Chinese television advertising increased by 17 percent (Schwankert 23). Although China continues to resist efforts by major media companies to invest in its emerging telecommunications infrastructure, the accelerating penetration of the Chinese media marketplace by global advertisers since the country joined the WTO suggests that the commercialization of Chinese television will continue. With a population of 1.3 billion people, 300 million TV homes, and 110 million basic cable homes, China offers a huge potential market for advertisers and television networks (Schwankert 23).

This paper analyzes the production, distribution, and consumption of *Survivor* in order to explain why reality television is a global staple of domestic and international prime time television.[9] It argues that intensifying concentration of ownership in the television industry, the worldwide proliferation of commercial television, the fragmentation of the global television audience, and the design of *Survivor* as a thinly veiled advertisement account for its success.

The centrifugal trends of media industry ownership concentration and global television audience fragmentation exemplify post-Fordism. By implementing a post-Fordist strategy of diversifying their products and their marketing in order to incorporate diverse locales, media conglomerates use their marketplace power to design television shows for both a global audience and national and local niche audiences. Financed by advertisers interested in cultivating new consumers in America and abroad, *Survivor* weaves sponsors' products into a format that can be flexibly adapted on a nation-by-nation basis to appeal to local tastes.

Concentration of ownership in the media industry parallels this expansionary logic of post-Fordism. On the one hand, capitalists are continually penetrating new territories and markets in their relentless search for profits. On the other hand, capitalists seek ways to eliminate competition in order to reduce the costs and risks that competition creates. Therefore, even though competition constitutes a major and continuing force of change in a capitalist economy, the overriding tendency within capitalism is concentration.

The concentration of ownership that has accompanied the global expansion of the communications industry during the last 20 years exemplifies this point. In the 1980s and 1990s, the maturation of cable and other communications technologies created competition in the U.S. and other countries that fragmented the mass broadcast television audience. Simultaneously, lax anti-trust regulation and the loosening of regulatory restrictions on patterns of media ownership facilitated the television industry's vertical and horizontal integration as a handful of media conglomerates bought up competitors and consolidated their control over the U.S. media marketplace.[10]

The global concentration of media ownership, the advent of post-Fordist television production and distribution, and the design of *Survivor* as a virtual advertisement for global consumer goods companies raises a concern: even though viewers of the show and its adaptations maintain "citizenship" in global, national, and local communities, media consumption increasingly circumscribes these identities in terms of participation in consumer culture.

When *Survivor* is studied in this critical political economic context, it becomes clear that it circulates worldwide because it fits the needs of producers, networks, and advertisers in an age of global television. To explore the show in these terms avoids reifying it as an expression of audience demand or a cultural shift unrelated to the needs of those who run the television industry. Critical political economy provides a framework for analyzing the influence of media structures and performance on the television industry and its programs by shedding light on the role of politics in shaping these forces.

Critical Political Economy and the Contemporary Television Industry

Three areas of inquiry provide the foundation for critical political economy: the relation between the capitalist class and the state; the relationship between the logic of capital and state policies; and the state as a mediator of public and private interests in the media industry (Bettig 127). Critical political economic theory studies how concentration of ownership and control enables a class that owns and controls most of America's productive capital to disproportionately influence government policy planning and execution. In contrast to economists, who relegate politics to the periphery of their paradigm, political economists make politics a central focus of their research. Two questions provide a starting point for this investigation: "who owns the media?" and "who rules the state?"

The logic of capital theory answers these questions by contending that a mode of production designed to multiply capital by ceaselessly cultivating new markets inevitably gravitates towards concentration of ownership because of its relentless drive for profit. As a mediator of public and private interests, the state then must periodically intervene and break up monopolies, oligopolies, or trusts. From this examination, it follows that the logic of capital, if unchecked by government intervention, promotes the economics of cost efficiencies, product differentiation, and vertical integration, resulting in a reduction of independent media sources, concentration on the largest markets, and the neglect of smaller, poorer sectors (Litman 117–124). Critical political economy thus argues that the media marketplace is prone to failure because the constant drive for profit that defines the logic of capital results in a restricted range of media output.

Critics of the capital logic theory of the state argue that it is overly simplistic to assert that the interests of capital always prevail in class struggle because business simply uses the state as an instrument to advance its interests (Jessop 37). Critical political economists counter by arguing that class forces struggling in and through the state determine policies and action. Various sectors of industry and the public insert themselves into relevant policy-making arenas and exert pressure on the various departments of the state system in order to advance their interests.

The state thus dons the mantle of ideal collective capitalist by promoting the long-term interests of capital as a whole through discriminatory management of monopolistic competition. The interaction of the state, industry, and the public helps to shape the general political economic framework within which television production and distribution take place. However, while mediating the process of compromise, government is also sensitive to the threat of a capital investment strike because it is dependent on the capital accumulation process for tax revenue. This makes the state particularly sensitive to the threat of a capital investment strike (Bettig 130).[11]

The FCC retreated from regulating the communications industry by enacting the Telecommunications Act of 1996. The merging of Viacom and CBS in 1999 directly sprang from the Telecommunications Act's liberalization of FCC policy and took full advantage of the commission's subsequent relaxation of other rules. The commission's relaxation of the National Broadcast Ownership Cap, National Television Station Ownership Rule and the Cable Broadcast Cross-Ownership Rule removed impediments that prevented Viacom from owning a network. Of crucial significance was the broadcast networks' contention that they could not compete against pay and cable television unless the FCC relaxed these rules. NBC's top Washington lobbyist, Robert Okun, stated in1999 that "in order for free TV to survive against pay TV, we need deregulation of our industry"(qtd. in Stern 53).

The relaxation of the National Broadcast Cap from 35 percent to 39 percent permits CBS to maximize its domestic audience for *Survivor* (Carter B1).[12] Revision of the Cable Broadcast Cross-Ownership Rule allows Viacom to own a cable operator and a broadcast network in the same market, while relaxation of the National Television Station Ownership Rule eases limitations on the number of television stations that a single network can own. Not coincidentally, CBS President and Chief Executive Officer Les Moonves stated in 1999 that audience size is a key advantage the network offers advertisers in relation to cable television, which draws substantially fewer viewers than broadcast TV (Adalian, "Moonves" 58).

Soft money campaign contributions represent one means through which media company executives influence the policymaking process. In 1999 and 2000, for example, Viacom and CBS contributed over $41,000 in soft money donations to the Republican National Committee, the National Republican Congressional Committee, the Democratic National Committee, and the Democratic Congressional Campaign Committee (opensecrets.org).[13] Viacom CEO Sumner Redstone also wields tremendous influence over the conglomerate's business decisions through his ownership of 76 percent of the company's stock. In comparison to the millions of Viacom stockholders who own only a handful of shares, Redstone controls the proxy vote by default.

Interlocking board memberships are another means through which media giants submerge competitive instincts in favor of joint, cooperative action in political reform. Viacom's board of directors is a virtual "who's who" of business and industry that includes former government officials, financial investment advisors, and chairpersons of other global telecommunications companies. In 2003, for example, the Viacom board of directors included Joseph A. Califano, William S. Cohen, and Alan C. Greenberg. Califano is a former U.S. Secretary of Health, Education, and Welfare. Cohen, a former U.S. Secretary of Defense, is also a former three-term U.S. Senator and Congressman. Greenberg is Chairman of the Executive Committee of the Bear Stearns Companies, Inc., the parent company of Bear Stearns & Co., a Wall Street investment banking and securities trading firm. Ivan Seidenberg, Chairman and Chief Executive Officer of the global telecommunications corporation NYNEX, also served on the Viacom board of directors between 1995 and 2004. Outside members such as these, who are not involved in day-to-day operations of Viacom, promote the long-term stability and goals of the company by providing valuable ties to finance, big business, and government.

World Trade Organization (WTO) trade initiatives have also been instrumental in facilitating the penetration of foreign countries by media distributors interested in propagating new markets for reality television shows. Incumbent in the WTO's agenda are trade liberalization, export-oriented production, and privatization of state owned industries. The nations most vulnerable to the WTO are Third World countries that borrowed heavily from wealthier nations during the 1970s. The formation of public-private partnerships between state owned television networks and global media conglomerates illustrates the impact of the WTO. Mexico's Televisa and Brazil's Globo, both publicly owned networks, share ownership of the Latin Sky Broadcasting satellite television service with U.S.-based media conglomerates AT&T-TCI and News Corporation (McChesney 97). The accelerating privatization of formerly public broadcasting systems around the world provides an opportunity for global advertisers to cultivate markets in developing countries.

David Harvey notes that this globalization of media production, distribution, and consumption exemplifies a shift from Fordism to post-Fordism. The Fordist system of manufacturing and marketing strove to maximize profits by making one commodity appeal to as many consumers as possible for as long as possible (145). Under post-Fordism, capitalism responds to the global flow of labor and consumption markets within and between nation-states by transforming local and regional cultures into market segments and mobilizing citizens as consumers. By implementing a post-Fordist strategy of diversifying its products and their marketing in order to incorporate diverse locales, capitalism transforms a problem into an opportunity as it markets products for both global markets and niche segments to take advantage of the countervailing flows of localism and globalism (Fiske, "Global" 58).

Stuart Hall contends that post-Fordism promotes democracy by globally circulating media products and other consumer goods (62). Reality television programs thus flow both ways between the United States and other nations. As John Fiske argues, globalization thus provokes localization, multiplying histories through migration and diaspora and eroding a sense of nationalism built around the interests of dominant groups ("Global").

Fiske also challenges the Marxist contention that television simply delivers malleable audiences to advertisers by arguing that audiences maintain an active role in decoding television texts (*Television*). The advancement of the prime time episodic television narrative, in terms of a "real time" structure that mirrors the rhythm of daily life, makes it far more amenable to consumption through means of displaced gossip than other television genres. Various scholars (e.g. Ang; Feuer; Olson) celebrate episodic television shows as open texts from which active audiences derive meaningful interpretations.

Some critics thus praise *Survivor* as an open text on the basis of its similarity to episodic drama. In its assessment of *Survivor*'s glossy production values, *Variety* compared the show to episodic drama rather than reality TV, observing that Burnett eschewed the "cheap-is better" conventions of most reality shows by giving *Survivor* "a virtually cinematic look" ("TV's peeper producers").[14] Mary Beth Haralovich and Michael W. Trosset define *Survivor* on this basis as an open, hybrid text that uses chance to generate "unpredictability and pleasure" for viewers (77). As these scholars also observe, however, Burnett attributes the popularity of adventure programming, in part, to market research-defined lifestyle preferences (Haralovich and Trossett 78). The commercial success of *Survivor* thus stems in large part from its role as a virtual advertisement for sponsors' products. There are several reasons why *Survivor* was designed in this way.

Production of Reality Television: The Medium is the Advertiser's Message

Various researchers (e.g. Bagdikian; McChesney; Bettig and Hall) point out that, while the television industry historically has been an oligopoly, concentration of ownership of it has intensified during the last two decades. A small group of global media conglomerates now owns the six broadcast television networks. They are Time Warner (WB), Disney (ABC),

Viacom (CBS, UPN), News Corporation (FOX), and General Electric (NBC).

Several factors promote the concentration of ownership in the television industry. The competition created by cable television, satellite TV, videocassette recorders (VCR), and other new communications technologies during the 1980s and 1990s fragmented the mass television audience share and encouraged the assimilation of cable and broadcast television networks into large media conglomerates. Changes in audience measurement also arose as the proliferation of cable, VCRs, and first-run syndication challenged the broadcast networks' economic domination of the television industry. Production budget cuts occurred as the conglomerates that purchased the big three networks during the 1990s incurred high levels of corporate debt and advertiser-driven changes in audience measurement techniques designed to identify specific market segments produced dramatically lower ratings for the networks (Raphael 121).

As the marketplace fragmented and audience measurement techniques changed, there arose more potential networks for producers to sell programs to, but less money from networks to cover the costs of program production. Although the number of television channels increased, the amount each network was willing to advance in deficit financing for program production shrank. Access to prime time television increasingly depended on an independent producer's ability to secure enough production financing from a third-party source to supply a network with low-cost programming that would nonetheless be of sufficient quality to garner high ratings.

Charlie Parsons and former rock band singer Bob Geldof developed the concept that became *Survivor* at their British TV production company, Planet 24. When Parsons and Geldof sold Planet 24 in 1999, they retained the rights to *Survive!,* which was being produced in Sweden by the duo's Castaway Productions under the name *Expedition: Robinson*. The next year, Parsons and Geldof licensed the *Survive!* concept to Mark Burnett for a U.S. version that ended up launching the reality TV craze in America.

As an independent producer, Burnett faced an uphill battle in gaining access to prime time because the relaxation of government regulations in the 1990s made it possible for networks to produce many of their own shows. In 2000, all six broadcast networks either owned or co-owned more than half of their new shows, and three of them (ABC, CBS, and WB) owned or co-owned more than 75 percent of their new programs (Schneider and Adalian 70).

Survivor appealed to CBS because the co-production deal it struck with Burnett required no deficit financing, yet offered the network a program with the high quality production values audiences expect of prime time television. Instead of paying Burnett a fee to license the show, CBS agreed to share the show's advertising revenue with him if he pre-sold sponsorship of the program. By pre-selling the show, Burnett raised the capital necessary to produce *Survivor*, provided CBS with essentially free prime time programming, and enjoyed a hefty share of the show's advertising revenue.

Advertisers readily sponsored *Survivor* because of its design as a virtual commercial for their products. Burnett acquired eight sponsors before the commencement of principal photography during the first season, selling not only 30-second spots but also sponsorship space in the show itself. Anheuser-Busch, General Motors, Visa, Frito-Lay, Reebok, and Target paid approximately $4 million each for advertising time, product placement in the show, and a website link (McCarthy, "Sponsors" B1). Even though *Survivor* is one of the most expensive reality shows to date, with production costs escalating from $1 million an episode for the first season to $1.5 million an episode for subsequent editions, it is profitable. With pre-sold sponsorships covering production costs and 30-second spots commanding $445,000 during the 2001–2002 season, *Survivor* proved that lavishly produced reality television shows could be low-risk and lucrative (Raphael 122).

Burnett's success in pitching *Survivor* to advertisers enabled the producer to circumvent the role of the advertising agency as a liaison between program creator and sponsor, making it even more cost efficient for sponsors. Producers started working directly with products' brand managers, moving away from shows such as *Temptation Island* with overt sexual innuendo and towards shows such as *Survivor* (see Littleton). Praised by CBS President Les Moonves as a "great pitchman," Burnett steered away from sexual sensationalism and towards themes of competitive merit by explaining to advertisers "how much sense it would make for someone on an island a million miles from home to crave a soft drink or something to eat from home"("Burnett Likes Mad Ave" 3).

At one time, advertisers balked at the insertion of a bag of chips or a soda into a situation comedy or drama because it might break the audience's suspension of disbelief. However, *Survivor* host Jeff Probst's act of rewarding winners of the show's challenges with Doritos and Mountain Dew integrated the products into a circumstance that abstracted the line between programming and advertising by associating them with adventure and heroism. During *Survivor: Africa*, for example, the word "avalanche" was the answer to a reward challenge. Viewers then saw the winner driving a Chevrolet Avalanche across the African plain to deliver medical supplies to hospitals treating AIDS patients (McCarthy "Sponsors" B1). In 2001, Burnett received $14 million from marketers such as Mountain Dew and General Motors for the production of *Survivor: Africa* (McCarthy, "Also Starring" B1).

The design of *Survivor* as a virtual advertisement raises the issue of how television's goal of selling audiences to advertisers shapes the program. According to Sut Jhally, a television program must be able to attract large numbers of people. Second, it has to attract the "right" kinds of people. Not all parts of the audience are of equal value to advertisers. Television programs will also have to reflect this targeting, excluding demographic groups that lack the spending power to satisfy advertisers. Third, television must not only be able to deliver a large number of the correct people to advertisers, but must also deliver them in the right frame of mind. Programs should be designed to enhance the effectiveness of the ads in them (Jhally 76).

Survivor accomplishes all of these goals. Broadcast during prime time, it attracts a teen demographic sought by advertisers as well as a huge national audience composed of other age groups. According to *Variety*, *Survivor* delivered during its initial season more teens than *WWF Smackdown*, more young adults than *Friends*, more children than *Wonderful World of Disney*, and more 50-plus viewers than *60 Minutes* (Kissell 19). Rejecting the jittery, hand-held camera style of public television documentaries of the 1970s, *Survivor* also boasts high quality production values that associate products woven into its text with adventure, heroism, and escape.

Survivor thus appeals to networks and advertisers because it combines high ratings with relatively low cost in comparison to comedies and dramas. The escalating cost of must-have sport and movie properties and the success of special effects-driven docudramas such as BBC-Discovery's *Walking with Dinosaurs* during the 2000 television season put drama budgets under scrutiny and encouraged U.S. producers to co-produce much more drama on the terms of European networks. Compounding the shift away from half-hour comedy shows and towards low-cost reality-entertainment hybrids was the lack of obvious successors to prime time smash hits such as *Seinfeld* [1989 -1998] and *Friends* [1994 — 2004] (Fry M4). High quality production values and exotic locations became means through which *Survivor* targeted the prime time audience sought by advertisers, distinguished itself from cheaper crime-based reality shows, and blurred the line between prime time drama and reality shows ("TV's Peeper Producers Are Powerhouses" 1).

Reality television shows have thus proliferated on prime time television in recent years because they pose little financial risk for networks, yet offer prime-time-friendly production values and generate huge ratings. The use of the Internet and cable television networks also attracts a young audience prized by advertisers. On this basis, *Survivor* became a valuable addition to Viacom's cradle-to-the-grave programming spectrum by enabling CBS, known for its primarily elderly audience, to capture a huge mass audience as well as a slice of the highly coveted youth audience.

Distribution of *Survivor:*
Creating a Global Franchise

Access to a nationwide audience plays a key role in advancing the networks' goal of enclosing new markets in the United States by facilitating economies of scale in television production that make the medium cost efficient for advertisers. As a fixed-cost product supported by advertising, a television program is a "public good" that costs the same to make independent of the number of people who consume it. As such, a television program does not diminish in available quantity because one person consumes it. The larger the audience a single television program attracts, the more cost efficiently and profitably a network can sell it to advertisers.

For mass advertisers, there is no cost-effective alternative to the broadcast networks. Network television remains the only place advertisers can reach large groups of people quickly. The relaxation of the National Television Station Ownership Rule, the Cable Broadcast Cross-Ownership Rule, and the National Broadcast Cap enables CBS to deliver a national audience of unprecedented size to advertisers and to promote synergies between cable and broadcast TV. *Survivor* is thus enormously profitable. In 2004, an average 30-second spot on the show cost $405,000, outstripping the $372,000 cost of a 30-second spot on *Friends,* previously the most expensive TV show for advertisers (McClintock 15). However, advertisers sponsor *Survivor* for reasons besides its ability to garner a huge audience.

Although more expensive than airing re-runs, *Survivor* proved that original network prime-time programming could curtail the loss of network audience share to cable during the summer months, when the networks typically re-broadcast the previous season's fare. Between 1999 and 2000, the four largest cable networks suffered a six percent revenue loss, while cable's overall share of the national viewing audience during summer 2000 rose only one percent, a major slowdown from an annual three-to-five point jump that occurred during the 1990s (Adalian "Webs" 9).

A tracking study by Lieberman Research Worldwide also revealed that, during summer 2000, *Survivor* ranked as the number two show of the year among adults ages18 to 49, second only to *E.R. Variety* proclaimed that "the idea that the networks can't attract large-scale audiences in the summertime with regular series—first challenged last year by 'Who Wants to Be a Millionaire,' doesn't hold much credence anymore. Nor does the notion that young viewers simply refuse to visit CBS' address" (Kissell and Schneider 19). Network programmers who once argued that it cost too much to put out new shows when so few viewers were available and reruns of fall programming were "free" were suddenly converts to reality television. NBC West Coast Operations President Scott Sassa opined that "as numbers for repeats get lower, the risk of replacement programming becomes less, and it becomes more advantageous to produce original programming. There's a greater opportunity to improve your performance" (Adalian, "Webs" 9).

While network television enables advertisers to target a huge audience, cable and the Internet can target specific viewer demographics and deliver them to advertisers at a lower cost. Viacom's cross-promotion of *Survivor* on CBS, its cable networks MTV and VH1, and its Internet websites CBS.com and MTV Networks Online enabled CBS to capture a young audience during the show's first episode and deliver it to advertisers along with a mass audience of 15.5 million. During its second week, the show attracted 18.1 million viewers, a 17 percent gain. (Schneider and Adalian 70). According to *Variety*, *Survivor* "gave CBS and Viacom tangible proof that corporate synergy works" by being the first CBS program to get the full marketing treatment from Viacom's youthful properties MTV and VH1 (Kissell and Schneider 19).

CBS's use of the Internet also promoted interactivity between viewers and *Survivor*, allowing the network to extend the program beyond the confines of the television set by encouraging audiences to participate in its dramatic trajectory by using other media to stay in touch with the show. Viewers stayed in touch with the program through the official *Survivor* website. Prolific coverage from established news outlets also generated several unsanctioned online homages as the websites *Survivor* Junkie and Megadice offered winner predictions, plot spoilers, conspiracy theories, and other information of varying quality (Bing and Oppelaar 5). Mobile media such as cellular telephones offer additional means of promoting this interactivity and provide valuable information about the audience that is impossible to gather from any other source. Text-based advertising campaigns have been conducted in various countries by major brands, including Coca-Cola, Nike, and McDonald's (McCartney C1).

The ability of Viacom to endlessly promote *Survivor* across multiple media improved CBS's ability to quickly capture a large audience during an era in which the network practice of ordering shows in small batches makes it imperative to transform a new show into a smash hit as quickly as possible. *Variety* observed that "the numbers for *Survivor* are all the more amazing given that *Survivor* had only 13 weeks to generate viewer interest and such a rabid following. Conversely, some of the top-rated programs of all time are finales of series—like all-time champ 'MASH'—that were on the air for many years" (Kissell and Schneider 19).

Survivor's relatively low cost and high ratings potential made the show imminently marketable worldwide, especially in the wake of CBS's purchase of television syndication giant King World in 1999. King World collaborates closely with international partners to produce shows carefully tailored to specific national markets, and creates customized promotional advertisements for international licensees (Compaine and Gomery 218). Overseas broadcasters that have licensed the American format of *Survivor* and created their own versions include China's CCTV, the Middle East satellite platform Gulf DTH, South Africa's SABC, Mexico's Televisa, and stations in Scandinavia, Eastern Europe, and throughout Asia (Guider 1).

The global popularity of *Survivor* is attributable, in part, to CBS's use of the economies of scale provided by the size of the U.S. television audience to sell the program cheaply in developing countries. The proven commercial appeal of *Survivor*'s format and the relatively low cost of reality television production also encourage foreign broadcasters to create their own versions of the program. Clarin, the Argentinian distributor of *Expedicion Robinson*, licensed *Survivor*'s format for these reasons. The modest cost of producing reality television proved very appealing in Argentina, where a global recession in 2002 led broadcasters to seek inexpensive programming with high ratings potential (Sutter M20). Local adaptations of reality television formats also typically satisfy quotas requiring a certain amount of locally produced programming (Magder 147). U.S. distributors typically make between $50,000 and $100,000 per episode from foreign sales of reality shows, but they can make more as a co-partner on localized, formatted versions. In 2004, Europe represented 75 percent of the revenues American television distributors pocketed from licensing their shows around the world (Hopewell and Guider 17).

The disappearance of American dramas and situation comedies from European prime time has led U.S. studios to focus on exporting reality shows to make up for the overall shortfall in their foreign revenues. Because almost 90 percent of U.S. exports are directed to North America, East Asia, and Western Europe, United States involvement in the WTO focuses on reducing tariffs and trade barriers in these regions. The U.S. version of *Survivor* is a Friday night mainstay of Sony Pictures Entertainment's AXN Action TV network, which airs in Singapore and Hong Kong (Osborne 32).

Although *Survivor* is a revenue bonanza for CBS, the origination of the show in England illustrates that European suppliers of reality television have also made inroads into the U.S. television market. Companies capable of producing a steady supply of low-cost programming nonetheless dominate the global distribution of reality television. Sold in 2000 to Telefonica, the Spanish telecommunications giant, reality television production company Endemol maintains partnerships with broadcasters in 22 countries in Asia, Europe, Latin America and North America.

The formation of Endemol Mexico in 2001 through a partnership with Mexico's state-owned Televisa network exemplifies how Endemol's ability to supply a high volume of low-cost programming raises market entry barriers and eliminates competitors by facilitating a strategic alliance with an established distributor. Endemol annually produces more than 25,000 hours of television, spread over approximately 400 different program series. The Endemol library also contains over 500 program formats (Endemol website). Televisa agreed under the partnership to purchase content from Endemol Mexico for five years, largely because Endemol's ability to deliver a steady stream of reality television shows neatly fits with Televisa's position as the world's largest producer and exporter of TV programming. Televisa also maintains a monopoly over Mexico's television market on the basis of its four national television networks and almost 260 affiliated stations, 225 of which the company owns either wholly or partially. Of every advertising dollar spent on television in Mexico, 70 cents goes to Televisa (Friedland and Millman A1). On this basis, Televisa also provides Endemol with access to a huge national audience.

The formation of advertising agencies with global reach provides evidence of the role of advertising in propagating the overseas proliferation of reality television. The largest advertising agency, Omnicon, has 14 major agencies in its portfolio, including BBDO Worldwide and DDB Needham Worldwide. Omnicon dominates the global advertising agency industry, along with WPP Group and Interpublic Group. Global consolidation is encouraged because the larger an advertising agency, the more leverage it has getting favorable terms for its clients with global commercial media (McChesney 86). "More and more, what [advertisers] want is to distribute their global dollars into fewer agency baskets," the *Wall Street Journal* observed in 1998 (Beatty 1).

The rise of transnational advertising agencies also enables sponsors such as Proctor & Gamble to penetrate developing countries with the offer of "free" programming, through which advertisers underwrite programming of general appeal and provide it free of charge to financially struggling broadcasters (Schiller 330). The top 10 global advertisers alone accounted for some 75 percent of the $36 billion spent by the 100 largest global marketers in 1997 (McChesney 84). Advertising sponsorship thus plays a pivotal role in determining the type of programming made and broadcast by foreign television producers in their native markets.

The competition for audiences and advertisers created by the proliferation of broadcast, cable, and satellite television overseas has led broadcasters in other countries to seek low-cost programming with immediate ratings potential attractive to advertisers. Nowhere has the commercialization of television been more rampant in recent years than in England, where declining public subsidization of TV has led to greater reliance on commercial means to support network activities. Peter Bazalgette, chairman of Endemol UK, observed in 2004 that "unlike the U.S., British networks used to have the time to grow a show because the competitive pressures weren't all that great. Now you've got three weeks to succeed or the show will be pulled from its slot" (qtd. in Clarke A1).

The consequence of an increasing number of channels in formerly public television markets competing for funding and audiences is that broadcasters must spend greater and greater sums on marketing to get their shows noticed, intensifying pressures on program funding. The pressures on overseas networks to control production costs has in turn led to the concentration of television production in the hands of companies most able to supply low-cost, high volume programming. *Variety* observed in 2004, for example, that Spain's independent production sector had in the past five years experienced rampant concentration, with 10 production companies turning out 33 percent of television programming (de Pablos A8). Television distribution is also tightly controlled in Spain.

The adaptability of reality television shows to local cultures and the convertibility of the format into a virtual infomercial for sponsors' products raises a concern about the role of reality television in propagating the culture of consumption in both the United States and other nations targeted by transnational capitalism. Herbert Schiller warns of the encroachment of advertising into such spheres as public television, the library, and nation-state relations, declaring that "the ultimate sponsor of the world's TV programming — the daily culture of the late twentieth century — will be transnational corporate enterprise" (330).

Consumption of Reality Television: Transforming Citizens into Consumers

The global success of reality television is attributable to the practice of licensing the format of a show to overseas broadcasters for adaptation to specific markets. The strategy of formatting springs from the principal of product differentiation, through which network executives attempt to replicate a successful show by blatantly imitating it. Hits are so rare on network television that network executives think that a bald imitation stands a better chance of getting ratings than a show that stands alone. This results in the repackaging of old forms in slightly different permutations (Gitlin 77–85). In the wake of *Survivor*'s success, television executives aggressively pursued imitations of it as the number of reality television hours on broadcast television skyrocketed from four-and-a-half to 19 hours a week between Fall, 2002 and Fall, 2004 (McNary 21).

Paralleling this proliferation of reality television programming was the repetition of what the *New York Times* called a "hamsters-in-a-box" narrative design. The strategy of casting individuals on the basis of type and forcing them to work and live together became cross-pollinated with various genres, including game shows, gross-out contests, makeovers, dating programs, situation comedies, and satires (Nussbaum 2). The minimal difference between these many shows stems from the pressure of the marketplace to duplicate a financially successful show.

Financed by advertisers interested in cultivating new consumers abroad, the development of reality television as a format that flexibly incorporates national ideologies on a nation-by-nation basis further suggests that reality TV is first and foremost a commodity. In licensing the *Survivor* format from a British production company, CBS found a program that can be tailored on a market-by-market basis around the world by integrating the game show and the adventure drama into a hybrid formula. Rather than democratizing global television programming, this trend organizes citizens into consumers by reifying capitalism as an ideology and a way of life. The design of *Survivor* as a game show/adventure/drama hybrid facilitates the placement of products in competitive circumstances that blend adventure and consumption.

In this way, the premise of the show — game show competitors seeking adventure in exotic locations that render global politics invisible — fuels demand for a lifestyle of conspicuous consumption around the world. The director of marketing for Sony's AXN Action TV Network, on which *Survivor* airs in East Asia, exclaimed that "the focus on action and adventure is something that's really picking up — it's a new lifestyle for the young in Asia, a fact borne out by the rise in sales of four-by-four vehicles, for example" (Osborne 32).

The design of *Survivor* also affirms consumption as a way of life both by attracting advertising and enabling its producers to develop lucrative licensing deals that extend its shelf life. By organizing leisure time around the consumption of both these programs and pricey ancillary merchandise, *Survivor* encourages viewers to participate in a commodified system of exchange. While merchandising tie-ins have been around since the advent of television, they are now far more commonplace. There are now 150 *Survivor*-themed products available, ranging from CDs to bug spray, to board games, and bandanas (Madger 150). Reality television's organization of the audience into consumers socializes the public into behaving like a market and as consumers rather than citizens.

Conclusion

This essay argues that the worldwide proliferation of reality television is a product of the increasing concentration of ownership in the television industry, the globalization of commercial TV, and the fragmentation of the worldwide audience. The dependence of the U.S. and other governments on capital investment has led to the implementation of policies that enable the largest media corporations to curtail access to prime time television through in-house production, co-production, and by favoring programs that offer the lowest risk and the highest potential for ratings. The privatization of formerly public overseas broadcasters has also led television programmers in developing nations to seek out inexpensive programming capable of attracting advertisers and viewers.

The first casualty of this trend is educational programming. Television producers, advertisers, and networks know that programs that are too long, too difficult to comprehend, or simply too boring will lead viewers to switch channels. In this way, reality television turns attention away from issues such as poverty in developing countries. The victory of a contestant from the African country of Makubale over a competitor from Tanzania on *Big Brother Africa* provided, according to *Variety*, "a welcome distraction from nationwide strikes in the impoverished country, where most people earn less than $1 a day" (DeJager 19). While some celebrate reality television's global popularity as a sign of the democratization of television production and distribution, a political economic study of reality television compels us to consider that economic determinism limits the possibilities of reality television's potential for democratic communication.

Works Cited

Adalian, Joseph. "Webs Storm Beach with Firstrun Fare." *Variety* 7–13 August 2000: 11.
_____. "Moonves Says CBS Ready to Go It Alone." *Variety* 18–24 January 1999: 58.
Adalian, Joseph and Michael Schneider. "'Survivor' Changes Webs' Reality." *Variety* 12–18 June 2000: 9.
Ang, Ien. *Watching Dallas: Soap Opera and the Melodramatic Imagination.* New York: Methuen, 1985.
Bagdikian, Ben H. *The Media Monopoly.* 4th ed. Boston: Beacon Press, 1992.
Beatty, Sally. "Survey Expects Pace of Mergers to Pick Up on Madison Avenue." *Wall Street Journal* 21 May 1998: 1.
_____. "Who Owns Prime Time? Industrial and Institutional Conflict over Television Programming and Broadcast Rights." *Framing Friction: Media and Social Conflict.* Ed. Mary S. Mander. Urbana: University of Illinois Press, 1999. 125–160.
Beatty, Sally and Jeanne Lynn Hall. *Big Media, Big Money: Cultural Texts and Political Economics.* Lanham, MD: Rowman and Littlefield, 2003.
Bettig, Ronald V. "Who Owns Prime Time?: Industrial and Institutional Conflict Over Television Programming and Broadcast Rights." *Framing Fiction: Media and Social Conflict.* Ed. Mary S. Mander. Urbana: University of Illinois Press, 1999. 125–60.
Bing, Jonathan and Justin Oppelaar. "'Rat' Race to Publish 1st Survivor Book Begins.'" *Variety* 28 August–3 September 2000: 4.
"Burnett Likes Mad Ave." *Advertising Age* 19 May 2003: 3.

Carter, Bill. "Amid Some Storms, CBS Finds a Surge." *New York Times* 24 November 2003: B1.

Clarke, Steve. "Quick Hits Are Key." *Variety* 22–28 November 2004: A1.

Compaine, Benjamin and Douglas Gomery. *Who Owns the Media?: Competition and Concentration in the Mass Media.* Mahwah, N.J.: Lawrence Erlbaum Associates, 2000.

De Jager, Christelle. "'Big Bro' Gives Reality New Meaning." *Variety* 15–21 September 2003: 19.

de Pablos, Emiliano. "Production Players." *Variety* 20–26 September 2004: A8.

"Endemol website." 15 May 2005 <www.endemol.com/index.xml>

Feuer, Jane. *Seeing Through the Eighties: Television and Reaganism.* Durham: Duke University Press, 1995.

Fiske, John. *Television Culture.* New York: Routledge, 1987.

_____. "Global, National, Local? Some Problems of Culture in a Postmodern World." *Velvet Light Trap* 40 (1997): 58–66.

Friedland, Jonathan and Joel Millman. "Fresh Lineup: Led By a Young Heir, Mexico's Televisa Puts a New Stress on Profits." *Wall Street Journal* 10 July 1998: A1.

Fry, Andy. "Europe Secure as Leader of Reality Programming." *Variety* 25 September–1 October 2000: M4.

Gitlin, Todd. *Inside Prime Time.* New York: Pantheon Books, 1983.

Guider, Elizabeth. "Eye Floats Survivor Worldwide." *Variety* 18 January 2001: 1.

Hall, Stuart. "Brave New World." *Socialist Review* 21.1 (1991): 57–64.

Haralovich, Mary Beth and Michael T. Trossett. "'Expect the Unexpected': Narrative Pleasure and Uncertainty Due to Chance in *Survivor*." *Reality TV: Remaking Television Culture.* Eds. Susan Murray and Laurie Ouellette. New York: New York University Press, 2004. 75–96.

Harvey, David. *The Condition of Postmodernity.* Boston: Blackwell, 1989.

Hopewell, John and Elizabeth Guider. "Reality's Two-Way Highway." *Variety* 19–25 July 2000:17.

Jessop, Bob. *State Theory: Putting Capitalist States in Their Place.* University Park, PA: Penn State Press, 1990.

Jhally, Sut. "The Political Economy of Culture." *Cultural Politics in Contemporary America*, Eds. Ian Angus and Sut Jhally. New York: Routledge, 1989. 65–81.

Kissell, Rick. "Survivor Fittest in All Demos." *Variety* 31 July-6 August 2000: 20.

Kissell, Rick and Schneider, M. "Summer Serves as Eye-Opener." *Variety* 28 August–3 September 2000:19.

Litman, Barry. "Network Oligopoly Power: An Economic Analysis." *Hollywood in the Age of Television.* Ed. Tino Balio. Boston: Unwin Hyman, 1990. 115–144.

Littleton, Cynthia. "Dialogue: Mark Burnett." *Hollywood Reporter.* 26 May 2004. 18 Aug. 2004 <www.hollywoodreporter.com/thr/crafts/feature/display.jsp?vnu_content_id =1000523184>

Madger, Ted. "The End of TV 101: Reality Programs, Formats, and the New Business of Television." *Reality TV: Remaking Television Culture*, Eds. Laurie Oullette and Susan Murray. New York: New York University Press, 2004. 137–156.

McCarthy, Michael. "Also Starring (Your Product Name Here); Brands Increasingly Make Presence Known in TV Shows." *USA Today* 12 August 2004: B1.

_____. "Sponsors Line Up for Survivor Sequel." *USA Today* 9 October 2004: B1.

McCartney, Neil. "Can You Hear It Now?" *Variety* 29 March — April 4 2004: C1.

McChesney, Robert W. *Rich Media, Poor Democracy: Communication Politics in Dubious Times.* New York: The New Press, 1999.

McClintock, Pamela. "Mad Ave's Firm Grasp on Reality." *Variety* 19–25 April 2004: 15.

McNary, Dave. "Coming to Terms with Reality." *Variety* 4–10 October 2004: 21.

Nussbaum, Emily. "The Woman Who Gave Birth to Reality TV." *Variety* 22 February 2004: 2.

Olson, Scott R. *Hollywood Planet: Global Media and the Comparative Advantage of Narrative Transparency.* Mahwah, NJ: Lawrence Erlbaum Associates, 1999.

"Opensecrets.org." 10 June 2005. <www.opensecrets.org>

Osborne, Magz. "AXN Packs Reality Fare, Hopes Viewers Will Follow." *Variety* 5–11 February 2001: 32.

Raphael, Chad. "The Political Economic Origins of Reali-TV." *Reality TV: Remaking Television Culture.* Eds. Susan Murray and Laurie Oullette, New York: New York University Press, 2004. 119–136.

Schiller, Herbert. "The Privatization of Culture." *Cultural Politics in Contemporary America.* Eds. Ian Angus and Sut Jhally. New York: Routledge, 1989. 317–332.

Schneider Michael and Joseph Adalian. "Nets Get It Together." *Variety* 22–28 May 2000: 15.

Schwankert, Steve. "China Opens Up Pay TV to Premium Tier." *Variety* 24–30 March 2003: 23.

Stern. Christopher. "Webs, Affils Scrap over O&O Caps." *Variety* 18–24 January 1999: 53.

Sutter, Mary. "Latins Like Ultra-Reality." *Variety* 26 March-1 April 2001: M20.

"TV's Peeper Producers are Powerhouses." *Variety* 25 September -1 October 2000: 1.

Notes

1. Prime time refers to a twenty-two hour weekly period spanning 8PM to 11PM Monday through Saturday, with an extra hour on Sunday.

2. Vertical integration refers to a system of organization that allows a single company or group of closely meshed companies to control at least two functions within the three principal activities of production, distribution, and exhibition. Horizontal integration refers to a system in which a single company or group of interrelated companies control multiple companies in one of these three areas of the media industry.

3. An example of an investment strike would be the refusal by networks to deficit finance programs as they faced more competition from cable programming. Deficit financing, a process under which networks advance only a percentage of the total cost of production to an independent producer, became during the 1950s a means of consolidating network control with respect to program suppliers. Under this practice, the networks leveraged producers into forfeiting up to 50 percent of the profits earned by a program or series from its network run in exchange for initial financing and eventual broadcast of it, as well as other rights, including the right to distribute the program in domestic and foreign markets and share in the profit from syndication sales in these markets (Litman 1990).

4. The number of 39 percent was not chosen randomly. Had the 35 percent limit been maintained, CBS would have been forced to sell off some stations to be in compliance. Access to 39 percent of the national television audience allows CBS to offer advertisers the largest possible television audience and better control program distribution by dominating relations with affiliate stations.

5. Opensecrets.org is the official website of The Center for Responsive Politics. According to its website, the center is "a non-partisan, non-profit research group based in Washington, D.C. that tracks money in politics, and its effect on elections and public policy. The center conducts computer-based research on campaign finance issues for the news media, academics, activists, and the public at large. The center's work is aimed at creating a more educated voter, an involved citizenry, and a more responsive government."

6. Surveying use of the word "quality" in the popular press, Jane Feuer defines quality pro-

duction values as innovative visual style, the use of film over video, actors with training in improvisational work rather than television, and a high degree of creative freedom. See Feuer, Jane. "The MTM Style." In *Television: The Critical View*, 4th ed, Ed. Horace Newcomb, New York: Oxford University Press, 1987, 52–84. *Survivor* arguably incorporates these traits. As Mary Beth Haralovich and Michael W. Trosset (76) note, the opening of *Survivor 1: Borneo* used seven hours of nonstop shooting coverage, one take, live, and 23 crewmembers. *Survivor* is also shot on film rather than video, and Executive Producer Mark Burnett oversees almost all aspects of the show, from "casting sessions to selecting specific musical interludes" ("TV's Peeper Producers Are Powerhouses" 40).

6

Domestication Incorporation: Cribs and The Osbournes as Narratives of Domestication

David S. Escoffery

Prologue: Going into Virginia Harned's Home

In the exquisite green and white and silver drawing room on the second floor of the Southern home, No. 37 W. 69th St., was a tall pearl and silver vase, from which flamed a dozen jacqueminot roses. When the interviewer was summoned to the library above, she found sitting before the fire, her hand shading her eyes from the firelight, her feet upon a leopard skin, a jacqueminot rose humanized [Patterson 94].

In the April, 1904 issue of *Theatre Magazine,* readers were treated to Ada Patterson's interview with then-famous Broadway actress Virginia Harned. Married to the even more successful actor E. H. Southern, Virginia Harned had often been criticized for her love of wealth and material gain, very un-womanly traits. The title of the article, "A 'Material' Actress," plays on the public perception of Harned and the interviewer's contrary impression that the "material" most important to this stage beauty is her marriage. Near the beginning of the article, Patterson says of Harned, "Her own marriage has been triumphantly successful, a very model of a marriage, that makes the necessary absences of herself and her star spouse from each other poignantly painful" (93).

The goal of this article is clearly to humanize Harned, to show her as a devoted, loving spouse, not a greedy actress. In order to accomplish this goal, the interviewer, Ada Patterson, spends a lot of time describing the details of the Southern home. Part of the appeal of these descriptions, of course, is wish-fulfillment for the readers who could not afford to live on West 69th Street in Manhattan. They thus love to hear about the expensive furniture and details like the "pearl and silver vase" (94) brimming with expensive roses. The effect of walking into Harned's home is more complex, however, than to simply satisfy the curiosity of those who long to know how the stars live. It was actually already a common narrative device used since the middle of the nineteenth century to humanize actresses by showing them in a domestic setting. Many interviews with successful actresses in nineteenth- and early twentieth-century America were depicted as taking place not on stage or in an office, but in the home.[1] Oftentimes, these articles were accompanied by photos of these famous women standing in the kitchen, the most domestic of home spaces.

Humanizing the actress was important at the time because working women, especially those making more than most men, were considered a threat to society.[2] One effect of articles like this interview with Virginia Harned was to take this threatening force and place it back — quite literally — into the domestic sphere. The narrative that runs through this article (and many others) is one of domestication. Ada Patterson goes out of her way to show Miss Harned as a traditional wife, a romantic woman very much in love with her husband. Even more, she takes us on a tour of Harned's home, focusing on details like furniture, fabrics, color choices, and decorative touches. She describes things like the "leopard skin" (94) rug on the floor of the library, and the color scheme in the drawing room. The collection of these detailed descriptions of the home serves to domesticate Virginia Harned, making her a traditional woman, not a threat to the male order.

Domestication as Incorporation

The same process of domestication visible in magazine interviews with actresses in the nineteenth and early twentieth centuries is still in use today, particularly in reality television shows like *Cribs* and *The Osbournes*. In order to demonstrate how this narrative of domestication works to take threatening forces and incorporate them back into the dominant order, I will make use of Raymond Williams' discussion of hegemony. In *Marxism and Literature*, Williams speaks of hegemony as something more than a simple system of beliefs and ideas, an ideology. For Williams, hegemony is a process, part of every aspect of our lives, something that we live deeply every single day. Ideology may be a system of ideas that could be dominant in a society, but ideas are not enough to control how we live and think. Hegemony, on the other hand, is a pervasive system, something much less definable than an ideology.

In much analysis, according to Williams, the terms ideology and hege-mony are used almost interchangeably. In Williams' work, however, he argues that hegemony operates on a deeper level than formal ideology. It is a lived experience of dominance, perhaps fueled and supported by a par-ticular ideology, but operating in every area of daily life. Williams claims,

> Hegemony, then, is not only the articulate upper level of "ideology," nor are its forms of control only those ordinarily seen as "manipulation" or "indoctrina-tion." It is a whole body of practices and expectations, over the whole of living: our senses and assignments of energy, our shaping perceptions of ourselves and our world [110].

Every aspect of our daily lives can function to create and reify the forces of dominance within a society. Control and power are not maintained sim-ply by force. Even Louis Althusser's notion of "ideological state appara-tuses"[3] ("Ideology") — those formal aspects of society like schools or churches that exercise control by shaping people's ideologies — do not pen-etrate deeply enough for Williams. Hegemony is a "lived system of mean-ings and values — constitutive and constituting — which as they are experienced as practices appear as reciprocally confirming" (110).

Not all practices, of course, be they systems of thought or works of art, necessarily support the dominant hegemony. Williams notes, "The reality of any hegemony, in the extended political and cultural sense, is that, while by definition it is always dominant, it is never either total or exclusive" (113). There is a continuous process of struggle and change as the domi-nant fights to maintain its position and alternative or oppositional forces threaten its place in society. Hegemony, then, is always active, never sta-ble. However, all oppositional or alternative tendencies can be seen in some ways as contributing to the dominant hegemony. The counter-culture is actually created and limited by the dominant culture in a continuous process that can be analyzed by examining complex examples such as works of art. At times, the oppositional culture may grow to be strong enough to actually threaten the dominant culture, and then "to the extent that [these counter-cultural forces] are significant the decisive hegemonic function is to control or transform or even incorporate them" (113).

Incorporation is an important term in cultural analysis. Generally, it is taken to refer to the process through which oppositional ideas or prac-tices are brought back into the mainstream. Of course, this process can occur in many different ways: by force, by indoctrination in schools or hos-pitals, or by more subtle means. Especially important in contemporary soci-ety is the role played by the mass media in the process of incorporation. Often media outlets like television are responsible for bringing alternative or oppositional points-of-view to a larger audience — hence the hostile reac-tion many parents and family groups had to the early years of MTV.[4] More complex, however, are the processes by which these counter-cultures are incorporated back into the mainstream. For Williams, what is most important about incorporation in contemporary society is the depth at which it occurs. True, schools and parents and churches perform their incorporative functions and teach people how to live "properly" in the dominant order. However, Williams claims,

> [I]n advanced capitalism, because of changes in the social character of labour, in the social character of communications, and in the social character of decision making, the dominant culture reaches much further than ever before in capitalist society into hitherto "reserved" or "resigned" areas of experience and practice and meaning [125–6].

It reaches all the way into our television sets, even on channels like MTV that seem to support alternative or even oppositional ideas.

I would like to put forward domestication as one of the means by which this incorporation of counter-cultural forces takes place. There are, of course, many such methods, but the rise of reality television has allowed for the narrative of domestication to be deployed very effectively. This narrative is the same one that was used in the past in interviews like the one with Virgina Harned with which I opened this paper. It involves several key features. First, this narrative always involves a very detailed description of the threatening celebrity's home. As I have said, these elaborate descriptions (be they verbal or pictoral) serve a dual purpose. They lure the audience in by giving them a glimpse of the luxury they probably cannot afford. However, they also set the stage for the domestication that will follow. The more details we are given about this home, the more "real" it becomes, the more we can see it as a place where this person really lives. It is not a setting, a fictitious place, at least in the mind of the audience. Details provide authenticity.

Along with these detailed descriptions of the home — the article on Harned goes so far as to provide her exact address — it is important to show the celebrity interacting with the space, living *in* it. The home must not be some place in which the celebrity is not comfortable. Thus, Harned is presented to us sitting in her library by the fire, her bare feet resting on the leopard skin rug. Often, this narrative goes out of its way to metaphorically link the celebrity to his or her home by depicting the home as somehow a reflection of the star's personality. We see this narrative trope very clearly in the interview with Virginia Harned. Ada Patterson spends time describing the beautiful jacqueminot roses blooming in a vase in Harned's drawing room. Later, she refers to Harned as "a jacqueminot rose humanized" (94). Thus, she belongs in this beautiful home, which sets her off in the same way that the pearl and silver vase in the drawing room sets off those roses.

Finally, this type of narrative of domestication always shows the threatening celebrity engaged in some sort of household activity. That is, it is not necessarily enough to show that this famous person feels comfortable in this domestic space, or even that he or she fits there in a metaphorical sense. In order to fully domesticate the celebrity, it is often necessary to show them actually doing something domestic. Thus, in the Harned interview, we hear about the dinner party she gave the previous night and how tired it made her. She says, "I gave a supper last night to a lot of clever people, and I enjoyed it very much, yet you see the result. I was so tired that I've been in bed nearly all day" (qtd. in Patterson 95). Not only do we get a sense of the housework she must have been doing, serving as hostess, but we also hear about her sleeping late, something that most women in the workforce would never have been able to do.

This narrative of domestication is a particularly effective tool of incorporation. On the one hand, it draws the reader or viewer in by offering them a glimpse of the good life, giving them a chance to see how the other half lives. On the other hand, it simultaneously humanizes that other, presenting him or her as "a regular person, just like me." Especially as we see the celebrity interact with the domestic environment, we (or society) can no longer be threatened by their money, their success, their race, or their background. They become part of the dominant order, in which everybody uses the same domestic products and shares in the same daily rituals of living. In other words, it is particularly difficult to be counter-cultural while brushing one's teeth or doing the dishes. Each domestic act that is depicted, then, incorporates the celebrity more and more into the mainstream culture.

Cribs *and the Domestication*
of Hip Hop Culture

One of the first reality programs to make use of the incorporative function of this narrative of domestication was MTV's *Cribs*. This program first aired on September 20, 2000, and from day one it has specialized in taking viewers through the homes of the bad boys and girls of rock and hip hop. In fact, the very first episode of *Cribs* featured the home of heavy metal icon Ozzy Osbourne. MTV was so impressed with the results of this show that they decided to create an entire reality program showing life in the Osbourne household, which will be discussed in the next section. Other notable celebrities who invited viewers into their homes during the first season of *Cribs* include heavy metal singer Sebastian Bach (front man for the band Skid Row), hip hop singer Sisqo (very popular that year with his hit single "The Thong Song"), and infamous rapper Snoop Doggy Dogg.

The show clearly follows the pattern of domestication visible in the interview with Virginia Harned and other articles on actresses from the nineteenth and early twentieth centuries. Each episode generally takes viewers into the homes of two or three celebrities, and for each crib visited, the camera pays particular attention to all of the details of the home that might interest viewers, from the size of the television to the colors of the walls and the style of the furniture. We see detailed views of almost every room in the celebrity's home, including bathrooms and walk-in closets. Artwork on the walls and decorative pieces on the shelves are revealed to viewers in an effort to showcase everything about the celebrity and his or her home. In keeping with the second part of the pattern, these decorative touches often reveal a lot about the artist's personality, connecting him or her with the home. It becomes clear that this is the place where the celebrity belongs, where he or she feels comfortable. Thus, a famous rapper may have pictures of star athletes on the wall, pictures that match the athletic jersey that he is wearing during the interview. Finally, each episode includes a number of moments in which the celebrity interacts with the domestic environment in significant ways. We see rappers cooking, rock stars cleaning up, and athletes decorating. In one episode, for example, rapper Ludacris opens his refrigerator and pulls out the only two things he keeps inside, Kentucky Fried Chicken and Corona Extra beer (both a statement of domestic life and a not-so-subtle advertisement for his album "Chicken and Beer").

For the purposes of this paper, I will focus on the depiction of hip hop and rap stars on *Cribs*, in part because they appear so often on the show, and in part because I will be dealing with the world of heavy metal in my discussion of *The Osbournes*. In particular, I will be discussing the representation of "gangsta" rappers Snoop Dogg and Ice-T. With the development of gangsta rap in the 1990s, along with its growing mainstream popularity, these artists posed a clear threat to the dominant order. One of the first gangsta rappers, Ice-T was born Tracy Morrow in Newark, New Jersey. After his parents died in a car accident, however, he moved in with an aunt in South Central Los Angeles and became inextricably linked with West Coast rap culture. He made a name for himself rapping about what he knew best, "the gang-infested, pimp-heavy streets of South Central" ("Official"). Snoop Doggy Dogg, the rap name of Calvin Broadus, was born and raised in southern California. He, too, was immersed in the world of gangs and drugs from an early age. Soon after high school, he was arrested for cocaine possession, and he has been in trouble with the law several times since then, including an arrest for accessory to murder in 1993 (by 1996, he was acquitted of all charges). Both Ice-T and Snoop Dogg used their knowledge of the streets as an entry into the music world, bringing a sense of authenticity to their music, and they both used music as a way to escape the cycle of poverty and gangs that they saw and rapped about.

The threat posed by these rappers can perhaps best be represented through the outcry that followed the 1992 release of the song "Cop Killer" by Ice-T's band Body Count. Ice-T, who styled himself the O.G., Original Gangster, created a storm of controversy with his outraged cry for black men to start shooting the police officers who harass them instead of helping them. The lyrics say,

> I got my twelve gauge sawed off.
> I got my headlights turned off.
> I'm 'bout to bust some shots off.
> I'm 'bout to dust some cops off.
> I'm a cop killer, better you than me.
> Cop killer, fuck police brutality!
> Cop Killer, I know your family's grieving
> (Fuck 'em!)
> Cop Killer, but tonight we get even [Ice-T].

Reactions to the song were so intense that Time Warner, Ice-T's record label, was eventually forced to remove the song "Cop Killer" from the album "Body Count."

Although Ice-T claimed to be merely "reporting from the front" (qtd. in Joseph D. Johnson "Cop Killer"), and defended his First Amendment right to express the anger of the black community who felt oppressed by the police, he was attacked by everybody from Pat Buchanan to Bill Clinton. Buchanan blamed the L.A. riots on gangsta rap songs like this one, saying, "[W]here did the mob come from ... it came out of rock concerts where rap music celebrates raw lust and cop killing" (qtd. in Johnson "Cop Killer"). The song engendered such a strong reaction not just because mainstream America feared that black people everywhere would start shooting police officers. A large part of the threat came from the song's "obvious popularity amongst white teenagers" (Johnson "Cop Killer"). When middle class white kids in the suburbs were screaming, "Fuck the police," the threat was really hitting home.

Given the level of fear Ice-T was able to generate during the summer of 1992, it may seem surprising that he now plays a police officer on the popular television show *Law and Order: Special Victims Unit*. How was this threatening force, the O.G. himself, transformed into a popular actor on a hit television show? Part of that transformation came from Ice's appearance on MTV's *Cribs* in March, 2001. Ice led MTV's cameras through his 10,000 square foot mansion in the Hollywood Hills, overlooking Beverly Hills, quite a home for someone who grew up in the projects of South Central. As he puts it during the interview,

> Considerin' when I was growin' up, I was living in South Central Los Angeles, lookin' up at these hills, like, saying, "I wonder what those people live like, up on…" Brother like me, as ignorant and as wild as I am to make it up here, that's a great accomplishment for myself [*Cribs: Hip Hop* DVD].

This gangsta rapper, then, is presented as an example of the American dream, someone who pulled himself out of poverty and can now afford a lavish lifestyle that includes exotic cars and a retractable roof over his pool. Of course, Ice then undermines that Horatio Alger tale when he calls out to Beverly Hills, "Kiss my ass!" (*Cribs*).

In fact, the entire *Cribs* segment with Ice-T functions on those two contrasting levels, part domestic tale of boy made good, and part outlandish flouting of mainstream values. I would argue, however, that showcasing Ice-T's oppositional attitudes as part of a trip through his house neutralizes those attitudes, making him seem like simply an extreme version of the average person. One controversial aspect of Ice-T's personality that we see here in this dual light is his association with sexuality and the pimp lifestyle. Ice-T claims to have been a pimp, and he has worked the attitude and language that go along with that profession into his image. So when he shows a picture of his young son, he is quick to note, "At one years [sic.] old, he had on his pimp boots" (*Cribs*). This comment could easily be considered offensive, as people wonder what sort of values this man is teaching his son. However, the picture of the little boy in his diaper is very cute, and it is shown as part of a montage of family pictures that Ice-T has displayed in his living room. Also, it is clear how much he loves his son, whom he calls the "leader and crown ruler of the domain" (*Cribs*).

Ice's own sexuality comes to the forefront when he takes the cameras into his bedroom. Here, however, the often threatening sexuality of the black man (and one who is a self-styled pimp, no less), is played for laughs. After claiming he does not remember what he did the night before, he opens the door to reveal a video camera pointed at the bed. There is then a moment of pure slapstick comedy, clearly scripted, as Ice tries to move the camera out of the way. He knocks the camera over and stumbles on the tripod, making himself look more like a bumbling clown than a bad-ass "playa." The humor of the moment humanizes Ice-T, turning him into someone like us, someone who can be embarrassed, someone who is not always suave and in control.

One signature moment on most segments of *Cribs* is the trip into the kitchen, our peek inside the star's cupboards and refrigerator. This moment really domesticates the subject, especially as we see and identify with many of the food products the interview subjects consume. Of course, many of them have expensive champagne like Dom Perignon or Cristal, but they also have milk and bread and assorted sugary breakfast cereals. In the Ice-T segment, however, we do not get to see his kitchen. We get a similar result, however, when Ice shows off the vending machine he has installed in his house. He explains why everybody should have a vending machine, saying, "'Cuz you know how your friends are always in your kitchen, tryin' to go through your cupboards and eat your cookies and stuff. You want some Skittles or somethin,' come down here. It's a buck. Stop beggin'" (*Cribs*). Once again, we see the trademark Ice-T attitude, tempered, however, by the domestic image of Ice using his street smarts to protect the cookies in his cupboard.

Nicknamed "Snoopy" by his mother because of his resemblance to Charlie Brown's beagle, rapper Snoop Doggy Dogg appeared on *Cribs* during its first season, in an episode that first aired on October 18, 2000. This segment shows the same duality we saw in the tour through Ice-T's home. Snoop is depicted as both a hardcore gangsta and a completely domesticated family man. On the one hand, he points out the "wall of fame" in his recording studio, saying, "Every gang bang homie I got come through here and sign the wall. Some of 'em still alive, some of 'em in jail for life, some of 'em still on the streets. But this is what we represent right here, this gangsta rap thing" (*Cribs*). Clearly, Snoop is demonstrating his credibility here, and an audience member familiar with his legal troubles will be reminded that Snoop himself has spent time in jail. It is difficult, however, to find even the "wall of fame" to be dangerous, given that it is shown to us right after Snoop has just shown off the very elegant formal sitting room in the front of his house. Although Snoop refers to this luxurious space as "the room where nobody get to kick it at" (*Cribs*), it is part of his house that he is proud of, and it clearly separates him from the gangsta life.

Snoop may claim that he brings "that ghetto environment out here to this nice neighborhood" (*Cribs*), but his house is much more plush than street. And throughout the interview, Snoop is depicted as a domesticated family man. He speaks lovingly of his wife, who seems to play the "proper" domestic role of homemaker and cook, and he very clearly loves his children. His living room features numerous family photos, and he makes a particular point of mentioning that his daughter does not appear in one of them because it was taken shortly before her birth. Snoop sounds very much like the doting father when he shows off his kids' rooms. Then, expressing a thought that every father has had, Snoop says, "She growin' up so fast" (*Cribs*), as we see him stroking his baby daughter's face.

As in many *Cribs* segments, except for the one with Ice-T, here we see extensive footage of the star's kitchen. Snoop's enormous kitchen is presented in great detail, and Snoop himself seems to really enjoy talking about the food he loves and showing off the contents of his fridge and pantry. In a funny moment of the same duality we see throughout *Cribs*, Snoop opens his freezer, saying, "We keep it gangsta up in here, man. Popsicles, leggo my eggo. [Laughs loudly.]" (*Cribs*). Here we see one of the most effective techniques of domestication in the *Cribs* repertoire, product placement. Even a gangsta rapper can hardly seem dangerous when we realize that he eats popular food like Eggos, just like everyone else in America. The footage shown to viewers reinforces this message. When Snoop opens his fridge, the camera pans up and down several times, giving us all an excellent look at the items inside. Although some of the labels have been turned so that we cannot see them, it is still easy to recognize a number of familiar brand names, including Sprite, Ocean Spray, Minute Made, and Heinz. We also get an excellent look inside Snoop's pantry, which is full of junk food like Ding Dongs. Of the junk food, he says, "S'posed to be for the kids, but I'm the biggest kid in the house" (*Cribs*). With that, Snoop is no longer a threatening force; he has been fully domesticated.

The Osbournes *and the Domestication of the Prince of Darkness*

Throughout the 1980s (and beyond, in legend if not in fact), who was considered a greater threat to the souls of Western children than Ozzy Osbourne? The former front man from the heavy metal band Black Sabbath, Ozzy went on to a hugely successful solo career and has courted controversy with each step in his career. He became infamous after biting the head off of a live bat at a concert in Des Moines, Iowa in 1981. In spite of the fact that Ozzy thought the bat, which someone had thrown on stage, was a rubber toy, it became a symbol of everything his critics hated about the man and his heavy metal music. Ozzy's notoriety was cemented after the 1984 death of a teenage fan who shot himself while listening to the song "Suicide Solution." Ozzy was eventually sued by the boy's parents, who claimed that the song included subliminal lyrics[5] and specially created musical tones, called hemisync tones, which make listeners more susceptible to influences and suggestions. Although the suit was eventually dismissed, Ozzy's reputation as the madman of metal was solidified. Indeed, based on this image, Ozzy came to call himself the Prince of Darkness.

When Ozzy and his family were featured on the first episode of *Cribs*, however, they began a phenomenon that was destined to alter Ozzy's image entirely. The episode was a great success, and the people at MTV were so taken with Ozzy's quirky clan that they developed an entire reality show about life in the Osbourne house. Thus, the reality program/mock *Father Knows Best*-style sitcom *The Osbournes* was born. When this show first aired on MTV on March 12, 2002, it was an instant ratings hit, spawning a near mania for all thighs Osbourne. Part of what people found so appealing about the show was its parodic skewering of the traditional family sitcom. From the opening credits, which are designed to resemble the opening from a typical sitcom, through the use of segment titles and cheesy music, the program is put together like a family sitcom in the vein of *Father Knows Best*, *Leave It to Beaver*, or *Ozzy and Harriet*. The joke, of course, is that this is *not* Ozzy and Harriet, but Ozzy Osbourne. The swearing and dysfunction presented provide a humorous contrast to the domestic sitcom setting.

As with *Cribs*, however, that domestic setting does a lot to reduce the threat posed by the heavy metal icon, incorporating him back into the mainstream. In fact, *The Osbournes* follows exactly the pattern of domestication I have been documenting here. First, we see the Osbourne house in great detail. The very first episode chronicles the family's move into their new home in Beverly Hills. Thus, we see the empty house begin to fill up with the family's possessions. The camera roams through each room, lingering on details like furniture, artwork, and decorative objects. As Ozzy's things are moved in, we get an excellent sense of the ways in which this house really reflects Ozzy's personality. They have painted crucifixes on the walls, and more are added to the front door. We also see boxes labeled "Devil Heads" and "Dead Things" along with those that say "Pots and Pans" and "Linens" (*Osbournes*). Finally, we also see many examples throughout the series of Ozzy interacting with his domestic environment, often in humorous ways. Near the beginning of the first episode, Ozzy tries to figure out how to work the remote control on his expensive new home entertainment system. When he fails completely, he is forced to call his son Jack to help him get the TV working so that he can watch the History Channel. He is depicted, then, as a man who just wants to watch documentaries on TV, but one who cannot even get his remote control to work.

Many of the other tropes of domestication used in *Cribs* can be seen in episodes of *The Osbournes* as well. For example, food and kitchen activity are featured prominently. In one short scene from the fourth episode of Season One, Ozzy sees some trash on the kitchen floor and goes to throw it away. He is unhappy to find that all three of the kitchen trash cans have no bags in them. Grumbling, he finds trash bags and re-lines the cans. It is such a simple act, one that normal people do all the time. However, seeing Ozzy Osbourne replacing trash bags, especially with silly whistling music in the background, really brings him down to our level. Furthermore, as on *Cribs*, many of the kitchen scenes feature name brand products that viewers are familiar with (and may even use themselves). One particularly conspicuous example is an episode from Season Two (originally aired January 7, 2003), which revolves almost entirely around Ozzy's love of the burritos served at the Tex-Mex chain restaurant Chipotle. He tries to force everyone in the family to eat them, and then buys enough burritos to fill up the freezer because he simply cannot eat just one of them. Chipotle got so much recognition from this episode that, over two years later, they still have Ozzy's recommendation posted on their website.[6]

Just as Ice-T and Snoop Dogg were presented as loving fathers and domesticated family men, Ozzy's fatherly duties are emphasized throughout this show. In the opening credits, he is the only one listed as playing a "role" in the show — "The Dad" (*Osbournes*) — whereas the other family members are simply listed by name. Throughout the credits, we see a large number of family pictures, featuring Ozzy and his kids at different ages. There are pictures on the walls of many of the rooms of the house, and they are even used by the show's producers as a motif to signal transitions between scenes. Of course, Ozzy Osbourne is not entirely a traditional father. He swears at his children, for example, and many parents would feel that he is too permissive (giving his teenagers a 2:30 AM curfew or allowing his daughter Kelly to get a tattoo). Here is an example of the fatherly advice Ozzy gives to Jack and Kelly in the first episode as they prepare to go out that night, "Please don't uh get drunk or get stoned tonight. Don't fuckin' piss off like that. Don't be ... don't drink or take drugs ... Please. And if you have sex, wear a condom" (*Osbournes*). Many parents in mainstream America might object to the last part of his exhortation, and they might not believe the first part, given Ozzy's long and well documented history of substance abuse. Throughout the show, however, one thing is always clear; Ozzy loves his kids. He later tells his son Jack, "Thing is, Jack ... I love you all. I love you more than life itself. [But] you're all fucking mad" (*Osbournes*).

Not only does Ozzy love his children, but he loves the family pets as well. Episode Two centers primarily on the problems the family has with the seven dogs and multiple cats who share the house with them. Ozzy's wife Sharon clearly loves the animals, introducing each by name (and by their place in the family pecking order). She feeds them from her own plate, even allowing them to lick food from her fork. Ozzy, though, seems more upset with the animals because they are not fully housebroken. Like any concerned homeowner, he gets angry when the dogs mess up his house, saying, "We might as well just live in a fucking sewer because the dogs just piss everywhere" (*Osbournes*). After we see him clean up after the dogs a number of times, only to find more dog feces on the floor, Ozzy says, "I'm not picking up another turd. I'm a rock star" (*Osbournes*). It is another example of the kind of humorous duality that was so effective in *Cribs*. We have already seen Ozzy picking up turds, so his status as "rock star" has been diminished. In spite of all his cursing and swearing, however, Ozzy loves the animals as much as his wife and kids do. He loves even Jack's bulldog Lola, who chews up several pieces of furniture. Though Sharon and Ozzy decide at one point that Lola must go, Ozzy has a change or heart. Sharon describes it, saying, "As Ozzy's walking down the stairs to leave, he goes, 'Don't get rid of Lola. I love her'" (*Osbournes*). How, then, can the man who loves the dog that destroyed his house, a man who loves his wife and kids and just wants to watch the History Channel, be considered a serious threat to society?

Conclusion: Incorporation and MTV

When MTV first came on the air on August 1, 1981, it was simply the development and expansion of a program originally offered by Warner Amex Cable in Columbus, Ohio. It was hardly a force to be reckoned with in society, let alone a threat to the dominant order. By the mid 1980s, however, many people in the United States came to think of MTV as a threat, especially as its videos made popular artists who questioned society's ideas about women (Madonna), gender and sexuality (Culture Club's Boy George), and eventually even race.[7] Continuing the long tradition of criticism of rock and roll music, people saw MTV as promoting sex and violence among America's youth. In fact, MTV was considered even more dangerous than rock music in general because it combined suggestive lyrics with powerful visual images.

As late as 1989, in fact, concerns about MTV were appearing in the mainstream American press. James L. Hall's article, "MTV Rocks (and Rolls) American Youth," summarizes several studies that had been conducted to determine the effects of MTV on young people. He notes a number of troubling questions these studies have raised, in particular the fear that images in rock videos, combined with the lyrics of the songs, may form "a complex communication system known only to the rock subculture" (88). MTV, then, is clearly depicted as forming part of a subculture that is alternative, if not yet completely oppositional. The fact that it promotes a particular kind of communication among members of that subculture, the sort of communication that contributes to revolutionary unrest perhaps, is particularly disturbing. It is especially problematic that MTV reaches so many of the nation's young people; the article at the very least encourages more study of the phenomenon in order to assess the extent of the danger. Hall claims, "If MTV is communicating potentially harmful, suggestive content to the youth of America, then the indictment of this programming genre appears justified. Throughout the period of additional research and investigation, concerned parents must take decisive steps in monitoring MTV" (88).

Of course, this article and the studies that prompted it were written long before reality programs like *Cribs* and *The Osbournes* came to dominate MTV's schedule. Perhaps MTV was truly alternative — or even oppositional — in its early years (that argument would be interesting to explore in another paper). With programs like *Cribs* and *The Osbournes*, however, MTV now has a very different set of effects on its viewers. One important effect of these shows is to incorporate the threatening figures presented back into the mainstream of American society. Although these shows appear to continue MTV's tradition of countering the mainstream, given the appearance of gangsta rappers and heavy metal icons, in actuality, *Cribs* and *The Osbournes* are part of the continuing process whereby the alternative is incorporated back into the mainstream.

I would argue that MTV's position as historically associated with alternative voices makes it the ideal site for this cultural work. The fact that studies have warned the American public for years about the dangers of MTV gives it a certain anti-mainstream credibility. In his article in *USA Today*, Hall mentions, "[t]he oft-quoted National Coalition on Television Study (NCTV) [which] analyzed 518 videos…. The results, which included both acts and threats of violence, indicated significant aggression in 40% of the videos; 39% of the violent acts were sexually related" (88). In spite of the fact that MTV is now owned by Viacom, one of the largest media conglomerates in the world, people still associate it with this sort of dangerous cultural agenda. The fact that *Cribs* and *The Osbournes* depict personalities who are outside the mainstream contributes to that impression, continuing the basic view that MTV is a site for alternative voices.

The cultural work of these two shows,[8] however, clearly involves the use of domestication to bring these alternative figures back into the mainstream. In a process that has been effective since the days when women in the workforce first were considered a threat to society, these shows use domestication to make extreme figures seem to be just like you and me. Peeking into the home of a gangsta rapper or a metal madman turns out to be less of a journey into the exotic and more of a trip to a familiar space. The kitchens may be bigger and nicer than the ones we see every day, but there are still dishes to be done, trash cans to be emptied, and familiar foods to be eaten. Mixed in with bottles of the most expensive champagne are the familiar brands of food that the rest of us eat every day. On the walls are family pictures that are actually not so different from the ones seen in any American household. It turns out that Ice-T, Snoop Dogg, and Ozzy Osbourne do many of the same things that the rest of us do, from watching TV to vacuuming the living room. Seeing their domestication takes away from the threat they may once have posed to society. In other words, how can Ozzy Osbourne lead us into hell when he cannot even figure out how to work his remote control?

Works Cited

Althusser, Louis. "Ideology and Ideological State Apparatuses." *Lenin and Philosophy, And Other Essays.* Trans. Ben Brewster. New York: Monthly Review Press, 2001. 127–88.

Cribs: Hip Hop. Perf. Ice-T and Snoop Dogg. DVD. Paramount Home Video, 2003.

Greenspan, Sam. "Media Effects on Kids: Music and Videos." *Preteenagers Today.* iParenting, LLC. 15 Sept. 2005 <preteenagerstoday.com/resources/articles/mediaand-kids.html>

Hall, James L. "MTV Rocks (and Rolls) American Youth." *USA Today* Ice-T. "Cop Killer." *Body Count.* Sire Records, 1992. Lyrics accessed online. 9 Sept. 2005 <lyrics.rockmagic.net/lyrics/body_count/body_count_1992.html#18>

Johnson, Claudia. *American Actress: Perspective on the Nineteenth Century.* Chicago: Nelson-Hall, 1984.

Johnson, Joseph P. "Cop Killer." *Daily Egyptian.* Originally pub. 19 Feb. 2002. Accessed 9 Sept. 2005 <newshound.de.siu.edu/online/stories/storyReader$1472>

"Learn." 15 Sept. 2005 <www.chipotle.com>

"The Official Website for Ice-T." 15 Sept. 2005 <www.icet.com/bio.html>

The Osbournes: The First Season. Perf. Ozzy Osbourne, Sharon Osbourne, Kelly Osbourne, Jack Osbourne. DVD. Miramax Home Entertainment, 2003.

"Ozzy Osbourne: Biography." 14 Sept. 2005 < www.veinotte.com/ozzy/madness.htm>

Patterson, Ada. "Virginia Harned — A 'Material' Actress." *Theatre Magazine* Apr. 1904: 93–5.

Williams, Raymond. *Marxism and Literature.* Oxford: Oxford UP, 1977.

Notes

1. There are too many examples to cite them all here. Typical would be the article "Stage Favorites at Home," from *Harper's Bazaar* 35 (Oct. 1901): 576–9. Even articles that claim to be about an actress' craft deal extensively with domestic details. See, for example, George T. Ferris' article, "Charlotte Cushman," in *Appletons' Journal of Literature, Science and Art* 11.261 (1874): 353–58.

2. For a discussion of the various social forces calling for women to remain at home, see Claudia Johnson's *American Actress: Perspective on the Nineteenth Century,* Chicago: Nelson Hall, 1984.

3. For a full understanding of the difference between ideological state apparatuses and repressive state apparatuses (i.e. the police or the military), see Althusser's essay "Ideology and Ideological State Apparatuses," in *Lenin and Philosophy and Other Essays,* from Monthly Review Press.

4. Speaking of parental disapproval of rock and roll in general, Sam Greenspan notes, "The advent of Music Television (MTV) in the early '80s fanned the flames. Songs with mes-

sages of violence, sex, hate, rebellion and anarchy were accompanied by moving pictures" (par. 7).

5. They claimed to hear, "Why try, why try? Get the gun and shoot it! Shoot, shoot, shoot" (qtd. in "Ozzy").

6. In the section "Learn" on www.chipotle.com, they quote Ozzy as saying, "This is my favorite burrito joint."

7. After having been criticized in its early days for playing predominantly white artists, MTV came to embrace rap and hip hop, as with the premier of *Yo! MTV Raps* in 1988.

8. I would include here other shows like *Newlyweds*, *The Ashlee Simpson Show*, and a host of "Celebreality" programs on MTV's sister network VH1, including *Celebrity Fit Club*, *The Surreal Life*, and *Hogan Knows Best*.

Part III
Representation and Gender
How Does Reality TV Represent Women?

7

How Women Really Are: Disturbing Parallels between Reality Television and 18th Century Fiction

ELIZABETH JOHNSTON

Since the introduction of MTV's *The Real World*, at least 318 different reality shows have aired in the US alone.[1] Seemingly, the public cannot get enough. A 2001 survey conducted by *American Demographics* found that "[f]orty-five percent of all Americans watch reality television programs. Of those, 27 percent consider themselves die-hard fans…. In fact, 37 percent of all Americans prefer to watch real people on television rather than scripted characters" (Gardyn). The reality television show phenomenon has launched a debate as to whether the genre evidences our society's moral decay and the increasing debasement of entertainment culture.[2] However, the purpose of this essay is not to measure the moral or aesthetic value of reality television programming but to explore its ideological significance. We know that the low-production costs of reality shows appeal to network execs,[3] but what draws *viewers* to this genre? What desires do these shows target? What appetites do they feed? We have always been a voyeuristic society, so why now, more than ever, do we crave viewing, ad nauseum, the minutia of people's daily lives?

To answer these questions, modern day web cam and television technology can be usefully compared to innovations in eighteenth-century printing which provided readers with that which was similarly hot off the press. Not since then has our society been so privy to the *immediacy* of what goes on behind closed doors. In an attempt to decipher what drives our desire for the "real," this paper compares today's cultural preoccupation with representing reality with a parallel obsession in the eighteenth-century. In particular, I want to consider the similarities between reality television shows and works of eighteenth-century fiction which focus specifically on domestic concerns and to explore how both genres work to inform our cultural understanding of gender.

Until recently, the field of cultural studies seemed relatively uninterested in the phenomenon of reality television. Laura Grindstaff has suggested that academia has overlooked reality shows because, like daytime television, they have been devalued as "low culture" watched primarily by women. It follows, then, that reality shows which focus on what might be considered feminine concerns—courtship, marriage, domesticity—would be considered the lowest of the low, eliciting even less critical attention. Indeed, a search for articles on dating shows like *The Bachelor, For Love or Money,* or *Joe Millionaire* turns up few, if any, hits on any academic search engine — in stark contrast to a search for works on shows like *COPS, Survivor,* and *The Apprentice.*[4] The latter all target a more heterogeneous audience and perform very explicit ideological work in the areas of class and race. The absence of scholarly work on what women watch no doubt can be blamed on the traditional assumption that what goes on in the privacy of the home ("women's space") is less important than what goes on outside it ("men's space").

Similarly, the eighteenth century novel was often disparaged by literary critics, shunned as "low" art because of its thematic focus on domestic experience and its obvious appeal to a female readership, as well as the fact that many eighteenth-century novels were written by women.[5] Only in the 1980's, on the heels of the 1970's feminist movement, did new scholarship begin to emerge suggesting that works about courtship and family did, indeed, perform important political work which both impacted and reflected the cultural imagination.[6] Importantly, many eighteenth-century scholars have linked domestic fiction to the success of an emergent middle-class ethos and nascent capitalism.[7] Likewise, I posit that a critical inquiry of reality television shows which focus on love, courtship, and marriage, yields a provocative, if often disturbing, insight into gender identity and its link to class consciousness. To date, an analysis of the political dimensions of reality dating shows remains oversimplified or simply unexplored. In turning our attention to these shows and drawing connections between the ideological work they perform and that exercised by eighteenth-century domestic fiction, we can better understand the ways in which both patriarchy and capitalism sustain themselves by marketing their fictions, in particular that of an idealized femininity, as "real."

Eighteenth-Century Fiction, Reality Television, and the Epistemology of the "Real"

One obvious parallel between eighteenth-century fiction and reality television is that both ask what is "reality," and how can it be most accurately represented? In the eighteenth-century, as now, "reality" was mapped out in fiction. Most critics agree that what we have come to understand as the modern novel emerged in the eighteenth century, and that its earliest defining characteristic was an emphasis on realism, evident in the novel's commitment to empirical detail, focus on the everyday, and exploration of the psychological complexity of its characters.[8] Hence, readers of the eighteenth-century novel endure Robinson Crusoe's painful detailing of every item he finds on his island, the notorious prostitute Moll Flander's fastidious notation of each street she travels, and Samuel Richardson's record-breaking, million-word novel *Clarissa*, in which the eponymous heroine tediously records her thoughts, feelings, distresses, fears, etc. These fictions shared a common frame which attested to its commitment to realism. Sometimes the story was from a first-person perspective, allegedly autobiographical, as in Daniel Defoe's *Moll Flanders,* Delarivier Manley's *The Adventures of Rivella,* or John Cleland's pornographic *Memoirs of a Woman of Pleasure.* Alternatively, the story could begin with a letter from someone, usually a male editor (often given a fictional name other than the author's), who had stumbled on the text at hand; sometimes it was willed to him, as in Samuel Richardson's *Clarissa,* and sometimes it was narrated to him, as in Sarah Scott's *Millenium Hall.* Alternatively, the author could claim to have found the story and translated it, as in Horace Walpole's *The Castle of Otranto.* Often, the enclosed story manifested itself as letters passed between one character and another; such is the case with Richardson's *Clarissa* and Frances Burney's *Evelina.* The epistolary form, making readers privy to private information, lent further credibility to the narrative. The story could also appear as memoirs, translated or edited by the author, as in Maria Edgeworth's *Castle Rackrent.*[9] Most readers recognized that the letters/memoirs were fictional. Nevertheless, the frame was still necessitated; the fiction needed the *appearance* of reality.

Emphasis on distinguishing fact from fiction is a distinctly modern phenomenon. Literary historian Lennard Davis explains that, in contrast to earlier modes of fiction, the eighteenth-century novel needed to assert its veracity in order to promote the moral improvement of its readers. In effect, the reader was split into a gullible reader who first believed in the work's veracity, and then a savvy reader, who recognized its necessary fictionality (Davis 23). He or she was forced into a sort of ambivalence, a willing suspension of their suspension of disbelief, believing, ultimately, that the fiction contained elements of truth about the human condition. Explains Davis, "[T]he surface is the alibi for the genuine material it conceals" (150). Literary critic Michael McKeon agrees that "the claim to historicity [realism] means to assert not brute factuality — an unattainable ideal — but a relative fidelity of narration" (121). One was not a "liar" if one's fictions were first, realistic, and then morally useful.

Similarly, the term "reality" in reality television is commonly accepted as a misnomer. Audiences recognize that the jungle-setting and dangerous tasks assigned to *Survivor* contestants are not "realistic." They know, as any single person knows, that neither the fantasy dates of *The Bachelor* nor the opportunity to choose from twenty-five aesthetically flawless women are plausible. No one expects to win a lucrative internship under Donald Trump like the guests on *The Apprentice*. And yet all accept that what happens in these shows *really* is *real* on some level. In other words, audiences acknowledge the shows' artifices, but believe that their content reveals moments of intimate truth about real people. Comments one avid viewer: "How the players feel is real. You can see their true emotions, their frustrations, their joy. That's real enough for me. If some of the smaller details aren't so real, so be it" (qtd. in Gardyn). Viewers consent to being "deceived" because they believe they are not *really* being tricked; they *allow* the shows to manipulate them and their emotions because they believe, ultimately, that some good will come of it. They believe they will learn more about human nature, about what kinds of people to trust, and whom to avoid.

A new addition to reality television, the ability to read the contestants' weekly updated diaries online at the official series' websites, further testifies to both the "realness" and immediacy of the action. Just as eighteenth-century domestic fiction often relied upon letters and diary entries to lend its stories veracity, so too do these television shows suggest that we can get inside the minds of the contestants on the show — and in doing so, to empathize with them. And, as in the eighteenth century, our ability to trust the narrative's claim to realism necessitates our trust in the teller's (here, the diary writer's) sensibility and genuineness. As McKeon has argued of eighteenth-century fiction, a claim to historicity depends on our ability to empathize with the characters' actions and motivations, and we can do so by identifying with the emotions they express. Richardson's *Clarissa* had to persuade her readers that she did not desire Lovelace's advances, and she did so in her oh-so-lengthy letters to her confidante, Anna — letters to which readers of the novel were made privy by its "editor." Readers felt sorry for her because they *liked* her and identified with her plight. When she cried, they cried. Richardson's friend, Susanna Highmore, wrote of her experience reading *Clarissa*: "I laid down the Book, and felt.... I verily think as much Affliction as such a Friend in real Life so circumstanc'd could feel ...

I see, I hear, I feel the same, and am for the present, as unhappy, as if it were all true..." (qtd. in Knights 228).[10] Similarly, because the diary entries of Jen Scheft of *The Bachelor* and *The Bachelorette* fame seem to evidence a compelling psychic struggle, moreover, because we *see* her crying on the show, we willingly suspend our disbelief. We *agree* to identify with her.

Both eighteenth-century fiction and reality television also tend to celebrate the everyday, focusing on both domestic experience and the lives of "ordinary" people. Importantly, fictional "realism" as it was understood in the eighteenth-century meant reality as it applied to the lives of the professional and entrepreneurial gentry, a growing population dependent on a burgeoning economic market. This shift in emphasis can be witnessed in the preface to *The Adventures of Lindamira* (1702), which declares its wish to turn from "the histories of foreign amours and scenes laid beyond the seas' to 'domestic intrigues,' aiming not at fabulous knight errantry but at 'real matter of fact'" (qtd. in Todd 49). Tales about the aristocracy and court intrigue slowly came to be understood as "romance"—far removed from the reality of the gentry's everyday life.[11] However, while eighteenth-century fiction detailed the realities of the economic market in an emergent capitalist state, its version of "reality" was often based in an idealized domestic space. Domestic fiction imagined the home as the moral anchor of society — the safe refuge to which the modern, capitalist man could return after a hard day in the greed-driven public sphere.[12] Even Robinson Crusoe, trapped on an island after being shipwrecked, works to transform the native land and people into an idealized domestic space. Indeed, the middle-class home was not only the moral anchor of society, but the defining space of eighteenth-century reality. As both the title and thematic content of Maria Edgeworth's eighteenth-century novel, *Belinda, Abroad and at Home,* implies, outside the home, people behave as public actors; within it they are themselves.

In today's reality programming, we see a similar push to celebrate the average Joe, the phrase, in fact, the name of a popular series. Most of the contestants on reality television shows come from working class backgrounds. While they may be aspiring actors or models, they are nevertheless still struggling — and reality shows force them to struggle all the more. In fact, the plot of *Survivor*, now in its tenth season, depends on reducing all of its contestants, modern day Robinson Crusoes, to the bare necessities of life, stripping them of markers of class, status, and wealth. Stuck in remote jungles without access to cell phones or ATMs, they must resort to the basics. *Survivor* makes explicit that to get at the "real" of the human condition, to allow for the genuine cooperation and authentic competition ostensibly missing from most people's lived reality, one must level the playing fields.

Not only are the contestants "ordinary folks"; many of the most popular reality shows focus on everyday experiences. While *Survivor* is not set in domestic space, although the contestants certainly learn how to recreate a sense of home and family out of the wilderness, many other reality shows are. Shows like *Supernanny*, *The Nanny*, *Trading Spouses*, *Wife Swap*, and *A Baby Story* offer viewers familiar glimpses into the domestic chaos (and, sometimes, bliss) of working-class families. Dating shows like *The Bachelor*, *Average Joe*, *Joe Millionaire*, and *Bachelorettes in Alaska* focus on that with which everyone can identify — the search for true love. Even shows whose protagonists are celebrities — like MTV's *Newlyweds*, featuring pop princess Jessica Simpson and husband Nick Lachey, and its much talked about *The Osbournes* — work to normalize the lifestyles of the featured celebrities. Now, we are as likely to see a photo of "Plain Jane Jen" Scheft on the cover of tabloid magazines as we are Jennifer Anniston.[13] Our society has long been entranced with celebrity; what do we make of the sudden celebration of the everyday?

As has been argued, the eighteenth-century shift in emphasis away from aristocratic values can be explained by economic changes: growing international trade began to offer the working class opportunities to garner some of the power until then held exclusively by the elite; hence the middle class was growing rapidly.[14] In turn, domestic fiction tended to focus on the lives of everyday people while ridiculing the excesses of the wealthy. But this was at the dawn of capitalism, when its democratizing promises seemed possible. Why now, when the middle-class is shrinking, do we celebrate the everyday?

Indeed, while television might privilege the middle-class, the economy does not. Since the 1980's, the income of the wealthy has steadily grown (Tyson 32). A federal inquiry by the Economic Policy Institute found that as of 2003, the top 1% of households control 33% of the national wealth and that the average rate of pay for a CEO is 185 times the salary of an average worker (Mishel, Bernstein, and Allegretto 277, 7). While the average American worker's salary rose by only 2.9% between 2004 and 2005, a rise offset by inflation and rising healthcare costs, the average CEO's compensation rose 15.6% (LaVelle 1). Meanwhile, the number of unemployed Americans has continued to grow, demonstrating a rate increase from 4% in 2000 to 6% in 2004 (Mishel, Bernstein, and Allegretto 220). One would think that we would be fed up with reality, that we would recognize the limits of the American Dream and capitalism's promise. One would think we would turn from reality television to fantasy.

Arguably, Americans simply do not recognize how bad things *really* are. An editorial in *The Economist* speculates, "This may be because they are deluded: a survey for Time/CNN in 2000 showed that 19% of Americans believed they were in the top 1% of earners. Or perhaps it is optimism: almost uniquely among nations, a majority of Americans think their success is largely determined by factors within their control, according to the Pew Research Centre in 2003" ("Poor" 13). Several critics have suggested that the appeal of today's reality television speaks to a desire to control an economy that has become increasingly out of control; ironically, the fantastic reality offered by these shows works to keep economic control in the hands of the elite. Critic Mark Andrejevic offers as evidence a Tivo commercial in which two working class men toss a network exec out a window. This is the democratizing promise of reality television — the working-class underdog can upset the status quo. Of course, this just entails the "collapse of the role of citizen into that of consumer" (Andrejevic 14). As Andrejevic wisely notes, if the industry supports this revolution, it cannot possibly be revolutionary.

Despite the parallel desires driving the epistemology of the real in both the eighteenth century and modern society, there is a significant difference between how readers received domestic fiction's reality and how viewers today understand the reality of reality television. In the eighteenth century, the reality circulated in domestic fiction signified optimism about the future; readers understood the depictions in these tales as representations of a reality they desired. They understood it as fiction, but believed that it might become reality. Domestic fiction, it has been argued, actually worked to promote the values which helped to topple the elite. Today, however, viewers tend to privilege the *representation* of reality on television over their own lived reality. In other words, as Baudrillard has articulated, the teleological drive of capitalism is an increasing emphasis on the sign and a decreasing emphasis on the signified. Our real experience (the signified), becomes less visible, less important as it is gradually replaced by the representation of "reality" (the sign). Baudrillard suggests that because "[c]apital was the first to play at deterrence, abstraction, disconnection, and if it is the one that fostered reality, the reality principle, it was also the first to liquidate it by exterminating all use value..." (22); thereafter, "[w]hat every society looks for in continuing to produce, and to overproduce, is to restore the real that escapes it" (23).[15] We keep trying to "restore" to ourselves a reality that does not exist; we pass into what Baudrillard terms the "hyperreal." Television, as the medium, disappears out of sight. If on television it *appears* that the playing fields are leveled, if it *seems* that the good guy (the working underdog) comes out on top — then that must be how things *really* are.

"*The Angel in* The Bachelor's *House*": Constructions of Ideal Femininity in Eighteenth-Century Fiction and Reality Television

THE GOOD GIRL/BAD GIRL BINARY AND THEMES OF FEMALE RIVALRY

I teach a semiotic analysis of media in my English 101 class, and I often begin with the example of reality television, challenging what I see as troubling stereotypes of femininity — weepiness, cattiness, and dependency upon men. Inevitably a student will shout out, "But that's how women really are!" If the "reality" which is defined by reality television functions as a vehicle for reproducing dominant ideology, naturalizing the real terms of capitalism, the effect is especially dangerous for women.

An important parallel between reality television and domestic fiction is that both are trenchantly invested in defining a monolithic version of femininity best suited to the purposes of capitalism. As the eighteenth-century novel tended to celebrate an idealized domestic space, a similarly idealized figure of womanhood came to represent the home. Significantly, eighteenth-century domestic fiction often involved a woman from the gentry or working-class reforming those in stations above her. We might think, for example, of Richardson's *Pamela*, in which a beautiful and virtuous servant uses her master's desire for her to transform his corrupt, aristocratic household into a decidedly middle-class home.[16] And while this idealized womanhood was a fictional construction, no less a fantasy than a domestic space untainted by the market, she and her home came to emblematize what was "real" in the cultural imagination.

Richardson's heroines became typical of what would come to be known in the nineteenth century as "the angel in the house," a woman who, while beautiful, eschewed beauty as her defining value, refused to be treated like a commodity, grudgingly attended festive masquerades, hated gambling, and despised coquetry. However, she also knew how to dance, sew, sing, and play the piano when the need arose (i.e., when a good-looking, wealthy bachelor happened to be in the room). Like a good middle-class exemplar, she turned up her nose at aristocratic values, rejected conspicuous consumption, and embraced instead absolute moderation. She was a woman who, although celebrating the rational autonomy heralded by enlightenment philosophy, inevitably married.

Often the "good" girl was defined in contrast to her other, the "bad" girl, who gamed, flirted shamelessly, and "painted." Often the bad girl is "bad" because she has turned her back on domesticity. She (or her editor/author) must describe her downfall, the sordid details rendering the fiction's realism most convincingly. Thus Fanny Hill, the prostitute narrator of Cleland's *Memoirs*, defends her scandalous storytelling, "Truth! Stark naked truth, is the word, and I will not so much as take the pains to bestow the strip of a gauze-wrapper on it, but paint situations such as they actually rose to me in nature, careless of violating those laws of decency...." (3). The popularity of works which detail the debauched behavior of anti-heroes and heroines does not attest to a liberated readership, nor does today's risqué reality programming implicate our society's increasing moral depravity — as is often asserted by the religious right. In fact, the "bad" behavior of these negative *exempla* reinforces society's restrictive sexual and social mores, both in the eighteenth century and now.

As popular in the eighteenth century as rogue fiction was, domestic or conduct-book fiction which pitted an innocent, good-hearted heroine against a multitude of corrupt women for the love of the hero; of course, he always chose the good girl in the end, and she, inevitably, reformed him with a middle-class ideology. In this way, as Nancy Armstrong has articulated, desire served a specifically politicized end. I suggest, additionally, that the trope of female rivalry which pervades eighteenth-century domestic fiction was also part of a larger ideological drive to alienate women from each other, the desire to do so rooted in anxieties raised by Enlightenment feminisms and women's increasing agency, especially on the literary market. In an April, 1756 letter to *The Universal Visitor*, Samuel Johnson responded to the growing presence of women writers:

> It is more difficult to know what can be done with the *ladies of the pen,* of whom this age has produced greater numbers than any former time.... I must therefore propose that they form a regiment of themselves, and garrison the town which is supposed to be in most danger of a *French* invasion. They will probably have no enemies to encounter; but if they are once shut up together, they will soon dis-encumber the public by tearing out the eyes of one another.

Here the trope of female rivalry is raised to reassure male writers of women's inherent inferiority; they can never rival male literary authority because they will be too busy "tearing out the eyes of one another." Similarly, today's dating reality shows figure as part of a trenchant backlash against the gains made by feminism in the last thirty years. The goals of feminism, one of which is to question the construction of womanhood, clearly threaten to destabilize the status quo. In turn, as in the eighteenth-century, ideology must retaliate by reconstructing a figure of femininity which best serves the interest of capitalism.

As with eighteenth-century domestic fiction, marriage continues to be the end-goal of the dating reality show, the driving desire of all single women. All the dating shows depict women competing, often viciously, for the attention of a lackluster bachelor in the hopes that he may propose to her on national TV. Many, if not most, of these women are educated, have careers, own their own businesses. They are beautiful, seem smart, and profess independence. However, so desperate are they to wed, they jump at the chance to marry a man whom they have known for a matter of weeks and who was, in all *reality,* cheating on them up until the day he popped the question. As predicted, once shut up together in one mansion or another, they do indeed threaten to "tear out the eyes of one another." Rather than competing *with* man, they compete for him — certainly a giant step backwards for feminism. Moreover, the winners of shows like *The Bachelor, Joe Millionaire, For Love or Money?*, and the granddaddy of them all, *Who Wants to Marry a Millionaire?* become icons of the "right" kind of femininity, ostensibly embodying the traits that our culture finds most desirable. What, then, are these traits and in what ways do these shows work to stabilize patriarchy?

The women on these shows are, like most contestants of reality television, "ordinary folks." Of course, the man over whom they compete may be of quasi-celebrity status (Giants football player Jesse Palmer, tire heir Andrew Firestone, and most recently, Charlie O'Connell, actor Jerry O'Connell's brother), but the object is to win his love by demonstrating the value of the everyday while simultaneously humanizing him or bringing him down to the level of "ordinary folks." Just as in eighteenth-century fiction, in these programs the "angel in the house" wins the wealthy bachelor by demonstrating her moral superiority over his other choices — and, ultimately, by reforming him from a swinging playboy to solid, middle-class, husband material.[17]

They must first, however, demonstrate their commitment to middle-class values. Under clearly artificial circumstances, the show promises the bachelor will get to know what kind of women they *really* are. This means that sometimes they will have to shovel horse manure, as in *Joe Millionaire,* to disprove accusations of snobbery. Sometimes it means they will have to write him a poem or draw him a picture (rather than buy him an expensive gift). Most importantly, they will have to talk about their *feelings*; they have to prove that they can offer more than silicone arm candy. After all, *all* the contestants are beautiful. The woman who wins, wins on the basis of her *virtue* (i.e., her willingness to be humiliated on national TV in the name of love). Women who do not agree to these rules, who feel themselves above cleaning horse excrement, routinely get eliminated.

Additionally, the winners of these shows are, themselves, *real.* That is, they eschew artifice. Like their eighteenth-century counterparts they, too, do not "paint"; their beauty is natural, they look good first thing in the morning rolling out of bed or lounging around the house in sweatpants (ever intrusive cameras assure us of this). "Bad" girls, however, plaster their faces with make-up; worse, they flaunt excessively large breast implants. They traipse around in low-cut dresses, mini-skirts, and wobbly high-heels. Sometimes they get drunk and make fools of themselves in front of the bachelor, bursting into histrionic sobs, flirting shamelessly, (their advances seemingly unwanted by the bachelor), or revealing too much about their sexual history. Unlike the "good" girl, they do not practice moderation.

There are, of course, some differences between the eighteenth-century version of idealized femininity and her modern day counterpart. Today's "good" girl is not as virginal as a Clarissa or Pamela, but she is always redeemable, in contrast to villains like Trish from *The Bachelor,* season 5, who revealed on TV that she slept with more than thirty men, one of whom was married. The good girl does not, for example, try to sneak, lingerie-clad, into the unsuspecting bachelor's bungalow, as did Season 6's Krysta (whom the bachelor later referred to as a "stalker"). Casual sex does not interest the good girl; she wants a family, usually a large one, and plans to take time off work to raise them. The "bad" girl, however, thinks kids are messy. The good girl is willing to leave her home and job to move to the bachelor's hometown; admittedly she will need some time to make this transition. She is, after all, a modern woman. The bad girl wants to stay put. The good girl refuses to speak ill of her rivals; she understands and forgives them their shortcomings (although she acknowledges that she would not choose them as friends). The bad girl ruthlessly backstabs. Significantly, when men compete for a bachelorette, there are generally no such rivalries (unless, of course, one of the bachelors is highly feminized and, therein, his sexuality suspect); in fact, they spend their time together partying and playing football.

Perhaps most importantly (and most ironically), the good girl of reality television, like her eighteenth-century counterpart, is defined by her commitment to "real" love. She is not on these shows for celebrity, or so she declares. She does not care whether the bachelor is rich or poor; in fact, she prefers a man more like herself, with middle-class tastes. (Bad girl Trish, on the other hand, proudly sported a shirt with the words "gold-digger" splashed across the front). The good girl declares to the world in true pageant style that all she really needs is love.

And yet the glossy veneer of these shows is as transparent as that of their eighteenth-century counterparts. Richardson's humble Pamela, for example, was awarded for her good behavior with riches— a plot so deeply hypocritical that it inspired numerous spoofs, including Henry Fielding's *Shamela.* To save face, Richardson would have his next heroine, Clarissa, die a martyr's death rather than marry the wealthy rake she reformed! Most audiences today accept that reality shows are never *only* about true love.

The contestants do want fame; many of them are aspiring celebrities whose agents have told them to try the reality television circuit. And they do want the cash reward; even if the show itself does not offer them money, there is always the promise of endorsements, talk-show and sitcom guest appearances, book deals, recording contracts, and, of course, *Playboy* layouts. Trista Rehn, ABC's first *Bachelorette* was rewarded for her "good" behavior with a luxurious, four-million dollar wedding thrown by ABC. What becomes clear is that in late-capitalism, one can embrace conspicuous consumption *as long as* one professes not to *really* care about conspicuous consumption. In other words, these shows address a fundamental contradiction in capitalist ideology. Being too invested in materialistic things is always, to some extent, at odds with human values. The shows seem to critique this flaw, but then provide a way for audiences to imaginarily resolve it.

Hence, some shows, like *For Love or Money?* and *Joe Millionaire*, seem bent on unmasking women's "gold-digging" potential. The plot of FOX's *Joe Millionaire* was to bring a bunch of women to France, introduce them to a fake multi-millionaire, and let the good times roll. The bachelor, Evan, really a construction worker raking in a measly $19,000 a year, would decide which woman was right for him, i.e., who loved him for who he *really* was (a difficult task because, as it turned out, this particular bachelor had little to offer other than brawn). The contest came down to two women: Zora and Sarah. Zora was a small-town beauty, a substitute teacher, a woman so modest that she wore a t-shirt into the whirlpool; she also, appropriately, loved horses (and did not mind shoveling their manure). Her opponent was a bombshell blonde who smoked, turns out to have starred in dozens of bondage movies, and who did not like horses. Need I tell you whom the bachelor chose?

EXPLORING THE APPEAL OF THESE SHOWS TO WOMEN

When we look at these shows with a feminist sensibility, it seems impossible that they would succeed; their version of ideal femininity seems so grossly conventional, so utterly silly. However, the appeal of these shows to the masses, and to women in particular, is unquestionable. An *American Demographics* survey found "women are the die-hard fans, making up 64 percent of regular viewers (those who watch as many episodes as they can)" (Gardyn). It makes sense for networks, vying for advertisers, to cook up shows for women who continue to be the largest consumers. But here is another interesting parallel. Women were the target audience for domestic fiction, too. Women then, as now, seemed to gobble up tales of courtship, intrigue, and scandal — and swallow whole a disturbing and hardly altered version of idealized womanhood. Why? What desires are being sated?

These misogynistic narratives appeal to women on several levels. First, both genres appear to offer women agency. Cut off from the rest of the world, domestic fiction validated eighteenth-century women's experience in the home and granted to them the moral authority to reform the public sphere and its male agents. In essence, it marked the reality of their everyday lives as the defining "reality" of the eighteenth-century. Arguably, women today are drawn to "reality" television for similar reasons. 57.5% of adult women are in the workforce, and those in the low and middle income brackets (the primary viewers of reality television) have experienced an annual work-hour increase of 60–70% since 1979 (Mishel, Bernstein, and Allegretto 250, 102). Yet studies have shown that many continue mentally to divide their lives outside and inside the home — and to privilege their function inside the home over their careers. Sadly, while many men now participate in household chores, the bulk of housework and childrearing remains on women's shoulders.[18] Thus, "reality" for today's women continues to be largely defined by domestic concerns in a way that working men's lives are not. Women viewers must certainly feel validated when largely domestic concerns, for so long relegated to daytime soap and talk show slots, gain primetime attention.

However, we should pay careful attention to the narrative of femininity constructed by these shows. Significantly, *Supernanny* immediately follows *The Bachelor* on Monday nights. Both *The Bachelor* and *Supernanny* function like conduct book fiction, delineating a clear trajectory in women's lives from courtship to marriage and, along the way, instructing them in the epistemology of proper femininity and motherhood. In fact, TLC used to run a similar trajectory, a back-to-back daytime line-up of *A Makeover Story*, *A Dating Story*, *A Wedding Story*, and finally *A Baby Story* — a sequence since changed, perhaps because it was a bit too overtly conventional. The sequencing of these shows no doubt attests to the female viewers' recognition of two simultaneous realities: the reality of her desire to return to the courtship phase, perhaps to rethink her decisions, and the reality of her lived experience, years long past the courtship phase and now muddled with career and childrearing concerns. Susan Douglas and Meredith M. Michaels, authors of *The Mommy Myth*, suggest that the media is responsible for what they term the "'new momism' ... a highly romanticized and yet demanding view of motherhood in which the standards for success are impossible to meet" (4) and that in the last twenty years, the media has launched a "long-term propaganda campaign ... to redomesticate the women of America through motherhood" (9). Even *Supernanny* and *The Nanny*, which seem to empathize with the trials and tribulations of motherhood, ulti-

mately promise a magical, 30 minute clean up of the chaos, a way to reintegrate the wayward family into the domestic ideal.

Ironically, while the promise of compulsory heterosexuality has proven
false, women return to play out the fantasy over and again; rather than
questioning its very premise, they privatize its failures. In other words, they
do not point fingers at society when things do not work out "like they're
supposed to"; instead, they turn the blame inward, and the masculinist fantasies of femininity propagated by television enable their masochism. Jennifer Maher concurs that the pull of such shows "reveal[s] the discontent
of perfect love as we've been coached to feel and live it as well as the repetition compulsion such dissatisfaction engenders" (212). In other words,
women watch because they are dissatisfied, but instead of turning away
from the heterosexist narrative, they continue to tune into it.

Women's desire for agency is targeted in yet another way; both domestic fiction and reality television encourage the participation of their audiences in re-constructing reality. Samuel Richardson, for example, noted
that he felt harassed by his readers' desire to intervene in the creative
process. Nevertheless, he continued to elicit criticism and suggestions from
his largely female coterie, no doubt a strategy to increase his own authority and popularity. By granting them agency, but only under his terms and
conditions, Richardson contained and shaped the critical discourse of his
female readership.[19] Similarly, female viewers of reality television are
encouraged to "vote" off female contestants whom they dislike, yet the
woman whom they unanimously hate is clearly a scripted type.[20] In other
words, producers and network executives, rather than losing authority, gain
it by instructing their viewers in a specific version of proper (and improper)
femininity. The women who win on these shows, the ones with whom we
are urged to identify, embody a desirableness, as evidenced by the bachelor's choice of them, which bespeaks the rightness, the naturalness of their
version of femininity. Yet what we understand as likeable, i.e., desirable, is
always, already informed by our culture. In essence, we learn to desire, to
choose, to celebrate that which best sustains patriarchy.

Another reason women might be drawn to the reality constructed for
them in both domestic fiction and reality television is that both promise
them connections with other women. In the 18th century we witnessed the
move from feudal societies to the nuclear family, and an ensuing compartmentalization of private space evident especially in residential architecture.
Part of the appeal of domestic fiction was to enable women, isolated within
their homes, to connect with each other. While it might seem that the divide
between the private and public has since been collapsed by technology,
research shows that people today are feeling increasingly isolated. In the
21st century, individuals have moved increasingly apart from each other;

they work longer hours and thus depend on technology to communicate in absentia. Female viewers who feel pressured to hold the family together might be drawn to these shows as a means of connecting with other women who share similar desires. The ubiquity of *Bachelor* parties, reality show cha-trooms, and blogs dedicated to discussion of these shows then comes as no surprise; one is reminded of the epistolary exchanges between eighteenth-century women readers as they bemoaned the fate of various fictional hero-ines and berated their catty antagonists. Ironically, female community is gained, but at the cost of critical discourse, and only under the conditions of the patriarchal imperative.

Also attracting women is, of course, the flimsy promise of agency bound up in consumerism. Unhappily married, burdened by the double-pressures of work and home, unable to pay their bills, female viewers can flip on the TV and tune into one more fantasy date to an exclusive resort. Therein, they can imaginatively celebrate the thrill of conspicuous con-sumption denied them by the reality of recession. They might not be able to afford the plastic surgeons on *Extreme Makeover*, but they can afford the Crest Whitening Strips and Victoria's Secret Wonderbras advertised dur-ing its commercials. The message of these shows and of their commercial sponsors is that the value of women continues to be defined by both their beauty and their commitment to domesticity, and furthermore, what women lack in desirability can be purchased. These fantasies, the one on the screen and the one embodied by plastic credit, are both made possible because we identify them as "real." And, just as in the eighteenth-century, "reality" works to maintain the status-quo, to secure patriarchal privilege, to underpin the capitalist drive.

We may say that we know what we see on TV is not real; but ideology uses our own cynicism against us.

Works Cited

Adkins, Gary, et. al. "TV's Orneriest Villains." *People* 24 May 2004: 19.

Andrejevic, Mark. *Reality TV: The Work of Being Watched.* Lanham: Rowman Littlefield, 2004.

Armstrong, Nancy. *Desire and Domestic Fiction: A Political History of the Novel.* New York: New York UP, 1987.

Balkin, Karin, ed. *Reality Television.* San Diego: Greenhaven, 2004.

Baudrillard, Jean. *Simulacra and Simulation.* Trans. Sheila Faria Glaser. Ann Arbor: Uni-versity of Michigan Press, 1994.

Davidoff, Leonore, and Katherine Hall. *Family Fortunes: Men and Women of the English Middle Class 1780–1850.* 2nd ed. London: Routledge, 1992.

Davis, Lennard. *Factual Fictions: The Origins of the English Novel.* Philadelphia: Univer-sity of Pennsylvania Press, 1983.

Donovan, Josephine. *Women and the Rise of the Novel, 1405–1726*. New York: St. Martin's, 1999.

Douglas, Susan, and Meredith W. Michaels. *The Mommy Myth: The Idealization of Motherhood and How It Has Undermined Women*. New York: Free Press, 2004.

Eagleton, Terry. *The Rape of Clarissa: Writing, Sexuality, and Class Struggle in Samuel Richardson*. Minneapolis: University of Minnesota Press, 1982.

Gardyn, Rebecca. "The Tribe Has Spoken." *American Demographics* 23.9 (2001):34–41. *Academic Search Elite*. EBSCO. West Virginia University Lib. Morgantown, WV. 8 Aug. 2005 <http:/www.epnet.com/>

Grindstaff, Laura. "Trashy or Transgressive? 'Reality TV' and the Politics of Social Control." *Thresholds: Viewing Culture* 9 (1995): 46–55.

Habermas, Jurgen. *The Structural Transformation of the Public Sphere*. Cambridge: MIT, 1999.

Johnson, Samuel. "A Project for the Employment of Authors." *The Works of Samuel Johnson in Nine Volumes*. Part 7 of 9. 15 Aug. 2005. <www.fullbooks.com/The-Works-of-Samuel-Johnson-in-Nine-Volumes7.html>

Knights, Elspeth. "'Daring but to Touch the Hem of her Garment': Women Reading *Clarissa*." *Women's Writing* 7.2 (2000): 221–45.

Kuhn, Kathryn E. . "'It Had to be You': Narrative Themes in *A Wedding Story*." *Popular Culture Review* 14.2 (2003): 83–92.

LaVelle, Louis. "A Payday for Performance," *Business Week* 18 Apr. 2005: 1.

Magder, Ted. "The End of TV 101." *Reality TV: Remaking Television Culture*. Eds. Susan Murray and Laurie Oullette. New York: New York UP, 2004.

Maher, Jennifer. "What do Women Watch? Tuning into the Compulsory Heterosexuality Channel." *Reality TV: Remaking Television Culture*. Eds. Susan Murray and Laurie Oullette. New York: New York UP, 2004.

McKeon, Michael. *The Origins of the English Novel, 1600–1740*. Baltimore: Johns Hopkins UP, 1987.

Mishel, Lawrence, Jared Bernstein, and Sylvia Allegretto, Eds. *The State of Working America, 2004–2005*. Economic Policy Institute. Ithaca: Cornell UP, 2005.

Murray, Susan, and Laurie Ouellette, Eds. *Reality TV: Remaking Television Culture*. New York: New York UP, 2004.

"Poor Prospects." *Economist* 9 Oct. 2004: 13.

Raphael, Chad. "The Political Economic Origins of Reali-TV." *Reality TV: Remaking Television Culture*. Eds. Susan Murray and Laurie Oullette. New York: NewYork UP, 2004.

Reality Television Show Directory. Walker Marketing Inc. 2000–2005. 19 Sept. 2005 <http://www.realityTVlinks.com>.

Suskind, Ron. "Without a Doubt." *New York Times*. 17 October 2004. *NY Times.com*. 19 September 2005 <http://cscs.umich.edu/~crshalizi/sloth/2004–1016b.html>

Thompson, James. *Models of Value: Eighteenth-Century Political Economy and the Novel*. Durham: Duke UP, 1996.

Todd, Janet. *The Sign of Angellica: Women, Writing and Fiction, 1660–1800*. New York: Columbia UP, 1989.

Tomaselli, Sylvana. "The Most Public Sphere of All: the Family." *Women, Writing, and the Public Sphere: 1700–1800*. Eds. Elizabeth Eger, Charlotte Grant, Cliona O Gallchoir, and Penny Warburton. Cambridge: Cambridge UP, 2001.

Tyson, Laura D'Andrea. "How Bush Widened the Wealth Gap." *Business Week* 1 Nov. 2004: 32.

Wallace, Diana. *Sisters and Rivals in British Women's Fiction, 1913–39*. London: Macmillan, 2000.

Warner, Judith. *Perfect Madness: Motherhood in the Age of Anxiety.* New York: River-head Books, 2005.

Watt, Ian. *The Rise of the Novel: Studies in Defoe, Richardson, and Fielding.* Berkeley: University of California Press, 1957.

Wolf, Naomi. *Misconceptions: Truth, Lies, and the Unexpected on the Journey to Motherhood.* New York: Anchor Books, 2003.

Notes

1. No doubt this number has grown since I first began drafting this essay. See the website entitled *Reality Television Show Directory*. For the purposes of this essay, I use the word "reality television" to refer to those shows which explicitly market themselves as such.

2. In fact, Greenhaven press has just published a collection of opposing viewpoints on the subject edited by Karin Balkin.

3. For discussions of the economic underpinnings of reality television production, see essays by Chad Raphael and Ted Magder in the collection, *Reality TV: Remaking Television Culture*.

4. TLC's *A Baby Story* and *A Wedding Story* have been analyzed for their explicit heterosexism, but the analysis generally stops short of connecting the work of gender to class. See Jennifer Maher's essay on *Baby Story* and Kathryn E. Kuhn's article examining *A Wedding Story*. Reality television shows have also recently elicited a spate of essays discussing the portrayal of homosexual men. The absence of critical work on the portrayal (or lack thereof) of homosexual women in reality television is worth further analysis, although beyond the scope of this essay.

5. There is, of course, much critical debate as to when the novel "emerged." Michael McKeon, however, provides convincing logic as to why we might consider the novel an eighteenth-century "creation." McKeon acknowledges that "[t]he origins of the English novel occur at the end point of a long history of 'novelistic usage'" (19). Yet, he suggests that "[b]y the middle of the eighteenth century, the stabilizing of terminology — the increasing acceptance of 'the novel' as a canonic term, so that contemporaries 'speak of it *as such*'— signals the stability of the conceptual category and of the class of literary products that it encloses" (19). One might make the same argument about the "emergence" of reality television, which clearly has a long history (considering its shared discourse with news media, as well as game shows) but was not spoken of "as such" until the 1990's.

6. Jane Spencer is one of the first and most notable to address this problem in the introduction to her book-length study, *The Rise of the Woman Novelist*. Of course, Spencer acknowledges that her work is itself indebted to Gilbert and Gubar's landmark text, *The Madwoman in the Attic*, which focuses largely on the legitimation of nineteenth-century women's fiction.

7. See Nancy Armstrong's *Desire and Domestic Fiction*. For a more recent analysis of the connections between politics and family, see Sylvana Tomaselli's essay, "The Most Public Sphere of All: the Family."

8. See, for example, works by Ian Watt, Lennard Davis, Michael McKeon, Janet Todd, and Josephine Donovan.

9. So common was this convention that Frances Burney, in the preface to her epistolary novel *Evelina* (1778), termed herself the "editor" of the letters while simultaneously begging that her critics would forgive her novel its imperfections because of her own youth and inexperience as an artist.

10. See Elspeth Knights' essay on women readers' responses to Richardson's *Clarissa*.

11. For a more detailed discussion of this literary shift, see McKeon, ch. 4.

12. For an analysis of the epistemology of public and private spheres in the eighteenth century and this division's relationship to emergent capitalism, see Jurgen Habermas.

13. Ms. Scheft was deemed "Plain Jane Jen" by her catty rival on season 3 of *The Bache-*

lor, although those who witnessed her glamorous makeover upon her return on *The Bachelorette* season 3 might be less than willing to embrace her as the icon of ordinary.

14. This is, of course, an oversimplification necessary for the scope of this essay. See Davidoff and Hall's seminal work, *Family Fortunes* for a broader discussion of the making of the eighteenth- and nineteenth-century century middle-class.

15. Baudrillard discusses, among other elements of popular culture, the first reality television family, The Louds, whose daily activities for seven months were aired in 1971.

16. For a discussion of the eighteenth-century novel's valorization of a middle-class ethos see, among others, works by Nancy Armstrong, Leonore Davidoff and Katherine Hall, and James Thompson.

17. VH1's most recent variation on this theme, *Kept*, in which American middle-class men compete for the chance to be the "kept" man of British rock aristocracy Jerry Hall is a notable exception to this rule and, although outside the scope of this essay, worth further examination.

18. See, for example, Naomi Wolf's compelling work *Misconceptions: Truth, Lies, and the Unexpected on the Journey to Motherhood*, Susan Douglas' and Meredith Michael's *The Mommy Myth*, and Judith Warner's best-selling study, *Perfect Madness*.

19. See Elspeth Knights' article, as well as Terry Eagleton's analysis, p. 27.

20. Interestingly, a survey conducted by *People* magazine found that the top two "orneriest TV villains" were women: masculinized Omarosa of *Apprentice* (and now Burger King commercial) fame and gold-digger Trish of *The Bachelor*. See the article by Gary Adkins, et. al. "TV's Orneriest Villains."

8

Female Police Officers and Reality Television: Analyzing the Presentation of Police Work in Popular Culture

TODD M. CALLAIS AND MELISSA SZOZDA

Introduction

Reality television is fascinating because of its often-conflicting goals of exposing the world to authentic human behavior while entertaining audiences and maximizing profit. Past research has indicated the importance of television consumption in shaping consumer reality (e.g. O'Guinn and Shrum; Shrum, et al.). Throughout the last 15 years reality television has blurred the lines between entertainment and authenticity by allowing individuals to consume edited packages of non-rehearsed and non-scripted social interaction. The presentation of these "real" situations creates the illusion that people are consuming an authentic human experience (Balkin). These qualities make reality television a permutation of sitcom or drama and documentary, which in turn makes its veracity less questionable in the eye of the consumer.

In the past, television and other forms of media have been criticized for their stereotypical or absent presentation of disempowered groups. Throughout the years, groups have lobbied for a more fair representation of demographics other than the white male. Many of these efforts have focused on the under or mis-representation of racial minorities in popular television; however, trivialized portrayals of women have also been questioned. Specifically, groups claim that women are generally presented as subordinate to and less competent than males in social interaction and job capability. Recently, television viewers have seen an emerging population of women in reality television. The actions and consequences of these shows are intended to be real, while they are often times manufactured or manipulated presentations of genuine human action and interaction.

One of the first reality television programs, initially airing in 1989, was *COPS*. Currently *COPS* is in its seventeenth season and lauds itself as an accurate portrayal of "the real men and women of law enforcement" (Curry). Aside from this clear statement of intent that *COPS* is a reality television show, there are also subtle cues within the show, such as shaky cameras and hard breathing after a long pursuit, that suggest a genuine portrayal of actual police work. *COPS* has been a staple in FOX's Saturday line-up for nearly fifteen years and consistently brings in high ratings. *COPS* is produced by Langley Productions headed by John Langley, and according to the Langley Productions' website, 31 of the 35 members of the production team are men. *COPS* can best be described as a "filmed ride along with U.S. law enforcement officials" which offers a "video-cam perspective on police work" (Curry 169).

Since *COPS* is presented as an accurate portrayal of women in law enforcement, it is important to understand the effects that this particular show may have on viewers' perception of women's capabilities in performing police work. If viewers believe that *COPS* is reality or basically reality, and if *COPS* is presented as such, there is a danger that people will view the actions and consequences as being real and valid data about typical police work. The presentation of gender in *COPS* can potentially be used to form impressions about differential capabilities for performing police work. Thus, if there are false stereotypes and exaggerated gender roles provided, these will represent a serious barrier to women entering and succeeding in the field of law enforcement.

This paper examines the portrayal of gender on the reality television show *COPS*. This examination has relevance and is necessary because a great deal of research illustrates that consumption of popular culture is a tool used to form impressions about groups with which individuals have very little interaction. *COPS* represents one of the only outlets for individuals to gain any "real" view of what police officers encounter on a daily basis. This can effect not only the perception the public has on female police officers, but also how women perceive their chances and abilities in relation to becoming an officer. We examine stereotypes commonly applied to women in policing and attempt to see if these stereotypes are highlighted and illustrated as being true. In addition we examine what specific roles and interactions female officers are involved in on the show.

Literature Review

THE PROBLEM FOR WOMEN IN POLICING

Stereotypes regarding female police officers are numerous. Bequidenhout highlights the following stereotypes regarding women in policing:

> Female police officials cannot utilize physical defensive techniques because they are not strong and tough enough ... Female police officials expect special treatment and favors from male police officers ... Female police officials are more inclined to use "deadly force" (a firearm) during confrontations because they lack the physical power to wrestle or to have a fight ... Female police officials are emotionally unstable and easily resort to tears [4].

Moreover, a common stereotype regarding women in policing is that their best skills are interacting with people, sensitivity, and understanding (Wilkinson). These stereotypes are discussed in a negative light by male officers, even though they are arguably the best skills for a police officer to possess. The veracity of these stereotypes, however, has been questioned by numerous studies. Austin found that, of 86 newly trained male officers and 86 newly trained female officers, men and women encountered similar situations, performed patrol work with equivalent skill, and responded to calls in a similar fashion. Austin also found that males and females are equally effective in patrolling.

Another stereotype about female officers is that they cannot use physical defense techniques because they are neither strong, nor tough enough. While women are generally not as physically strong as men, there is no conclusive evidence that suggests female officers are less effective in using defensive techniques to defuse potentially harmful situations. Women are especially skillful in using conflict resolution and negotiating techniques to bring an end to the situation. Furthermore, many female officers want and prefer to be treated as equal to their male counterparts, expelling the stereotype that women seek and expect special treatment and favors. Regarding the stereotype the female officers are more likely to use deadly force, the contrary is actually true. In fact, female officers are more likely to try to negotiate or defuse the situation before using deadly force. The stereotype that female officers are more emotional can be attributed to the way in which females in general are socialized. While females are socialized that it is normal to show emotions, female officers report that they attempt to set themselves as equals to their male counterparts and try to have a high level of professionalism, so they are more controlling of their emotions (Bequidenhout). Finally, although females do exhibit high levels of negotiation and people skills, those are not the only skills the female officers have.

Aside from typical gender stereotypes, male officers' perceptions of female officers also play a role in creating barriers to women in policing. "Study after study concludes that the single largest barrier to increasing the numbers of women in policing is the attitudes and behavior of their male colleagues" (Harrington 2). There is no doubt that this barrier is due to the fact that policemen's attitudes are "almost always uniformly negative" (Wilkinson 3). Perpetuating these stereotypes is dangerous in many ways, not only for female officers, but also for women in general and for the viewers of *COPS*. For female officers, these stereotypes may limit them in what they are able to do. In Wilkinson's study of women and policing she addressed this, stating, "If female officers are perceived as less able than male officers to perform policing tasks, they cannot expect to be similarly deployed" (3). Moreover, the longer these stereotypes are allowed to grow, the more time it will take for females to gain equality on the police force. Another effect of stereotyping is that, due to the small proportion of women in the policing field, one poor performance by one woman is often generalized to many women (Wilkinson 3).

Perhaps because of these issues, the number of women in policing has actually been declining recently. In 1999, 14.3% of sworn law enforcement persons were women. In 2000, this number declined to 13.0%. There are many stereotypes associated with women in law enforcement, and the recent decline in the population of female officers could be related to the possible growth of stereotypes, which are set forth and can be exaggerated through television shows. As with all other stereotypes, these can be detrimental if they are perpetuated to the point at which people cannot escape them.

THE THEORETICAL IMPORTANCE OF POPULAR REALITY TELEVISION

Gerbner's Cultivation Theory states that heavy exposure to mass media leads to attitudes consistent with the "reality" that the media has created, which in turn leads to making assumptions about people, events, and other facets of life. Cultivation theorists focus primarily on continued consumption over the life-course, and how this consumption affects general beliefs about society. Gerbner's theory would support the thought that if viewers continuously watch stereotypical and weak portrayals of women, then that will greatly affect the view of the world those individuals will generally have. If *COPS* portrays women as incompetent or lacking knowledge in their job, that notion will be transferred to the mind of the viewer and will become "reality" to that particular viewer. While Gerbner might argue that watching *COPS* alone would not completely change someone's opinion on the topic of women in policing, it certainly could be part of a general television repertoire replete with negative images of women. The issue of whether or not portrayals of women in reality television are factual in one way or another may be less important than the perceived truth of what these television shows represent. This paper takes a step towards assessing whether viewing reality television is a way of validating dramatic representations of police work.

In a context where viewers are not provided with contrary evidence, the function of reality TV programs may become confused in the minds of the viewers with their value becoming the ability to represent the work of police officers as opposed to weekend television entertainment. Gottdiener proposes the idea of transfunctionalization, arguing that an object can mean one thing to a producer (typically a physical and monetary worth) and have another meaning to the user, such as a cultural or status symbol. Transfunctionalization occurs when one actor changes the function of an object from the function that another actor intended. Especially relevant for this analysis is his discussion of the user/object stage. Gottdiener explains:

> This second stage involves the creation of culture by the users of objects, a much-neglected aspect of the mass culture dynamic. One example of this aspect of meaning production is illustrated by the process of personalization, in which users modify objects of mass consumption in order to express certain cultural symbols, or in connection with specific group practices, or for use in subcultural activities [994].

Gottdiener gives the example of how many Chicano cultures change cars into a low-rider form. This change transfunctionalizes the purpose of the car from transportation to cultural symbol (994). Although the producer might create *COPS* with the intent of entertaining and gaining monetary compensation, the consumer can see the exchange value benefiting them in that it provides them insight into a group with which they previously felt out of touch, police officers. From this it could be hypothesized that the more involved a person is in the viewing of *COPS*, the more likely he or she is to buy into the legitimacy and representativeness of the television show; this has potentially dire consequences for the perception of police work by females.

Women in general may also be affected by these stereotypes. Women often feel that they are incapable of becoming officers because of the over-representation of highly physical and aggressive police work that is presented during the television show *COPS*. Furthermore, viewers who watch *COPS* are influenced and may feel that it is not necessary to think of women as serious officers of the law because generally they are not portrayed as being active officers who pose a true threat to offenders of the law. The images created by this show might be taken by the viewer as complete reality, and, therefore, heighten the risk of confirming, reinforcing, and perpetuating stereotypes.

The effect of males creating a barrier to women in policing is that it discourages females from becoming officers. If these barriers were diminished, a better opportunity would be provided for females in policing. Wilkinson argues, "If police leaders and police academics acknowledged that women have a contribution to make to all aspects of policing [in Australia], they can significantly increase both the quantity and the quality of women's contribution by their pubic support of women police" (3). Sullivan's Interpersonal Theory is based on the idea that person will often define characteristics necessary to participate in any behavior as favorably as possible for him or herself. This means that if male officers see female officers working at the same level that they are working at, it will question and possibly jeopardize their masculinity. Male officers, and perhaps the public in general, define police work in terms of physical prowess and intimidation, meaning that these stereotypes positively benefit their dominance in the field. This causes the man to distort his views and perceive women as not being "strong, competent, or courageous. Since most males do this, it is collectively reinforced" (Sullivan 47). Not only are these negative perceptions limited to patrol officers, but also to officers of higher ranks, such as sergeants who believe that women are better at diffusing potentially violent situations, but think men are more likely to quell these situations simply with their physical presence (Wilkinson 5).

The problems with the veracity of stereotypes about female police officers are clear, and the impact that these stereotypes have on women and society in general should be unquestioned. This study aims to examine the impact of a reality television program aimed at presenting a "realistic" vision of the work of police officers. Research indicating the importance of popular culture, and even reality television, in affecting the worldview of individuals is abundant. Examining the television show *COPS* allows us to see what worldview is being presented in relation to gender and police work.

Research Methods

We performed a content analysis of the FOX television series *COPS*. Content analysis is an appropriate method for our research questions because it allows us to measure the smaller components that create and contribute to the larger social issue that we are studying. Content analysis is also appropriate because of the size and nature of the data. Moreover, it provides a depth to understanding how we are socialized to see gender roles and work. We used this method because it allowed us to achieve the most inclusive and consistent results due to measuring a large number of the same variables for every episode.

COPS is an ideal show to analyze in this study because it is the most recognizable reality show focusing on police officers. The show's continued success illustrates an acceptance from the public. Furthermore, many times on *COPS* the officers are performing non-typical police duties, such as many physically challenging activities. In many of the scenes, there is some type of physical pursuit, while typically policing does not consist of multiple physical pursuits in one day. Many times in these on-camera pursuits, only male officers are shown performing strenuous physical work, which may have a serious consequence in that women may think that they are incapable of being an effective physical force. Moreover, viewers may take female officers less seriously, especially when it involves a physical matter.

Overall, we coded 114 police interactions from programming obtained through broadcasts on basic cable television. Approximately one-third of these episodes were double coded in order to ensure accuracy. First, we measured the objective data for each show, including the number and the sex of the officers present. We also recorded the time of day, the location, and the type of operation that was being illustrated, for example a call response or a traffic stop. Next we organized our analysis to include commonly established stereotypes of female officers, as defined by past research, in order to see if and to what extent these stereotypes are highlighted. In order to do this, we used smaller variables, which may contribute to defining stereotypes commonly associated with female officers. Specifically there were four main issues we examined: demographics, physicality, emotions, and male officer to female officer relationships. We also included a small number of open-ended analysis questions in order to record other commonalities not already defined in the analysis or specific situations that might add to or perpetuate these stereotypes. This content analysis sheet can be located in Appendix A.

In regards to all of the subject matter previously discussed, we have come to hypothesize that female police officers on the television show *COPS* will be portrayed in a stereotypical manner, rather than a manner that reflects the true professional nature of the female officer. This will be portrayed by first having minimal coverage of female officers, and when there is coverage, the coverage of the women officers will put them in roles that are typically associated with women, such as negotiators, as opposed to physical threats. Moreover, in scenes involving physical activities, women will not be involved or will not be the focus of the camera. Finally, certain "feminine" issue will be highlighted when female officers are focused upon, such as emotions and family involvement.

Results

UNDERREPRESENTATION OF FEMALE POLICE OFFICERS

In 2001 the National Center for Women and Policing reported that female police officers comprised approximately 12.7% of sworn in officers in forces of 100 or more people (Harrington). However, the percentage of female officers in *COPS* is much lower. In this study, two types of officers were defined and measured for. The first type of officer was labeled the primary officer. The primary officer was defined as having the most contact and interaction with the offender or victim if no offender was present. Female officers were only represented 11.2% of the time as the primary officer.

Secondary officers were defined as officers who had a helping role in the situation. While these officers did not have the most contact with the offender, they were actively involved in the situation as it presented itself. After combining the primary officers and the secondary officers, females accounted for 10.0% of all officers. While this does not represent a substantial statistical difference from the number of officers that exist in reality, the slight difference does represent a problem. Since negative actions by female police officers are typically attributed to female police officers on the whole, because they are so small in number, it is troubling that there is even less female representation in a television series as popular as *COPS*.

One large consequence of this underrepresentation is that females considering employment in the policing field may be deterred from this career because they feel that the policing field is not for women. The gross misrepresentation may also lead women to think that their chances of being accepted and being successful in the field are very small. This underrepresentation shows that women are not a significant part of the criminal justice system. Another consequence is that, by showing only a small number of female police officers to the general public, there is a larger negative generalizability. Therefore, every time that a female officer makes a mistake, it is easy to generalize her mistake to all female officers. If there are fewer female officers with positive portrayals, it is harder to offset those females who might make mistakes.

THE ROLE OF THE CAMERA

The camera and the editing of the police footage both seemed to play an important role in creating the portrayal of the female officer. Fifty-three percent of the time when a male and a female officer were involved in the same scene, the camera focused more on the male than the female, regardless of the amount of action both were performing. The viewer would be able to hear the female officer talking, but would not actually be able to see or locate her in the picture. In one scene, there was a briefing where in the beginning two female officers were clearly visible and were planning on partaking in the operation at hand. However, once the operation was actually in progress, one female was not visible at all, and the other female was just barely visible. The male officers seen in the briefing, however, were easily identifiable.

Moreover, sometimes the camera would seem to shift away and divert itself from the female officers. This often happened if a female officer was dealing with the offender and a male officer came into the scene. Almost immediately, the camera would shift away from the female to the male, regardless or whether or not there was a shift in involvement (as many times there was not). Sometimes this shift would even negate or devalue the female officers' work by not crediting her with the work she had done prior to the male officer arriving. Strong shifts in the camera away from the female officer to the male officer were apparent in seven of the twenty-two scenes involving officers of both sexes.

In one episode, there was an officer-offender foot pursuit. One male and one female officer chased the offender, and eventually the female officer caught the offender. The camera showed very briefly that she had captured the offender and then focused again on the male officer who was simply standing to catch his breath. Later in the scene, the male officer was shown again chasing another offender, and after he caught the offender there was a significant amount of time spent focused on the male officer and the offender he had caught. While the male officer was praised by the camera for catching the offender, the female officer was barely recognized and credited. This story is representative of a general trend towards glorifying male physical prowess while underplaying the prowess of females.

Aside from not focusing on female officers and shifting away from female officers, the camera also sometimes appeared to disengage the officer from her work. Particularly, one episode focused entirely on prostitution. The first scene and the last scene focused on arresting alleged prostitutes, while the second scene focused on arresting the alleged johns. During the first and last scene when the male officer was undercover, after the "bust," the camera showed him being very active in the arrest. He spoke to the offender and actually escorted her to the police car. Through his actions, it was clear that he was an officer. However, when the female officers went undercover, they were not shown to be active at all during the arrest. They were visible in the camera, yet the camera did not focus on the female officer confronting the offenders, as it did for the male officer. The female officers gave the signal for the other officers to move in and arrest the offender, and that was all that the viewer saw of the female officers for the rest of the scene. These instances are important because, even when women are succeeding at stereotypical police work, it is being underplayed and undervalued by the camera crew and film editors; this leads to a biased portrayal of gender and police work to the general public.

FEMALE OFFICERS AS CAREGIVERS

When the camera was generous in allotting time for female officers, many times these officers were shown in the role of caregiver. In some scenes, the female was shown serving solely as a shoulder to cry on. This role greatly perpetuates the stereotype of the woman as solely a caring and sympathetic person. In one scene, a grandmother and her grandson were involved in an altercation. The male officer handled all of the information relevant to the facts of the offense, and in the end the camera finally showed the female officer who had been present the entire time, as evident by her knowing every fact of the case. The way in which this scene was framed made it appear that the female officer was there only to comfort the grandmother. The only shots of the female officer were of her talking to the grandmother about how to better parent the child and how she felt sympathetic for her. The camera made it appear that the female officer had no significant business in the scene, other than to comfort the grandmother.

In another scene, a woman was very distraught after her friend was stabbed. The male officer advised the woman to calm down and to talk to one of the officers. Although there were many officers on the scene, he immediately pointed to the only female officer around. Later, the camera showed the female officer talking to the woman and zoomed in on the officer's hand on the woman's knee as a sign of her comforting the woman. The constant reiteration of female officers as caregivers can easily distract the viewers from recognizing that they are in fact relevant actors in police situations.

THE SEVERITY OF THE NATURE OF
THE CRIMES COVERED BY FEMALE OFFICERS

In the episodes of COPS studied, female officers tended to respond to and be assigned to crimes of a less severe nature. As the primary officer, females attended to the following crimes: assistance call, disturbances (4), narcotics, response to a robbery, street patrol, suspicious persons, theft, and traffic stop. In two scenes, there was a shared primary officer role, and in those two scenes the female officers were involved in an assistance call and a homicide investigation. Not inclusive of the homicide investigation, many of these crimes were not of a greatly severe nature. Moreover, female officers did not appear to be assigned to any large tasks as the male officers were. There were many scenes in which male officers were assigned to very compromising positions in order to catch narcotics offenders. Sometimes they were asked to go undercover to buy or sell drugs, and other times they would use forceful techniques to raid suspected drug houses. Aside from the other calls they attended to, primary male officers attended to: homicide calls (3), kidnapping (1), narcotics (17), shootings (6), stabbings (3), and vehicle pursuits (9). By showing female officers as responding to less severe crimes, it devalues their work, showing them to be less consequential in their duties.

FEMALE OFFICERS AND STEREOTYPES

The first stereotype, which seemed to be confirmed in the portrayal of female officers, was that female officers lacked physical prowess. Female officers were involved in physical pursuits in only 7 of the 114 scenes examined. Moreover, sometimes these female officers were portrayed in a negative light while completing these physical tasks. In one scene, a female officer was forced to chase an offender on foot. After she caught the offender, she scolded him for "making her run." In two of the seven scenes in which a female officer was involved in a physical pursuit, the female officer appeared to be struggling with the physical task. Since female officers were only involved in physical pursuits seven times, it does not appear to be beneficial to female officers that in two scenes they are struggling.

Another stereotype that was confirmed was that female officers are more likely to use negotiation techniques. In all reality and practicality, this seemed to benefit all parties involved and represent a better style of policing. In one scene, a mother and daughter were fighting, and two female officers were dispatched to handle the situation. While the female officers could have easily dismissed the feelings and the best interests of the mother and daughter, the officers attempted to mediate and negotiate between the parties involved. By using and applying these negotiating techniques, the officers were able to help the mother and daughter resolve their situation without anyone being hurt or arrested. In half of the scenes in which females were the primary officers, special negotiation techniques were used. These techniques seem to be greatly beneficial to all parties involved, yet this stereotype is generally treated as being negative when applied to female officers.

In dealing with the other stereotypes commonly associated with female officers, many of these stereotypes were not actually highlighted through the show. In analyzing 114 scenes, in no scenes did the female officer cry, appear overly sensitive, or ask special favors of her male counterparts.

Conclusions and Direction for Future Research

The purpose of this paper is to explain how the presentation of police work in popular television can serve to repress the representation of women on the police force. Adorno and other members of the Frankfurt school argue that the culture industry has subtly and successfully transfunctionalized the use value of reality television so that it is presented to a consuming audience as not just an entertaining form of television but also as an authentic law enforcement experience; this is an assumption of the paper. Cultural critics and actors close to reality television have argued that consumption of reality TV is different than consumption of other forms of television because of the cultural veracity attributed to its documentary style presentation. Conducting a content analysis of the themes presented in the television show *COPS* allows us to understand the potential impact of this phenomena.

Overall, the portrayal of female officers on reality television is not beneficial to female officers in general. While reality television may not intentionally be attempting to handicap female officers, the lack of numerous positive portrayals advances negative thoughts and stereotypes. The true problem posed by these inaccurate portrayals lies in the effects that these portrayals may potentially have on the viewers. Gerbner suggests that these portrayals will lead people to believe that the portrayals are reality. Therefore, viewers may believe that all female officers are like the ones they see on television — in this instance, female officers as care giving, secondary officers. Furthermore, these portrayals may also affect females wishing to enter into the policing field. Females might perceive their chances of being successful on the police force as more difficult than it may be in real life.

There a number of conclusions that can be drawn from this research. With such a variance in the beliefs about how representative reality television is of female police work, it is still clear that common past stereotypes about female police officers are predominantly represented in the given data. Second, the evidence indicates that when women are not playing into stereotypes about female police work and are succeeding at the more masculine rules of police work, it is underplayed or ignored by the film crew and editors. With all of this in mind, it would seem that the consumption of this form of reality television could fall in line with the beliefs of many cultural critics and sociologists alike that *COPS* is being perceived by many as a consumption of culture; thus reality television has become transfunctionalized.

The data on how people interpret *COPS* and reality television is for the most part inconclusive. The hard numbers show trends indicating that those who watch a great amount of television will view it as a cultural or political form and therefore are more likely consume *COPS* as an educational medium. A number of important implications for the study of reality television flow from these findings. Our research indicates that, despite attempting to appear real and valid, reality television often presents individuals in a stereotypical and inaccurate manner. Individuals attribute a great deal of veracity to popular forms of television that are associated with groups the consumer has little interaction with. We lay the groundwork for future research on the consumption of other types of reality television and assumptions about their corresponding groups (*American Idol* and popularity for example). In addition, future research could focus on more detailed measures of exposure and perception of television.

Furthermore, this research indicates that the messages in popular television reify stereotypical impressions about females and police work. Future research should focus on the general content of television stations to understand the framing of gender behavior and capabilities. An analysis of the content of popular television corresponding with viewership would illustrate the extent to which the producers of television cater to the consumption desire of those who view reality television. One possible opportunity for future research in this topic would be to analyze a greater number of episodes of *COPS* and also to analyze different reality television portrayals of female officers. However, this topic would have the most beneficial research by expanding the study of the effects of reality television to the actual psyche of the human being to see if there is a true correlation between reality television and viewers' thoughts and beliefs.

Although additional research is needed, the present study has set the stages for future studies in two important ways. First, it is one of the only current works that attempts to demonstrate the blatant misrepresentation of females and police work in reality television, laying the foundation for further discussion of the dangers of cultural consumption. Second, it indicates the importance of art in managing identities and countering dominant ideologies.

Appendix A

Episode #: _____ Location: _____ Time of Day: _____

Type of Operation: Call Response   Traffic Stop   Physical Altercation/Pursuit
Undercover Op.

Specifics: _____

Number of Officers: 1   2   3   4   5   6   7   8   9   10+

Sex of the Primary Officer (most contact with the offender):   M   F

Sex of the Secondary Officers: (1)M/F   (2)M/F   (3)M/F   (4)M/F   (5)M/F
(6)M/F   (7)M/F   (8)M/F   (9)M/F   (10)M/F

	Male	Female
Sex of the Primary Offender:	Male	Female

	Yes	No	NA
Is the male the primary narrator of the sequence (i.e.- speaks to the main camera at the beginning of the scene)?	Yes	No	NA
Does the female officer involve herself in any physical pursuits where extra effort is exerted?	Yes	No	NA
Running/chasing solely?	Yes	No	NA
Running plus another physical task(s)?	Yes	No	NA

If so, what:_____

	Yes	No	NA
Does the female officer appear to be struggling with the physical challenge?	Yes	No	NA
Is the female officer unable to assist others due to the physical challenge?	Yes	No	NA
Does the male officer involve himself in any physical pursuits where extra effort is exerted?	Yes	No	NA
Does the male officer appear to be struggling with the physical challenges?	Yes	No	NA
Does the female officer draw a weapon?	Yes	No	NA
Is there sufficient reason to believe that the officer may have perceived physical threat to her being?	Yes	No	NA
Does the male officer draw a weapon?	Yes	No	NA
Is there sufficient reason to believe that the officer may have perceived physical threat to his being?	Yes	No	NA
Does the female officer cry at any time?	Yes	No	NA
Does the female officer portray signs of emotion?	Yes	No	NA

If yes, how?_____

	Victim	Offender	NA
If the situation involves a victim and an offender, whom does the female officer primarily deal with?	Victim	Offender	NA

	Yes	No	NA
Does the female officer display sensitivity to the people involved (other than other officers)?	Yes	No	NA

	Facts	Feelings	NA
Does the female officer appear to focus more on the situation facts or situation feelings?	Facts	Feelings	NA

	Yes	No	NA
Does the female officer use techniques other than physical force to diffuse potentially violent situations?	Yes	No	NA
Does the female officer defer to the male officer in making decisions?	Yes	No	NA
Is there a strong shift in responsibility from the female to the male officer?	Yes	No	NA

Does the female officer experience great opposition from the people they arrest?	Yes	No	NA
Verbal opposition?	Yes	No	NA
Physical opposition?	Yes	No	NA
Does the male officer experience great opposition from the people they arrest?	Yes	No	NA
Verbal opposition?	Yes	No	NA
Physical opposition?	Yes	No	NA
Does the female officer seek out any "preferential" help from her male colleagues?	Yes	No	NA
Does the female officer seem subordinate to the male officer?	Yes	No	NA
Does the camera focus primarily on the male officer?	Yes	No	NA
Does the camera ever divert itself away from the female officer?	Yes	No	NA

At what point does this happen? _____

Is the maternal role of the female ever referenced or referred to?	Yes	No	NA
Is the paternal role of the male ever referenced or referred to?	Yes	No	NA

What do the female officers tend to do if they are not in primary contact with the offender?_____

What do the male officers tend to do if they are not in primary contact with the offender?_____

Comments:

Works Cited

Adorno, Theodor W. "Culture Industry Reconsidered." *New German Critique*. 6 (1975): 12–19.

_____. "Perennial Fashion-Jazz." *Prisms*. Cambridge, MA: MIT Press, 1981.

Austin, Wendy. "The Socialization of Women Police: Male Officer Hostility to Female Police Officers." First Australian Women in Policing Conference, 1996.

Balkin, Karen. *Reality TV*. San Diego: Greenhaven Press, 2004.

Bequidenhout, Christiaan. 2002. "Performance of Female Police Officers in a Male Dominated Environment: Replacing Myths with Reality." *Acta Criminologica: SA/Southern African Journal of Criminology* 15 (2), p 110–118.

Consalvo, Mia. "Hegemony, Domestic Violence, and *COPS*: A Critique of Concordance (The Shows of Violence)." *Journal of Popular Film and Television* Summer (1998): 1–9.

Curry, Kathleen. "Mediating *COPS*: An Analysis of Viewer Reaction to Reality TV." *Journal of Criminal Justice and Popular Culture* 8.3 (2001): 169–185.

Gerbner, George, et al. *Communications Technology and Social Policy: Understanding the New Cultural Revolution*. New York: Interscience Publication, 1973.

Gottdiener, M. "Hegemony and Mass Culture: A Semiotic Approach." *American Journal of Sociology*. 90.5. (1985): 979–1001.

Harris, R. J. *A Cognitive Psychology of Mass Communication*. 4th ed. Mahwah, NJ: Lawrence Erlbaum Associates. 2004.

Harrington, Penny. *Status of Women in Police Reporting: Equality Denied*. National Center for Women and Policing, 1997. <www.womenandpolicing.org/status.html>

Knox, George W. *Female Gang Members and the Rights of their Children.* National Gang Crime Research Center, 2001. <www.ngcrc.com/ngcrc/page16.htm>

Lonsway, Kim. *Equality Denied: The Status of Women in Policing 2001.* National Center For Women & Policing, 2002. <www.womenandpolicing.org/PDF/2002_Status_Report.pdf>

Martin, Leanne. *Women Police in the Media- Fiction Versus Reality.* Sydney: Australian Women Police Conference, 1996.

O'Guinn, Thomas C. and L.J. Shrum. "The Role of Television in the Construction of Consumer Reality." *The Journal of Consumer Research* 23.4 (1997) 278–94.

Schrum, L.J., Robert S. Wyer, Jr., and Thomas C. O'Guinn. "The Effects of Television Consumption on Social Perceptions: The Use of Priming Procedures to Investigate Psychological Processes." *The Journal of Consumer Research* 24.4 (1998): 447–58.

Sullivan, H. S. (1953). *The Interpersonal Theory of Psychiatry.* New York: Norton.

Wilkinson, Vicki, and Irene Froyland. "Women in Policing." *Trends and Issues in Crime and Criminal Justice* 58 (1996): 1–6.

9

The Cutting Room: Gendered American Dreams on Plastic Surgery TV

Shana Heinricy

Recently, plastic surgery has proliferated on television, including the fictional program *Nip/Tuck* on FX and reality programs such as *Extreme Makeover* on ABC, *Miami Slice* on Bravo, *The Swan* on FOX, *Dr. 90210* on E!, and TLC's *Body/Work*. Beauty has long been commodified, with endless tubes and tubs and jars of products to make someone (usually a woman or girl) beautiful. In addition, beauty has long been considered a site of labor, particularly for women. This labor is active, physical, and embodied, from tightening a corset, applying lipstick, plucking or shaving hairs, denying food, to exercising at the gym. However, television has constructed plastic surgery as a different sort of labor of beauty, one of passivity, but still mainly for women. Women are free to choose plastic surgery, but they have little active involvement in the transformation. Scholars studying plastic surgery have argued for the choice to have plastic surgery as a site of empowerment (e.g. Davis, *Dubious*; Davis, *Reshaping*). While this theory may in part be valid, it overlooks the ways in which the structures of plastic surgery seek to reduce choice and agency.

My specific project focuses on the constitution of labor in plastic surgery programs on television. I argue that a new form of the American Dream is evident in these programs, one in which hard work becomes a labor of passivity and suffering. The female body functions as a form of biological capital, which must be cut open by doctors in order to increase its value. The active labor of the doctors, one of sawing and hammering, is dwelled on by the cameras. A hegemonic discourse of the beauty economy is created, one in which women's work is again elided.

These shows clearly reflect a mostly feminine and female bodily transformation, usually performed by a male doctor on a female patient. According to the American Society of Plastic Surgeons (ASPS), more than 8.7 million Americans received cosmetic surgery in 2003, a 32% increase from 2002. This figure does not include 6.6 million reconstructive surgeries. Of the elective cosmetic surgery procedures, 86% were performed on women.[1] Unfortunately, I could not find plastic surgery statistics regarding the ethnicity or income of the patients. Nonetheless, these statistics illustrate the abundance of cosmetic surgeries performed and the gendered nature of the phenomenon.

Within the context of plastic surgery reality programs, men are quite literally creating beauty standards for women. The labor of men is one of activity, such as sawing through flesh, and of authority, declaring what is or is not beautiful. Women's labor, on the other hand, is one of passivity and suffering, both physical suffering and suffering of financial sacrifice. The job of women is to allow things to be done to their bodies, rather than doing things to other bodies, which mirrors traditional ideas about gendered relations and sexual behaviors. Women allow these things to be done to their bodies as a form of creation of capital and upkeep of capital. The female body thus becomes capital for women's participation in the American Dream. I argue that a new form of the American Dream is evident in these programs, one in which hard work becomes a labor of passivity and suffering.

I explain the history of the American Dream and the transformations that have occurred, arguing that reality television is a site illustrating a recent transformation. I argue that the capital necessary for plastic surgery is erased within these shows, thus constructing the appearance that everyone has access to plastic surgery. This exemplifies the myth of equality on which the American Dream is founded. A gendered division of labor is created within the shows which erases the hard work of beauty transformations.

I examine four of these shows, two on networks: *The Swan* (4 episodes) on FOX and *Extreme Makeover* (5 episodes) on ABC, and two on cable: *Dr. 90210* (7 episodes) on E! and *Body/Work* (2 episodes) on TLC. These programs were chosen primarily due to access. They were recently on the air, and thus I was able to record them. While watching the shows I looked specifically for how labor was constructed during the programs, including the verbal, textual, and aesthetic elements of the program which structured ideas about labor.

The Myth of the American Dream

American destiny was informed, in myth, by one central principle: America is a fresh place, a new beginning, an opportunity; it is the New World [Robertson 29].

Inherent in the mythic narrative of the United States is the idea of transformation, of striving for something better. As Robertson explains, the United States was founded on a revolution, which indicates a dissatisfaction with the ways things are and a concerted effort to improve the situation. Immigrants came, and still come, to the United States in the hopes of improving their lot in life, whether financially, politically, or both. The dream of the possibility of transformation is still alive in the United States, and is tied to the founding of the nation through American narratives.

I argue that there have been two major transformations of the American Dream, the second of which is my primary concern for this project. The original American Dream was tied to religious values of hard work leading to salvation. In the early to mid-twentieth century, the religious aspect of the dream was displaced onto consumerism. Hard work was not leading to a spiritual heaven, but a heaven on earth achieved through attainment of consumer goods. A second transformation has occurred recently, as evidenced in reality television, in which hard work is either eliminated from the equation or changed into a form different than the original conceptualization of work.

Many, perhaps most, narratives connected to the nation of the United States focus on a positive transformation which occurs through the efforts of an individual. Some scholars, such as Cullen, attribute this focus on the individual to the sort of Protestantism prevalent in the early years of the nation . These Puritan religious values focused on the monitoring of individual behaviors in order to determine if the person were going to heaven or hell. This heavy, personal control leads to the success of the individual. Therefore hard-work and self-discipline are often indistinguishable from each other. This sort of discipline would ultimately be rewarded with success. For the Puritans, this success was salvation. However, this success soon became linked with capitalism, giving rise to the more contemporary version of the American Dream.

An example of the American Dream, the narrative of Benjamin Franklin's life focuses on a poor boy who takes the initiative to educate himself and sets out from home at an early age to learn a trade (Franklin). According to the myth, with little help, solely through his own dedication and perseverance, he was able to become a successful inventor and politically important. Franklin's life story even served to further the distinction between the old world and the new world, since Franklin lived in London for a time and admittedly lacked self-control. While in London, he toiled in mediocrity and self-indulgence, only to come back to the United States and achieve success. Horatio Alger wrote similar fictional stories about independent young men who are able to pull themselves up by their bootstraps, finding success without much help.

Max Weber argues that capitalism, the focus on the individual, and Protestant religious values are ultimately connected. The early version of the American Dream, which focused on hard work and labor as a means of salvation and success, became transformed through capitalism to focus on a specific kind and degree of monetary success. Protestant values focused on self-restraint and labor of the individual as a means to salvation. Weber argues that labor therefore was not solely a way to attain material goods, but was also deemed good for the soul. Therefore, an individual's hard work was encouraged and rewarded in multiple ways, thus perpetuating the capitalist system. According to Weber, the motivation of a work force is necessary for capitalism to proliferate. The particular Protestant ethics on which the United States was founded served as a strong breeding ground for capitalism, and helped to create the American Dream.

As the United States became more secular, particularly in the twentieth century, the religious associations with hard work began to disappear, and the capitalist associations of hard work resulting in material wealth became more prevalent. The focus of the American Dream began to shift, from salvation to material gain. Cross argues that commercialism became the defining ideology of 20th century America, replacing and becoming inseparable from religion and democracy . The grounds for commercialism were paved around the turn of the century with the introduction of the means for mass production. Mass production allowed a link to be forged between democracy and commercialism. Goods could be produced to appear approximately the same and interchangeable with each other; thus theoretically everyone had access to the same goods. The ability to consume similar products as other people was an aspect of equality.

The Depression proved to be a challenge to the doctrine of consumption due to the lack of purchasing power of the masses, but it was one that was overcome. In their study of *Vogue* magazine, Lakoff and Scherr locate a change in the portrayal of beauty due to the Depression, resulting in the beginning of the commodification of female beauty. They argue that prior to the Depression, actual wealthy women, rather than models, graced most of the pages of *Vogue*. The magazine served to show the masses how wealthy people should look and act, thus reinforcing class difference. Beauty appeared to be a by-product of wealth. The images of these beautiful, wealthy people were used to titillate and entertain, but Lakoff and Scherr argue that they were not yet selling beauty to poor women. Being beautiful was not seen as possible for poor women, thus naturalizing class difference in terms of beauty. *Vogue* revised its image during the Depression, and began publishing stories on how women can look beautiful on a budget. In addition, models (who until this time were low-paid workers considered to be clothes-hangers) began to be viewed as bringing a certain sort of beauty to the magazine's pages. Efforts were made to transform these poor workers into elegant beauties via the work of the camera, thus indicating that any woman can be transformed into a beauty. Beauty was no longer simply inherent in the lives of the rich, a by-product of their lives of leisure, but was something to be bought by women.

While women's bodies have long been seen as commodities to be exchanged by men, such as in the marriage ceremony, this was the beginning of a commodification of the beautiful women's body which required women of all classes to purchase goods for the maintenance of their bodies. The female body became a form of capital as necessary of upkeep as any other capital, such as a house. The maintenance of beauty thus became part of women's work. Beauty was not something that was inherently possessed, but something that a woman must work at. According to the mythos of the American Dream, equality can be achieved through hard work, which leads to equal access to material goods. Beauty was one such good available to all under the mythos of commercialism. Thus, previously un-sellable products were converted into necessary products, particularly for women.

Television played a central role in spreading the doctrine of consumption as part of the American way, as necessary for the recovery of the economy after WWII. Consumption was part of the American Dream. Cohen argues that a "consumer's republic" was created in the United States, one in which buying products was seen as participating in democracy and aiding the nation. Consumption was the duty of American citizens; it would fuel the economy and save the nation. The ability to consume freely became the defining element of democracy, separating the United States from communists. Of course, this consumption was gendered and classed. Women were encouraged to buy certain sorts of goods, mostly household items, clothing for her family, and beauty products, while men purchased big ticket items, such as televisions, cars, appliances (usually to be used by women), and homes. Ultimately, husbands often had control over money, and many people did not have the money to buy many consumer goods at all.

Spigel helps to explain the gendered nature of women's labor and its relation to television. She argues that the separation between work and leisure has not always been differentiated for women, specifically because women's work has traditionally been done in the home. The home has been constructed as a site of leisure for men, and one of unpaid labor and leisure for women. This constituted women as always being at work, unclear when leisure time began. Thus, leisurely consumption and labor were always intertwined and often inseparable for women. Spigel's specific study focuses on how daytime television in the middle of the twentieth century was created specifically for women in a way that reflected cultural fears about

women being distracted from their labor in the home by having television
in the home. The fear was that women would not be able to control their
consumption of television, unable to discipline themselves to remain at
work in the home. Labor, then, is constructed as a corrective for women's
uncontrollable urge to consume.

However, despite the images on television, home and car ownership
were not possible for many people in the 1950s (or even today). White
women could possibly achieve these things through marriage, however, and
a better marriage was promised as the result of the work of beauty. Minorities had little opportunity to achieve these things, but they were alive as a
possibility. Home and car ownership were part of the American Dream,
which posed that attainment of these things was possible for every man if
he worked hard enough and utilized enough self-restraint. In this way, the
American Dream posed possibilities of a better life, which were within all
men's grasp due to the capitalist system at the "heart" of the nation. Personal transformation, striving for a "better" life, is at the heart of this American Dream. In addition, consumption was tied to aiding the nation, and
therefore those who had the money to consume were depicted as better citizens than the poor.

Contemporary reality television shows, particularly plastic surgery
programs, reveal a postfeminist[2] approach, equating the consumption of
expensive goods with equality. However, while the American Dream
appeared to focus on the attainment of material success through the hard
labor of the individual, reality television has begun to illustrate a version
of the American Dream which eliminates work from the equation. It is not
that no work is done, but that labor is erased from these programs, particularly the labor done by women. Some programs take a documentary style,
in which people are followed as they receive services from a plastic surgeon.
Often, the work necessary to acquire the money for the surgery is eliminated within the show. The women may be shown to be relatively poor
through images of their homes, but nonetheless, miraculously have the
money for the surgery, illustrating that all women can afford beauty. In
addition, the physical work of suffering is eliminated, with only the doctor's labor of surgery portrayed on the shows. In other sorts of programs,
people (mostly women) are chosen to receive surgery for free, thus indicating that they have access to the consumer product of beauty.

The new version of the American Dream, one that equates the personal
choice to consume with equality, is rhetorically produced for women
through the constitution of labor on television, which plastic surgery program help to illustrate. Reality television is particularly suited to this task,
since it is itself a form of gendered labor. Clearly, being watched and sur-
veiled, as occurs in reality television, is a sort of unpaid labor in itself

(Andrejevic). It is the unpaid labor of having an all-consuming, ever-present gaze upon the body. In short, it is women's work.

The American Dream has changed throughout American history. First, due to its ties to Puritan ethics, hard work of the individual was linked to salvation. This became the grounds for the dream. The goal of salvation was replaced by the goal of attainment of material wealth as a measure of success. Recently, hard work has begun to drop out of the equation. However, its erasure is not total. What counts as labor has become multifaceted and nuanced. While labor has generally been associated with activity, now a work of passivity, of allowing oneself to be transformed, is a new form of work which can still yield material success and thus achievement of the American Dream.

Erasure of Capital

Participation in the pursuit of any version of the American Dream requires some form of capital, whether economic, social, cultural, or biological. Plastic surgery TV stresses the body as a form of capital that can yield the fruits of the American Dream with proper upkeep. All other forms of capital are erased, thus positioning the body as the only form of capital necessary for the achievement of the American Dream for women. By eliminating the economic capital necessary to have these surgeries, the shows perpetuate the postfeminist tenet that personal choice and equal access to goods means that equality has been achieved.

Bourdieu discusses a variety of different kinds of capital, or those things that allow one to have access to commodities. Social capital is who one knows. Economic capital is the money one has. He focuses his research mostly on cultural capital, which includes taste. Cultural capital is an internalized body of knowledge regarding things such as what to like, how to dress, and how to speak. Cultural capital serves to differentiate different classes, prohibiting access to the upper class to working class people. For example, even though a working class person may somehow acquire enough economic capital to be able to go to a five-star restaurant, the person likely would not possess the cultural capital to know appropriate behavior at a fancy restaurant. The person thus may stand out as not belonging. Cultural capital is usually elided from the American Dream, which operates on the assumption that economic capital is all that is necessary to take part in all aspects of American culture.

Cultural capital becomes embodied through habit, which is important to my argument. Through implication in Bourdieu's theory, the social world resides within the body. I argue that for women, the body itself (not just knowing how to adorn the body) is a form of capital (biological capital) and thus is positioned as a way for women to attain commodities. The body as capital for women is one of the key ways that the American Dream is gendered, and is constituted in part through these plastic surgery reality shows.

Within Bourdieu's theory, all human bodies function in some way as capital. Nonetheless, within the discourse of these reality shows on plastic surgery, male bodies physically work to attain commodities, and female bodies suffer. Therefore, not only capital but also labor itself becomes an internally directed passive state of the body for women, not outward directed labor. Therefore, plastic surgery as it is presented on television is constructed as an important site for the upkeep of capital for women.

While labor (as a form of merit) is stressed within these shows, the capital needed to participate in this postfeminist American Dream is negated. *Dr. 90210* is a documentary-style reality program about an actual plastic surgery clinic in Beverly Hills. Dr. Rey, the featured doctor of the series, who was brought to the United States by missionaries from a childhood of poverty in Brazil, is shown working long hours and operating. He stated, "I'm living proof of the American Dream." It is not shown who helped him set up his practice (social capital) or who paid for his college education (economic capital).

A patient of Dr. Rey's, a young single mother, received a tummy tuck from him. Her meager home is shown very quickly, not lingered over like those of the rich, good-looking doctors. She stated that she had wanted the surgery since her son was born four years ago. The show never mentioned why she did not receive the surgery sooner, which is likely because she was saving up for four years. Any discussions of the economic capital needed for the surgery, and thus for participation in the American Dream, is elided. However, this segment shows a woman who is clearly poor receiving surgery, indicating that it is accessible to all.

Minorities are portrayed as participating in the male or female version of the dream, but not creating a dream specifically for themselves. Therefore, gender difference is somewhat celebrated in the shows, but race and class differences are eliminated. This is because the surgery is supposed to function to erase ethnicity and class by giving the patients greater cultural capital. One of the unspoken tenets of the American Dream is highlighted through this elision: that race and class distinctions need to be erased in order to have cultural capital. Jhally and Lewis' study of *The Cosby Show*, for example, illustrated that the Cosby family needed to be culturally whitened in order to appear as pinnacles of the American Dream.

Labor

Throughout the cable documentary-style reality television shows *Dr. 90210* and *Body/Work*, labor and the fruits of labor are heavily emphasized. The doctors, who are often minorities, are presented as achieving every American "man's" dream: to have respect, large amounts of money, and a beautiful partner. Both *Body/Work* and *Dr. 90210* have one female surgeon (who is also Asian in each case); all the other doctors on the documentary-style plastic surgery programs are male. The camera lingers over the possessions of these men, showing long expansive shots of their houses, with close ups on their cars to clearly show the expensive brand. The gaze hangs on their wives and girlfriends, exploring their perfect bodies. However, these doctors are shown as worthy recipients of these prizes, since the camera also dwells on their labor. In contrast, the female doctor's possessions are rarely shown, thus illustrating the gendered ways that this version of the American Dream is constructed.

Within these shows, the gore of the surgery is shown in detail. Surgery is depicted as labor. The surgeons are forceful and physical in order to make their patients beautiful. They literally hammer on noses and saw bones. They push and pull and shove implants into a variety of orifices created by the surgeons. This is "manly" work, which indicates that they have earned their possessions and thus attained the American Dream. This construction is particularly significant since it is on television, coupled with a flow of advertisements which attempt to create lack in the audience which can only be filled by consumption.

The labor of the doctors, then, which is depicted as forceful hammering and sawing of the human body, is gendered male, except when performed by female surgeons. On *Extreme Makeover*, the narrator explains that the female surgeon uses terms of nuturing, in order to further portray this gendered difference. When Heather goes in for her surgery with Dr. Hayden, the narrator states, "She in good hands, caring hands, a surgeon's hands." Interviews with patients are intercut with scenes of Dr. Hayden working, in which the patients explain that it is very different to have a female plastic surgeon because she is much more caring than the men. This stresses the way in which her labor is gendered differently from men's labor.

With the exception of *Extreme Makeover*, almost all of the people receiving plastic surgery on these programs are female. As was expressed previously, 86% of cosmetic surgery patients are female (www.plastic-surgery.com). In addition to this fact, the narrative of the shows serves to further reinforce the gendered divide regarding who should receive plastic surgery. In *Dr. 90210*, Dr. Rey repeatedly stresses the gendered nature of his clientele by stating that he went into this field of medicine because he likes women and enjoys working with them. This tension is further accentuated when Dr. Rey learned that his unborn child would be a boy, and he directly expressed discomfort with how to behave around a son. Dr. Rey's comfort is clearly working with women, who are almost his only clientele.

Extreme Makeover, however, attempts to pretend that these gendered distinctions are not salient by giving plastic surgery to men and including a female surgeon. *Extreme Makeover* is not a documentary of a real plastic surgery clinic. Instead, they seek out the truly "ugly" and those who claim to be miserable due to their appearance. They then give them many procedures at once to make them over. The men in the show who receive the surgery, however, are positioned differently from the women. They are able to reject the objectification of the gaze of reality television and also the objectification of their bodies.

While the doctor's labor is forceful and active, the labor of the patient is one of passivity and suffering. On *Extreme Makeover*, some men are in the role of the patient, and the emasculating nature of the patient's labor must be negotiated. For example, in the first season, a man named Bubba was chosen to receive surgery, but he maintained an active role. Bubba's voice consistently directs the camera off of him and on to women around him as he objectifies these women. When Bubba found out he would be on *Extreme Makeover*, he was at a party. He grabbed a male friend and said, "You pick one of these and all the rest of it is for me." He was referring to the women at the party, indicating that he would be able to get "the rest of it" with his soon-to-be good looks. As he said this, the camera moved off of Bubba and onto the bodies of the women at the party. Similarly, when he was in the limousine on Rodeo Drive, he whistled at the women on the street. The camera then moved to shots of various female passersby's body parts, in particular boobs and butts. Women within the show are never shown objectifying men or women, and are not similarly allowed to escape the gaze.

Within a traditional notion of the American Dream, hard work yields rewards. The doctor's labor, which is one of activity, positions the doctors as deserving the fruits of their labor. They are explicitly discussed as having achieved the American Dream. The patients, on the other hand, are forging the possibility of participating in the American Dream through allowing work to be done to them. Common ideas about what constitutes "hard work" are eliminated, replaced with the conceptualization of "hard work" as passivity and suffering, illustrating a transformation of what the American Dream has been.

Science

The labor of passivity and suffering requires a certain degree of surrender to someone working upon the individual. That sort of surrender seems to be the antithesis of American rugged individualism, which is particularly characteristic of the mythos of the American Dream. However, the surrender of patients to their doctors becomes sanctioned under the guise of science, and specifically in the case of plastic surgery, of therapy. Plastic surgery has long been considered a corrective for psychological disorders. Many consider plastic surgeons to be going against the Hippocratic Oath to do no harm, particularly because they are cutting into otherwise healthy bodies. Plastic surgeons claim, on the other hand, that they are fixing mental problems, such as poor self-image, with the surgery (Gilman). Therefore, the body is characterized as mutable and capable of being changed, while the mind is fixed (Hausman). The correct course is intervention on the body to reflect what is in the mind.

On these shows featuring plastic surgery, the doctors and narrators are established as authorities on beauty, and gain submission of their patients on that ground. This is different from other authorities on beauty such as beauticians, makeup artists, and stylists, since it places beauty within the discourse of science, and therefore rationality and objectivity. Beauty is no longer in the eye of the beholder. Instead, beauty is measured and objectively verified. This creates standards of beauty that are deemed scientific, and due to the currency that science has in our culture, these standards become "truth" and are naturalized. This is problematic for people, and particularly for women, since these standards are rarely achievable.

The ideal of beauty is based on a degree of perfection which is only attainable for a few people. As can be seen on television, even those who generally would be considered gorgeous are still lacking by this assessment. Even models come in for a little "tweaking." As Dr. Rey said of one beautiful patient, "This is a very, very beautiful girl with a few defects." While *The Swan* and *Extreme Makeover* transform generally ugly people, the documentary-style programs portray relatively attractive or beautiful people as most of the people receiving plastic surgery.

Dr. Rey, the featured doctor on *Dr. 90210*, expressed the contrived nature of his beauty standards when he was asked if he had had plastic surgery. His response was, "Yes. Do you think this profile is found in nature?" Here Dr. Rey clearly acknowledged that these standards of the human body are not "natural," but created through science. Therefore these standards exist within science and are superior to standards created from non-surgically altered bodies. In a later episode, he commented that "we" had created a generation of breastless women, since breasts do not exist on women with such low body fat as is currently in fashion. His job was to put the breasts back on women.

On *Body/Work*, Dr. Mani, who is starting a new practice, stated, "A lot of them see plastic surgery as a way to achieve perfection. I hope my new practice will reflect my ideals of perfection." People pay him to implement these ideals of perfection on their bodies, allowing their bodies to be cut into. These ideals appear to be neutral, since race and ethnicity are not discussed. Dr. Mani never claims that he wants to implement "white" ideals on these bodies in order to make all races look more ethnically white. Of course, it would be scandalous if he said this. However, this is clearly what is happening in many cases. Gilman notes that cosmetic surgery was created as a field in part due to the demand of Jewish people to have their ethnically Jewish noses erased. Kaw addresses the phenomenon of Asian American women trying to make their faces "whiter" through surgery by creating rounder eyes. Within these plastic surgery shows, the doctor's authority to decide these standards of beauty is never questioned, in part due to his status as a scientist and a man.

Susan Bordo critiques plastic surgery in part due to the promise it contains, of changing the "inside" by changing the "outside," thus offering the benefits of therapy through incisions. The inside/outside dichotomy of the body is yet another manifestation of mind/body dualism. As Grosz argues, the body itself is situated as an outside which is subordinate to and inhabited by the mind which lives inside the body. The body is thus the border through which the real "I" is supposedly bounded from the world. Gimlin argues that, in part due to mind/body dualism, the body has become a signifier of the self and moral character. It is a sign of the failure of the mind if the mind cannot properly control the body. Gimlin argues that work on the body, such as the work of beauty culture, is thus work on the self. Exercise, makeup, and plastic surgery are actually ways of correcting a wayward moral character, one that excessively consumes or lacks discipline. However, much of the body work discussed by Gimlin requires an active labor, instead of the passive labor of surrender and suffering available to patients of cosmetic surgery.

On *Extreme Makeover* and *The Swan*, doctors continually lament the difficulty of their task, as if belaboring the ugliness of their patients and instructing the viewer and the women on what should be beautiful. On *The Swan*, when making over a deaf woman named Gina Davis, the doctor repeatedly commented on how "crooked" and "asymmetrical" her face was, and therefore how difficult the surgery would be. On the same episode, the doctor claimed Lorrie's tummy tuck was the most difficult he had ever performed. It was repeatedly stressed that she was "receiving" more procedures than any other woman had on *The Swan*. When Christina had her *Swan* makeover, the doctor stated, "Your nose is completely crooked." The doctors' voices are established as authorities on beauty, and thus help to gain the submission of the patients and the viewers. Beauty is therefore taken out of the realm of art and relegated to science and rationality. Beauty is no longer in the eye of the beholder, but instead can be scientifically determined.

The standards expressed by the doctors are not questioned within the shows. No patient ever speaks up and says, "Isn't my nose supposed to look like this?" or "I like my nose just fine." On *Extreme Makeover* and *The Swan*, the doctor's authority is wholeheartedly accepted. Of course, these people are volunteering for free complete body makeovers and therefore are interested in the doctor's authority. On *Body/Work*, which is not contestant-based, a woman came in to see Dr. Mani about getting her nose fixed. The doctor refused to work on her nose, saying that it was fine, but that he would be willing to operate on her lips instead. This illustrates the positioning of the doctor as authority and the power that the doctor has to enforce his ideals of beauty, refusing to operate in ways that go against his standards. In addition, the doctor was positioned as able to see a flaw (the woman's lips) that the woman was not able to see on her own. Thus the doctor was rendered an authority on this women's body, needing to control it and manage it for the woman.

On one episode of *Dr. 90210*, there was a momentary questioning of authority. Ana came to Dr. Rey for breast implants. She had previously had breast implants and then had them taken out. She was unhappy with how deflated and saggy her breasts now looked, since the breast tissue must be cut and damaged in order to insert the implant. She wanted only a B cup implant, but Dr. Rey was urging her to receive a D or larger implant. He was very uncomfortable with performing this surgery with such small implants. He stated that her breasts would not sit close enough on her chest, and that "there's nothing uglier than a wide cleavage." She insisted on the B implants, and he hesitantly performed the surgery. During the actual operation, he repeatedly complained that the implants were so small they would only look like bee stings on her chest. He stated, "She picked such tiny little implants. It broke my heart." At the end of the episode, after Ana had recovered, she stated that she was very happy with her breasts, noting that "breast size is a very personal choice," thus affirming the postfeminist ideal of choice. While Ana was able to resist Dr. Rey's medical authority, this also shows the power that the surgeons hold. Dr. Rey was hesitant about performing the surgery. He could have refused to operate on her if she did not consent to get the larger implants.

The male narrator is also used to establish authority on these shows, particularly on *Extreme Makeover* and *The Swan*. These male narrators emphasize the difficult lives of the participants in order to serve as a justification for the transformation, indicating the way the surgeries serve as a form of therapy. When Heather, a 33 year-old-woman seeking an *Extreme Makeover* is first shown on screen, the narrator states, "She's young but can only dream of looking sexy." Within media, the voice of a narrator is almost always a voice of authority, the voice of someone who knows more than the viewer does. These narrators appear to be authorities on justifiable reasons to get plastic surgery. For example, the narrator of *Extreme Makeover* proclaimed on one episode that "these are three of our most deserving extreme makeovers yet." Apparently, it was the individuals' suffering due to their ugliness that made them deserving. In order to end their psychological suffering, these patients consent to additional physical suffering, which the network gets millions of people to watch.

Both the doctors and narrators are established as voices of authority on these programs, guiding the viewer to discern which parts of bodies are beautiful and what needs to be changed. This is similar to assessing which parts of a house should be updated. This constitutes the labor of the doctors as both active and labor of the mind, in which the doctors need to intervene on wayward bodies of women. The women thus become objects for the doctors to work upon. Their own agency in their bodily transformation is minimized, just as the agency of a car at the mechanics is nonexistent. The body is capital being made over for a woman. As this capital is made over, women have a greater chance of acquiring the commodities necessary to be deemed successful in American culture, thus being better able to participate in the American Dream.

Conclusions

Plastic surgery reality television illustrates an instance of a new form of the American Dream, one which focuses on the labor of suffering and passivity. People's lives are transformed by transforming their bodies through surgery, increasing the value of their biological capital. Beauty renders access to the American Dream for women, as it is supposed to be accompanied by wealth, success, and the ideal heterosexual union. The body is the capital that allows access to these things, and thus needs to be maintained through constant work. While labor for men is labor of the mind and performed with the body, labor for women is constructed as allowing things to be done to the body. Perhaps this is the crux of the argument. What should be seen as part of "women's work," the labor of beauty, is instead seen not really as labor, but as creation of capital. Thus, women's work is yet again elided, as it has been historically.

Women's bodies become capital on these shows, a fact that becomes natural and scientific, as if relegating woman to her "true" or "real" role. By accepting these constructions of women's labor and bodies, a hegemonic discourse is created which attempts to limit women's access to other versions of the American Dreams, ones which may not require her to have such invasive procedures done upon her body. In addition, they render all women "equal," despite ethnic or class structural barriers. The category of "woman" is deemed to trump all others, thus ignoring the ways that many women throughout the United States and the globe are left out of even this hegemonic version of the American Dream.

Works Cited

Andrejevic, Mark. *Reality TV: The Work of Being Watched*. Lanham, MD: Rowman & Littlefield, 2004.

Blum, Virginia L. *Flesh Wounds: The Culture of Cosmetic Surgery*. Berkeley: University of California Press, 2003.

Bordo, Susan. *Unbearable Weight: Feminism, Western Culture, and the Body*. 10th anniversary ed. Berkeley: University of California Press, 2003.

Bourdieu. *Distinction: A Social Critique of the Judgment of Taste*. Trans. Richard Nice. Cambridge, MA: Harvard University Press, 1979/1984.

Cohen, Lizabeth. *A Consumer's Republic: The Politics of Mass Consumption in Postwar America*. New York: Alfred A. Knopf, 2003.

Cross, Gary. *An All-Consuming Century: Why Commercialism Won in Modern America*. New York: Columbia University Press, 2000.

Cullen, Jim. *The American Dream: A Short History of an Idea That Shaped a Nation*. New York: Oxford University Press, 2003.

Davis, Kathy. *Dubious Equalities and Embodied Differences: Cultural Studies on Cosmetic Surgery*. Lanham, MD: Rowman & Littlefield, 2003.

_____. *Reshaping the Female Body: The Dilemma of Cosmetic Surgery*. New York: Routledge, 1995.

Dow, Bonnie J. *Prime-Time Feminism: Television, Media Culture, and the Women's Movement since 1970*. Philadelphia: University of Pennsylvania Press, 1996.

Franklin, Benjamin. *The Autobiography of Benjamin Franklin*. Mineola, NY: Dover Publications, 1868/1996.

Gilman, Sander L. *Creating Beauty to Cure the Soul: Race and Psychology in the Shaping of Aesthetic Surgery*. Durham, NC: Duke University Press, 1998.

_____. *Making the Body Beautiful: A Cultural History of Aesthetic Surgery*. Princeton, NJ: Princeton University Press, 1999.

Gimlin, Debra L. *Body Work: Beauty and Self-Image in American Culture*. Berkeley: University of California Press, 2002.

Grosz, Elizabeth. *Volatile Bodies: Toward a Corporeal Feminism*. Bloomington: Indiana University Press, 1994.

Hausman, Bernice. "Plastic Ideologies and Plastic Transformations." *Changing Sex: Transexualism, Technology, and the Idea of Gender*. Durham: Duke University Press, 1995. 49–71.

Jhally, Sut, and Justin Lewis. *Enlightened Racism: The Cosby Show, Racism, and the Myth of the American Dream*. Boulder, CO: Westview Press, 1992.

Kaw, Eugenia. "Opening Faces: The Politics of Plastic Surgery and Asian-American Women." *Many Mirrors: Body Image and Social Relations.* Ed. Nicole Sault. New Brunswick, NJ: Rutgers University Press, 1994.

Lakoff, Robin Tolmach, and Raquel L. Scherr. *Face Value: The Politics of Beauty.* Boston: Routledge and Kegan Paul, 1984.

Oulette, Laurie. "Victims No More: Postfeminism, Television, and Ally Mcbeal." *Communication Review* 5.4 (2002): 315–36.

Plato. *Phaedrus.* Trans. W.C. Helmbold and W.G. Rabinowitz. Upper Saddle River, NJ: Prentice Hall, 1952.

Robertson, James Oliver. *American Myth, American Reality.* New York: Hill and Wang, 1980.

Spigel, Lynn. *Welcome to the Dreamhouse: Popular Media and Postwar Suburbs.* Durham, NC: Duke University Press, 2001.

_____. "Women's Work." *Television: The Critical View.* Ed. Horace Newcomb. 6th ed. New York: Oxford University Press, 2000. 73–99.

Weber, Max. "The Protestant Work Ethic and the Spirit of Capitalism." (1958/2003).

Notes

1. See the official website of the ASPS, www.plasticsurgery.org.

2. See Dow for a complete discussion of postfeminism, which holds that feminism is no longer needed because equality has been achieved. Part of this belief stems from the equal purchasing power women have in our consumer society, equating consumer equality with political equality.

Part IV

Representation and Difference

How Does Reality TV Represent "the Other?"

10

Playing with Hooks: Neo-tribal Style, Commodification and Resistance

Andrea Schuld-Ergil

> Dress is, in part, frequently in large part, about cultural capital;
> it often serves political designs; it consorts with hegemonic
> norms and domination; its regulating force incites mainly con-
> formity but sometimes resistance. To adopt a style (or uniform)
> is to choose a socio-economic milieu and a future (Leitch 112).

Niedzviecki suggested that we are in a "New Age of New Conformity" (14), a time of unprecedented mass cultural conformity to individuality, above all else. "Essentially, in our ongoing bid to demonstrate that we are special individuals, we require an endless supply of limited-edition, hand-made, one-time-only products ... capable of conveying at least some partial sense of our uniqueness to everyone..." (19). This chapter will examine the above idea related to a reality television depiction of the unique, controversial subculture of Modern Primitivism (ModPrim); it will explore issues of subcultural representation and co-optation by mainstream cultural forces.

To locate actual and "reality" representations of Modern Primitivism on the (sub)cultural map, it will be useful to contemplate the example of a Modern Primitive character, Art Aguirre, who appeared in the 2004 reality/game show, *Mad Mad House.*[1] The culture industry (as fashion apparatus) will be addressed as operating in relation to current (sub)cultural fragments. The process of commodification will be outlined as it relates to representations of alterity. Finally, the suitability of the term "subculture" in relation to Modern Primitive modes and meanings will be addressed.[2]

Overall, the issue of cultural co-optation of this group by televisual means will be considered, and it will be argued that, by and large, Modern Primitivism is able to elude the machinations of the culture industry in an age of conformist individuality.

A brief précis of the television show on which Art the Modern Primitive appeared provides a useful context:

> SCI FI's newest reality series [is] Mad Mad House. This 10-episode weekly series chronicles the unhinging of 10 everyday people who move into a house run by a Vampire, a Wiccan, a Naturist, a Voodoo Priestess, and a Modern Primitive to compete for a $100,000 prize. Part reality and part game.... In this Survivor-meetsThe Real World–meets–The Osbournes series, five genuine practitioners of "alternative lifestyles," referred to collectively as the ALTS, rule the roost. Their ten more "conventional" GUESTS strap in for the ride of their lives as they undergo a number of tolerance-testing activities. The Guests are judged by the Alts to determine their openness to and tolerance of alternative lifestyles. From their participation in House activities, to their willingness to get to know the Alts, the Guests are subject to constant evaluation. The Alts determine which of their Guests will be banished in the weekly elimination ceremony ... and which one will ultimately walk away with the six-figure prize [Jax].

Mad Mad House, aired also by Canada's Space Channel in March and April 2004, was capped by a two-hour finale. The major concluding challenge for final participants consisted of an endurance test to see how long competitors could hang in the embrace of Art the Modern Primitive during his suspension from a frame via hooks through his back. The hanging flesh-hook ritual, which has many variations, has become one of the more commonly shared practices among Modern Primitives, derived from the Sun Dance and O-Kee-Pa rituals of Native American tribes (Vale and Juno).

Culture Industry → *Fashion Apparatus*

Horkheimer and Adorno's theory of the culture industry centres on the "massification" of a society's cultural imagination by way of a formulaic culture- and meaning-making process, controlled by a small elite. The authors warned against the consumption of standardized material that would "deaden the masses"; individuals' potential for critical thought would be "drowned by the peddling of endlessly bland and repetitive cultural commodities" (Dant 110). According to the authors' theory, cultural commodities— those ideas manufactured into the form of things for sale — are aimed by producers not to satisfy consumers' physical needs but to influence consumers' conscious and subconscious selves. This commodification process was seen to utilize propaganda techniques with the aim of manipulating "the audience, forcing them to follow the plot and giving them no space in which to reflect or use their own imagination" (Dant 111). The process whereby ideas are processed into commodified material is discussed below.

Emberley's theory of the fashion apparatus parallels the theory of the culture industry. While the culture industry creates bored, passive, distracted consumers of a seeming taste, the fashion apparatus manufactures alienated, self-loathing consumers of alleged style. The fashion apparatus

> ... operates on the basis of a primary contradiction: it claims to fabricate within you your being, your individual sense of expression, while at the same time forcing you, through its freedom of choices, to conform to the market uniformity of seasonal products; what is produced here is alienation, alienation from self and one another because of the way fashion negates life, by becoming the dominant repository of what it means to live and to have a "life-style" [49].

Both theories, fashion apparatus and culture industry alike, elicit wariness of the systematic production of mass images and goods, and accordingly, a homogenized and homogenizing mass taste. The only response to the pressures of the "post-modern pace," in Emberley's view, is a final, burnt-out "collapse and implosion of the body" (59).

As if in response to Emberley, Arnold describes a type of speed consumption that became endemic in the late twentieth century Western world. An increasingly rapid pace occurring within the cycle of desire, consumption and disinterest was found not only in the fashion apparatus but also, more broadly, within the products of the culture industry. "The shallow satisfaction of the act of shopping further speeded up the desire to consume, the blurring of real feeling, real status into the fantasy of image and commodity adding to the sense of confusion" (Arnold 10). Throughout the twentieth century there was a tradition for Western intellectuals and artists to shun the "constantly shifting whims of fashion," opting instead for simpler self-decoration as a way to distance oneself from conspicuous consumption. In congruence with the professed aims of some Modern Primitives (Rosenblatt), acts of disaffection demonstrate "contempt for capitalist pressures to conform" (Arnold 18).

> ... In the relentless search for satisfaction ... the consumer has been continually assailed by images promising newer, greater experiences that may provide opportunities for creating new identities but which also have a brutalising effect. People are reduced to generic consumers, labelled and defined by market research into lifestyle groups, and individuality is sought in vain in a marketplace that is carefully stratified and driven by forecasting trends [34].

In light of Emberley's and Arnold's assessments, it is worth considering that Modern Primitivism is a negative response to the fashion apparatus' aims and effects; it relates to the idea of identity implosion into the body as opposed to only upon the body, as is the case with fashion. The history of the Western fashion apparatus reveals a fluctuating fascination with "other" cultures, where ethnic elements have been routinely appropriated to add an exotic flair for the typically white, status-seeking consumer. Arnold describes exoticised fashion as "a new 'skin,' a costume that appropriated for the over-exposed white body connotations of mystery and eroticism.... Just like the tradition of exoticism itself, fashion 'grew up rich and a little bored'" (95–96). Always on the hunt for a fresh infusion of the perfect, special detail to keep the apparatus turning, fashion tastemakers cannot adhere too heavily, or for too long, to one influence. In contrast, ModPrim relates to slow and carefully planned evolution of identity via the body; a search for a time of permanence, stability, and ritual; and the effort to find a simpler, less artificial way of becoming as a self.

In an effort to remain vital, the fashion apparatus and the culture industry have become highly adaptable in responding to the changing moods of consumers. Where individuals have noticeably opted out of regular consumption patterns, new marketing and merchandising techniques have been quickly upgraded in order to reintegrate the disaffected consumer. Taste or niche marketing caters to the fragmented masses in all their "specialness" (e.g. Niedzviecki; Louw).[3] For example, in Western culture's current phase of "conformist individuality," a general trend in consumer purchasing is the rejection of corporate branding strategies. Niedzviecki describes how an increasing proportion of consumers are

> ... spending more and more time trolling malls and box stores for semi-individualistic purchase.... They don't want prepackaged. They want special. And yet they generally have little interest in making their own clothes or doing anything other than buying a look. Here, the conformity of individuality is obvious. It's no coincidence that, as [the trend for] the logo fades, the single trend in fashion these days is custom-made ... "a lifestyle without the effort involved in a life" [17].

Regardless of trends being positioned either toward or against something, the fashion apparatus and culture industries are ready to deliver. In contemporary Western culture, one can witness ceaseless cultural production: "Codifying, simplifying, and sometimes even diversifying subcultural styles for the market-place ... the fashion industry stimulates its own markets and drains the energy from its subcultural prey" (Connor 216). This leads to consideration of the process of co-optation that routinely occurs within culture industries and fashion apparatus.

Commodification / Co-optation

The term commodity can refer either to a material item or element that actually functions in a particular way, or to something that has been transformed into an "emotionally charged totem of an imagined lifestyle" (Budd, Craig, and Steinman 158). It is the second use of the word — the inferred commodity — that requires primary deliberation here. A key concern within the term commodification, then, is related to the process of how something becomes a commodity. Commodification is bound to the process by which a thing is imbued with meaning so as to create within it a type of cultural identity. This alteration occurs via an individual's (or culture's) mental projection or encoding of certain qualities or essences into the perception of that good or service. These acts of alteration aid in the construction of our cultural environment, and are powerful determinants of the manner by which a culture composes shared meanings (152–53).

Examples of commodification are pervasive within the fashion apparatus, such as the alleged purchasability of taste. Arnold, in describing Otto Dix's 1920s paintings, posits that "...fashion is the dialectical switching station between the woman and the commodity..." (59). Elsewhere, Arnold states, "The web of meanings and emotions that attaches both to products and the images that are used to entice the consumer has great impact in Western culture, where identity is so often judged by appearance" (3). In terms of commodification, the perceived characteristics of one's identity may become a surrogate for the actual identity of an individual who appears in a certain light via ensembles of dress. Where the actual commodity is clothing, hair or makeup, the inferred commodity has become the wearer's qualities of self, which is often couched in terms of taste, or lack thereof.

Horkheimer and Adorno state, "[A]ny trace of spontaneity from the public in official broadcasting is controlled and absorbed by talent scouts, studio competitions and official programs of every kind selected by professionals" (72). This process of absorption by media industry talent scouts has been increasingly employed within the fashion apparatus, most notably since the early 1990s in Western markets. Fashion here includes not only clothing styles but also extends to commodifiable goods and behaviours, such as the latest in tattoo styles, music, beverages, colours, zeitgeist, high-tech dating practices, and so forth. Within the fashion apparatus, it is a new breed of talent scout, "undercover market researchers known as cool-hunters"— routinely street-style savvy teenagers— who are proffering information on emerging trends, typically those fashions plundered from creative youth cultures (Goodman 27).[4]

> Market researchers send out culture spies to study the young consumers, hoping to learn how to convince them of what they should crave.... Once the marketers discover cool, they force it to change into something else. The teens drive themselves to extremes to create new spaces in which to be themselves. But each time teenagers create their own unprocessed expressions of pleasure and angst

... these expressions are appropriated and sold back to them in the malls as products to consume [29].

Brooks describes the cycle of consumption as a site of cannibalism, saying, "Young people are the primary subjects of these images as well as the principal consumers [and] ... through a cultural feasting, they are invited to devour themselves" (9).

This is the launch-point for the commodification process of (sub)cultures, by way of stripping their styles and perceived meanings—the point at which ideas and ideologies begin transformational disintegration into a purchasable thing. This is the location wherein the impetus of difference from the mainstream becomes identified as something desirable, and solidified into a marketable commodity for a broader range of consumers. Controllers of the fashion apparatus, as with other culture industry tastemakers, have become keenly adept at interpreting street-level zeitgeist and translating it into items ready for purchase at the mall. Has Modern Primitivism joined the spiral into a seemingly inevitable commodification process?

(Sub)cultural Representation(s)

It is significant that *Mad Mad House* included as one of its main 'Alt' characters a person with the moniker Art the Modern Primitive. This marked the first time that a member of the Modern Primitive[5] (sub)culture[6] appeared within a genre other than the documentary,[7] or through written documentation available mainly from academic scholarship. Atkinson states that, "because such factions of body modifiers typically emerge in 'hidden' areas of large urban centres and tend to maintain close in-group boundaries, outsiders usually learn of such behaviours through academic research or special documentaries" (375). The novelty of *Mad Mad House*'s inclusion of Art Aguirre, a heavily tattooed and modified body piercer and practicing ModPrim, was precisely that it worked to emphasize the rarity of media representation of the (sub)culture. However, did the debut of a ModPrim on mainstream cable TV signal the group's waning marginality? Does this representation mean that the Modern Primitive subculture has been co-opted by image-making industries?

Mad Mad House character Art the Modern Primitive has been described as such:

Art Aguirre looks like an intricately detailed Mayan painting....
    Art is a professional piercing artist and body modifier. His San Diego-based "Church of Steel" body piercing and tattoo shop specializes in a relaxed and tranquil experience. Professionally, his goal is to use his knowledge to enlighten and

educate people about the practice of body modification. When preparing for his own modifications, such as ritual suspension, Art endeavors to reach a higher realm of consciousness by perfecting his mind's ability to control his body. Diagnosed with cancer at an early age, Art developed a new outlook on the mind's power in overcoming physical pain and also in overcoming illness. After surviving cancer, Art threw himself into living life "to the fullest," as he puts it. "It's all about a love of life," Art explains, "a primal urge I strongly have. It has to do with what's inside you, what your heart is about. Our exterior is just a form of expression of our individuality." Art's ultimate goal is to seek out higher levels of consciousness, inner peace, tranquillity and strength [Jax].

A brief history of ModPrim, and a description of aesthetics, practices, and some meanings will aid in contextualizing the odd moment of the group's television debut, via Art Aguirre's representation on *Mad Mad House*. A Californian advertising executive called Fakir Musafar, self-named after a 19th-century Sufi, originally coined the term "Modern Primitivism" in 1967 to describe a group of body modification devotees emerging in San Francisco's underground scene (Vale and Juno). Fakir, exposed at a young age to cross-cultural tribal rituals printed in National Geographic Magazine, is now regarded internationally as ModPrim's godfather figure. His efforts via publications, public appearances, and his Piercing Intensives School have been elemental in spreading awareness of ModPrim. A second important source of identification and dissemination about the group was the 1989 publication of the seminal text *Modern Primitives* by Vale and Juno. The Internet has been a third important source for the spread of ModPrim; online discussions and photographs from innumerable locations around the globe attest to a growing awareness and activity of the (sub)culture.[8]

The ModPrim aesthetic is tied to significant amounts of body modification on an individual. Examples include tattooing, body piercing, subcutaneous incision, branding, corsetry, body moulding, and a growing list of other experimental modifications. Many ModPrims take part in temporary modification practices, termed "body play" (Vale and Juno 14–15). Furthermore, for many ModPrims, various ritual practices are as important as the aesthetic of the body modifications, which may be one way to separate dedicated individuals from the merely interested. Practices are derived mainly from non-Western rituals, including:

> ... body modification (tattooing, piercing, branding, scarring, etc.) as a means of achieving spiritual growth. Ritual suspension and other traditions of the modern primitive are based on Indian rites of passage and are accomplished through yoga, meditation and special breathing techniques [Jax].

The meaningfulness of the aforementioned modifications, through aesthetic, technique, and practice, is central to ModPrim identity and ideology; mention of personal significance is cited time and again in a high proportion of personal accounts (e.g. Pitts). A common expression by Mod-Prims centres on deeply felt needs, "for meaning, fulfilment, and experiences that can confirm the existence of a genuine self — that drive ModPrims to reject consumer society and to valorize the primitive" (Rosenblatt 323). Ongoing body projects represent a desire for other forms of knowing the self and being in the world and act as a means toward "expression of a basic human need for rituals that give life meaning" (303). Creation of a hybrid body may help to secure a sense of permanence, significance and stability as an embodied, true self; at the same time, viewing this composite body as an evolving work of art may signify a more fluid mode of identity (Schuld-Ergil).

In discussing ModPrim until this point, the term subculture has been avoided, as have notions of mainstream versus marginal. While one can point to the continuing existence and emergence of some groups that can be unambiguously termed subcultural,[9] ModPrim does not fit neatly within such polarized categorization; it is fundamentally ambiguous. It goes against the standard of "subculture," which is generally defined (following the CCCS[10]) as usually deviant "stylistic responses of working-class youth" against the norms of the parent-culture (Bennett and Kahn-Harris 5).

Atkinson suggests conceptualizing the ModPrim movement as figurational, a concept favouring "the study of interdependent human agents embedded in complex webs of social interaction" (376). Chaney (qtd. in Bennett and Kahn-Harris) views the distinction of subculture as being no longer relevant "because the type of investment that the notion of subculture [once] labelled is becoming more general, and therefore the varieties of modes of symbolization and involvement are more common in everyday life" (37). Rather, the current supermarket of style points to Western culture's growing fragmentation. This is reminiscent of Niedzviecki's thesis that everyone is a "special individual."

Maffesoli's use of tribus or "neo-tribes" is a term that better describes the current, increasing fragmentation found in Western culture. "Neo-tribe" aptly portrays our cultural landscape wherein a pluralism of lifestyle preferences and interests has replaced a previously rigid, binary distinction between sub- and dominant cultures. ModPrim fits into this reconceptualized cultural neo-tribalism, in that it has fuzzy boundaries, does not have internal group cohesion, and "has become increasingly heterogeneous and fluid in terms of ... membership and style" (Bennett and Kahn-Harris 79). ModPrim, itself, can be understood as an oppositional response to a multiphrenic hyper-modernity in tandem with the speed consumption of late capitalism.

Resistance and Awareness

While ModPrim does not identify itself as one homogeneous group, neither is there a unified response to commodification by every ModPrim individual. That is to say, in an effort against co-option by the fashion apparatus, some individuals might resist by quiet avoidance, while others might display overt disaffection; indeed, even a singular individual might not show a consistent response pattern. In keeping with the group's ideology of personal choice at a meaningful level, it is not surprising that a spectrum of non-uniform responses can be found across individuals' accounts, via various media forms, and in personal communications.

Leitch discusses the machinations of the fashion apparatus as a "general ideological appeal to a purchasable 'new you'" (114). Similar efforts on the part of the advertising industry are discussed by Czitrom: "The term lifestyle best captures the essence of the current version of the ideology of consumerism.... It reduces all life to a style, equating how one lives with what one consumes" (qtd. in Goldman 54). It is this purchasable self-transforming and reifying process of the modern identity-as-commodity that is refuted by ModPrims. The incessantly shifting elements that comprise the dominant Western cultural landscape — that is, those elements that constitute the reigning symbolic order — are viewed by ModPrims as emblems of a defunct culture. The will to transform one's body and to self-create by re-ordering the "natural" body is seen by ModPrims as "an experience [of] liberation from one's own society and to become human rather than Western" (Rosenblatt 320).

ModPrim, in a way similar to punk, attempts to "subvert the currency of appearances" (Goldman 57). Unlike the schism between hippy and punk styles, however, ModPrims attempt to both "withdraw from consumerism ... [as well as to] ... shatter the ensemble of signs and recombine its elements" (57), as an effort to escape the cycle of commodification. ModPrim style also works at a deeper level of ideology on and under the skin, both literally and figuratively. The flesh marks a dual metaphorical and actual site of the private and public (i.e. inner and outer). Atkinson and Young confirm that the flesh is "simultaneously an accessible canvas to be manipulated in a deeply personal, private way, and a billboard to be displayed socially" (128).

While the culture industry and fashion apparatus move quickly to appropriate and re-package style for mass consumption, ModPrim will not be so easily commodifiable. Although the appearance of Art the Modern Primitive on *Mad Mad House* might indicate growing awareness of the ModPrim aesthetic, the fact of its inseparable rituals, meanings and ideologies might preclude a full-scale co-optation by culture industries. This unlikelihood is further amplified by the fact of its irreversible corporeality. The fashion apparatus is entirely characterized by and concerned with constant change, while ModPrim aesthetics and practices "are thus used to maintain the illusion, if not the reality, of social and cultural stability" (Sweetman 62). ModPrim bodily adornment is not only anti-fashion; it is antithetical to the fashion apparatus. "Its adoption in a modern social context represent[s] a deliberate attempt to symbolically defy ... change" (62).

Sweetman states,

> As corporeal artefacts then, tattoos and piercings differ remarkably from sartorial accessories: part of the body rather than simply an adjunct to it, there is something in both which escapes the flow of commodification.... The modified body produces itself. A pair of jeans, or a new pair of training shoes, can be consumed and displayed as a "pure sign" ... Tattoos and piercings, in contrast, demand one's presence as producer, consumer and living frame for the corporeal artefact thus acquired [64].

While a mainstream reading of ModPrim body modification may only take into account the aesthetic physical appearance, it is an individual's significant experience of the painful, planned, ritual process of such modifications that places ModPrim outside the realm of commodification. One's body projects work at many different levels beyond that of visual, fashionable signifiers: as corporeal artefacts they "continue to refer to the manner of their production, and in this sense to resist full incorporation ... however popular related imagery becomes" (70).

ModPrims place great importance on the deeply personal aspects of their modifications, citing them as outward signifiers of a particular worldview (Vale and Juno). The heavy modifications of ModPrims indicate a lifelong commitment to a particular lifestyle as well as an adherence to non-mainstream ideologies. Through publicly displayed bodywork,

> ... the radically modified body [acts] as a political billboard of protest, dissent and dialogue [that] also underscores how corporeality is tactically manipulated to symbolize a threatened personal identity or cultural position.... [It also] has established a new cultural discourse about the body [Atkinson 378–79].

If an individual chooses not to overtly display modifications, it could be argued that the body acts instead to elude, rather than protest, and works rather as a form of private resistance. In either case, although there can be elements of fashion in body modification styles, the heavily modified body — and accompanying mindset — moves ModPrim far beyond existing "simply as [a] fashionable product in the 'supermarket of style'" (Sweetman 72).

The ModPrim neo-tribe acts in multiple ways. It is a loosely grouped site for a discourse of disaffection against an alienating, fragmenting, commodifying late-modern culture; it moves against the fashion apparatus and those cultural forces that would popularize it. It is also an attempt towards a more integrated, meaningful existence; it attempts to reconceptualize and reintegrate personal and shared identity. ModPrim does not merely zap past the culture industry's manipulative "production of sign values based on fetishized codes" (Goldman 58); rather, it unplugs and rejects the whole apparatus.

Concluding Thoughts

Did the debut of Art the Modern Primitive herald the culture industry's co-optation of Modern Primitivism? Or was his appearance just a blip on our cultural radar screen, perhaps a mere curiosity? It remains to be seen whether this neo-tribe will continue its ability to resist and/or evade further commodification. Further work will broadly aid comprehension of "attempts to re-ground or anchor the self through a more or less specific commitment to a particular narrative" (Sweetman, qtd. in Bennett and Kahn-Harris 90).

Taste/niche marketing within the fashion apparatus and the culture industry has been gaining momentum in recent years in the attempt to cater to the growing number of cultural fragments or neo-tribes, described by Maffesoli. It is possible that the appearance of Art the Modern Primitive on the TV show *Mad Mad House* was an effort to capture the interest of a perceived emerging audience segment. It remains to be seen, however, whether or not ModPrim will be a viable market segment to warrant further targeting by the fashion apparatus and culture industry. While following the evolution of ModPrim in years to come, it will be worthwhile to remember that the neo-tribe's identity and ideology is deeply enmeshed with aesthetic, technique, and practice. What is underneath the skin is much more than display of a style, or representation of an individual's taste.

Works Cited

Arnold, Rebecca. *Fashion, Desire and Anxiety: Image and Morality in the Twentieth Century.* New Brunswick, NJ: Rutgers UP, 2001.

Atkinson, Michael. "Figuring Out Body Modification Cultures: Interdependence and Radical Body Modification Processes." *Health: An Interdisciplinary Journal for the Social Study of Health, Illness and Medicine* 8.3 (2004): 373–86.

Atkinson, Michael, and Kevin Young. "Flesh Journeys: Neo Primitives and the Contemporary Rediscovery of Radical Body Modification." *Deviant Behavior: An Interdisciplinary Journal* 22 (2001): 117–46.

Bennett, Andy, and Keith Kahn-Harris, eds. *After Subculture: Critical Studies in Contemporary Youth Culture.* New York: Palgrave Macmillan, 2004.

Brooks, Karen. "Nothing Sells Like Teen Spirit: The Commodification of Youth Culture." *Youth Cultures: Text, Images, and Identities*. Eds. K. Mallan & S. Pearce. Westport, CN: Praeger, 2003.

Budd, Mike, Steve Craig, and Clayton Steinman. *Consuming Environments: Television and Commercial Culture*. New Brunswick, NJ: Rutgers UP, 1999.

Connor, Steven. *Postmodernist Culture*. 2nd ed. Baltimore, MA: The Johns Hopkins UP, 1997.

Dant, Tim. *Critical Social Theory: Culture, Society and Critique*. Thousand Oaks, CA: Sage, 2003.

Emberley, Julia. "The Fashion Apparatus and the Deconstruction of Postmodern Subjectivity." *Body Invaders: Panic Sex in America*. Eds. A. Kroker & M. Kroker. New York: St. Martin's, 1987.

Eubanks, Virginia. "Zones of Dither: Writing the Postmodern Body." *Body and Society* 2.3 (1996): 73–88.

Goldman, Robert. *Reading Ads Socially*. New York: Routledge, Chapman & Hall, 1992.

Goodman, Steven. *Teaching Youth Media: A Critical Guide to Literacy, Video Production and Social Change*. New York: Teachers College, 2003.

Horkheimer, Max, and Theodor Adorno. "The Culture Industry: Enlightenment as Mass Deception." *Media and Cultural Studies: Keyworks*. Eds. D. Kellner & M. Durham. Malden, MA: Blackwell, 2001. (Original work published 1972).

Jax. "'Mad Mad House' Premieres." *MediaFiends*. Mar. 2004. 30 Apr. 2005 <www.mediafiends.com/modules.php?op=modload&name=News&file=article&sid=3589>

Kinsella, Sharon. "What's Behind the Fetishism of Japanese School Uniforms?" *Fashion Theory* 6.2 (2002): 215–38.

Leitch, Vincent. "Costly Compensations: Postmodern Fashion, Politics, Identity." *Modern Fiction Studies* 42.1 (1996): 111–28.

Louw, Eric. *The Media and Cultural Production*. London: Sage, 2001.

Maffesoli, Michel. *The Time of the Tribes: The Decline of Individualism in Mass Society*. Thousand Oaks, CA: Sage, 1996.

The Merchants of Cool. Dir. Neil Docherty. Boston, MA: WGBH Educational Foundation, 1999.

Negrin, Llewellyn. "Some Thoughts on 'Primitive' Body Decoration." *Postcolonial Studies* 3.3 (2000): 331–35.

Niedzviecki, Hal. *Hello, I'm Special: How Individuality Became the New Conformity*. Toronto, ON: Penguin Canada, 2004.

Parker, Ginny. "The Little-girl Look is Big in Japan Now." *The Wall Street Journal* 17 Sept. 2004.

Pitts, Victoria. *In the Flesh: The Cultural Politics of Body Modification*. New York: Palgrave Macmillan, 2003.

Rosenblatt, Daniel. "The Antisocial Skin: Structure, Resistance, and 'Modern Primitive' Adornment in the United States." *Cultural Anthropology* 12.3 (1997): 287–334.

Schuld-Ergil, Andrea. "Bricolage or Appropriation?: Exploring Meaning in Modern Primitive Adornment." Congress of the Social Sciences and Humanities, University of Alberta, Edmonton, AB. 29 May 2000.

Sweetman, Paul. "Anchoring the (Postmodern) Self? Body Modification, Fashion and Identity." *Body and Society* 5.2–3 (1999): 51–76.

Turner, Bryan. "The Possibility of Primitiveness: Towards a Sociology of Body Marks in Cool Societies." *Body and Society* 5.2–3 (1999): 39–50.

Vale, V. and Andrea Juno, eds. Re/Search #12: *Modern Primitives: An Investigation of Contemporary Adornment and Ritual*. San Francisco, CA: Re/Search Publications, 1989.

Notes

1. For images of Art, see his official website, http://www.churchofsteel.com/art.html.

2. There is not room here to discuss problematic aspects of Modern Primitivism, specifically, accusations of cultural appropriation from its surface to its depth. Examples include the seemingly contradictory terminology of the group, and its ideologically driven practices and aesthetics. For discussion of such issues, see Eubanks, Negrin, Pitts, and Turner.

3. Fragmentation and 'neo-tribes,' as per Maffesoli, shall be discussed below.

4. *The Merchants of Cool* provides an excellent view into some technique of 'cool-hunting.'

5. Hereafter referred to as ModPrim, rather than modern primitive/ primitivism/ primitivist.

6. Some ideas regarding the difficulties with the term subculture are discussed below.

7. Interviews on Canadian TV, such as Life Network's '*Skin Deep*' and Bravo Channel's '*Richler, Ink*' have included the major players in Canada's body modification and/or ModPrim scene: Daemon Rowanchilde, who popularised 'tribal style' tattooing in Canada; Shannon Larratt, founder of internationally (in)famous '*Body Modification E-Zine*'; and Michael Atkinson, sociology professor and tattoo aficionado at McMaster University.

8. One example is the extensive www.BMEzine.com site (*Body Modification E-zine*), created and maintained by Shannon Larratt of Canada (mentioned above).

9. For example, the recent Japanese *kogal* subculture of young, highly visible, street- and media-savvy school girls (Kinsella); and the current "*Gothic Lolita*" subculture, started in Japan and spreading globally (Parker).

10. That is, the Birmingham Centre for Contemporary Cultural Studies, whose work has proven essential as a base for subcultural theory, especially around the late 1970s and early 1980s.

11

"Sexual Racism" and Reality Television: Privileging the White Male Prerogative on MTV's The Real World: Philadelphia

ELIZABETH R. SCHROEDER

One cannot consider the vast social implications of reality television without looking, critically, at a primary spear header of the genre — MTV's *The Real World*. Now in its fifteenth season, MTV's *The Real World* thrusts viewers into a peculiar type of voyeurism characteristic of what dominates the majority of Americans' television screens, that beast named reality television. Reality television has had little meaningful analytical attention; frequently such shows are stigmatized as "trash television," reinforcing narrow critical views and lending to the paucity of its appearance in academic debates. This paper hopes to provoke a serious discussion over reality television. The paper aims to treat MTV's popular docu-drama, *The Real World: Philadelphia*, as a complex media construction and to explore the importance of viewers' and characters' relationship to imagery and representation in a program that proclaims to "tell the true story of seven strangers, picked to live in a house and have their lives taped, and find out what happens when people stop being polite and start getting real."[1]

In particular, this paper explores *The Real World: Philadelphia*'s representation of black male sexuality. The show's only homosexual cast members are also the only two men of color present — one African American male and one Puerto Rican American male. Using Kevin J. Mumford's concept of "sexual racism," I understand MTV's rendering of these characters' sexuality as an intersection of sexism and racism that works to the advan-

180

tage of the white male cast members and viewers.[2] Such a representation satisfies reality television's project — the manufacture of what Arild Fetveit calls "comfort zones," televisual spaces where the most problematic aspects of reality find erasure (799). The relegation of homosexuality to the non-white male body creates a comfortable space for the homosexual and heterosexual white male viewer where race trumps sexuality and hyper-masculinizes the white male body. Such characterization allows viewers to comfortably reflect on their own identity through the observation of the behaviors of the nearly fictional characters on screen. As a result, these comfort zones provide viewers with a euphoric "tuning out" to the very real and deeply problematic expressions of sexual racism.

Sexual racisms express themselves through myriad aspects of daily life and find reproduction through various popular culture apparatuses— literature, cinema, film, music, and television in all its various forms, such as reality television. One definition of reality television is: "non-fictional programming in which the portrayal is presumed to present current or historical events or circumstances. The production presents itself as being a realistic account" (Baker 57). This interpretation is broad, including news and public affairs programming, talk shows, entertainment programs, sports coverage, news magazines, documentaries, docu-dramas, movies "inspired by real events," and cinéma vérité formats. Another definition is: "the edited footage of unscripted interactions, broadcast as a television series about participants' naturally occurring social life" (Goddard 73). The common bond between these definitions is the supposed naturalness of social interaction. The casts, who participate with almost no scripted dialogue, interact in patterns that can be described with the same theoretical statements that describe social life in any setting. While the settings are atypical—for example, Ellis Goddard writes, *The Real World*'s cast typically lives in a plush urban loft courtesy of the television network— the social life is theoretically ordinary (73). Viewers are attracted to reality programming for what it represents: the drama of this ordinary human condition readily available to viewer's scrutiny. I would like to propose a blending of these definitions to define reality programming as the manipulated portrayal of unscripted actions to create a politically and ideologically scripted viewer response.

Reality television's mechanisms encourage viewers to perceive the behind-the-scene mechanisms and on-screen elements of reality television programming as the subjects of severe criticism and objects of ridicule in an effort to discover the "real." Viewers learn how not-to-be and reinforce normative aspects of their own identities when they watch reality television because, rather than easily identifying with the people on screen, viewers are encouraged to find fault in nearly everything the cast members do.

In "The Perversity of (Real)ity TV: A Symptom of Our Times," Jan Jan-godozinki argues that these shows:

> become a way to vent anger and hatred against those who are held up to be the evil perpetrators of society, those who are immoral in their behavior and criminal in their intent, in order that we, their audience and moral judges, can deny and disavow these same tendencies within ourselves. That is to say, they allow us to confirm that we really are not racists, homophobes, or sexists as long as the distance between them and us is preserved [326].

When viewers engage in a reality show, they are encouraged to distance themselves from the bodies on the screen to preserve critique of a racialized and sexualized Other in order to produce a comfort zone. By keeping the immoral and the criminal on the other side of the screen, viewers are safe — safe from the Other and safe from their own immoral and criminal potential. Engaging in a process of anti-identification by negation, viewers preserve their own prejudices and intolerances. Viewers remain comfortable and oblivious to the injustices their viewing perpetuates. Fetveit argues that this logic "points to an increasing compartmentalization of society in which we build up 'safe environments' where we no longer need to share physical room with the underprivileged, where the more problematic aspects of reality are locked out" (799). Fetveit's comments are important in that they show the lengths to which viewers will go to keep actual physical spaces and representations of these spaces void of contact with those perceived and labeled as Other. Not only do viewers lock out the physical presence of Others, but they refuse to tolerate the presence of Others or narratives about Others in fictional, televisual worlds. Television's worlds, even those proclaimed to be "the real," are dominated by and privilege narratives holding intact oppositions of masculine and feminine, white and black, and heterosexual and homosexual. With its focus on rescuing us from nature and technology gone astray, and protecting us from criminals, reality TV could easily be interpreted as conveying an ideology tailored to such a development (Fetveit 799).

At the same time, viewers identify with the possibility of being on TV, like the "real" people on screen; they identify with the actions of the characters on screen, yet they are simultaneously encouraged to distance themselves from the action on the screen, because television, as a fictional, contrived world, could not, by its very nature, be real. Viewers are caught between what "is" and what "could be" (Chvasta and Fassett 215). This space, between the real and fictional, is the project of reality television. So close to the real, reality television engenders a comfortable space in which viewers can meander between the virtual and the actual. The viewers are not on screen, so they will never be objects of scrutiny; as a result they can keep their prejudices intact. Too frequently, however, because it never falls under public scrutiny, this space is used for the domination and oppression of others.

The under-theorization of this space makes explicit the need for its examination. We must begin to ask crucial and difficult questions of reality television. Kevin J. Mumford asks the important question, "What happens when sexism and racism intersect?" Sexual racism, a concept explored by Mumford in *Interzones: Black/White Sex Districts in Chicago and New York in the Early Twentieth Century*, refers to a pervasive theory of racial difference relying on the intersection of racism and sexism through the dynamics of racial inferiority and sexual attraction. In 1933, black novelist James Weldon Johnson argued that "in the core of the heart of American race problems the sex factor is rooted" (qtd. in Mumford xvi). Mumford reflects on this statement by employing interracial sex as a category of analysis and then, with an eye for phenomena related to intercultural or interracial relations, moves his interpretive lens across the historical landscape of the early twentieth century (xi). His purpose is to write a history of black/white sexuality, to situate cultures often regarded as marginal at the center of historical analysis. Mumford's story is ultimately about the cultural forms and social life that emerged in what he calls "interzones: the spaces, both geographic and cultural, where black and white, homosexual and heterosexual, mixed and played and, in the process, created an intense and vibrant cultural life" (Gilman Srebnick 1328). Mumford argues that "sex across the color line always represents more than just sex" (Mumford xi).

I would like to explore the dynamics and significance of this "more than" as it applies to the pervasive narrative of white privilege that fuels and manipulates social structures and personal attitudes and action, the three being intertwined in the public and private realm. This narrative of whiteness expresses itself in ideology, institutions, and human interactions. It influences culture through symbols, myths, mechanisms of social control, and technologies of every day life — such as television. Mumford writes, "In both sexual racism and homophobia, the center of oppression is the stigmatization of people because of the nature or direction of their sexual desire" (179). Such stigmatization reinforces the white male prerogative, severely punishing and vehemently pushing homosexual men of color to the margins.

My analysis of *The Real World: Philadelphia* will show the mechanisms used by dominant groups to preserve racial distinction and sexual orientation; I will also demonstrate the degree to which sexual racism serves as an integral factor in their success. Several episodes from the fifteenth season illustrate producers' cunning use of editing mechanisms to preserve racial distinction and sexual orientation to the advantage of one group over another. Racism and homophobia intersect through the intricate, intimate encounters between people designated as different. *The Real World: Philadelphia* meets at this intersection with cameras rolling and viewers eagerly waiting.

MTV launched its first season of *The Real World* in 1992 in New York City (MTV.com). The show has since enjoyed great success with fourteen subsequent seasons exploring the drama unfolding between its young casts in cities all across the nation and globe. The casts of *The Real World* are selected to fit the youthful demographic of MTV's audience and generally range between 18 and 24 years old. Each season, the cast is comprised of seven people from various socioeconomic backgrounds. *The Real World* casts live together for as many as four months. Not only is there sufficient intimacy for love and marriage to develop, but also sufficient relational histories to generate a condition for violence as well as settlement within the context of the show (Goddard 89). The cast of *The Real World: Philadelphia* has two white women, Melanie and Sarah; one African American woman, Shavonda; one African American man, Karamo; one Puerto Rican man, Willie; and two white men, Landon and MJ.

As noted earlier, *The Real World: Philadelphia*'s only homosexual cast members are the African American man, Karamo, and the Puerto Rican American man, Willie. The series' first cast, the New York cast, had one homosexual white male: Norman. His sexual orientation took center stage a few times during the season when he developed a serious relationship and had to deal with the issues that arose. Since Norman's debut, producers have followed a trend in having at least one homosexual male or female cast member on each season; but never, in the show's 14 seasons, have there been more than one homosexual man, and neither has the show ever included two homosexual men of color. *The Real World: Philadelphia*'s homosexuals are men of color, and, vice versa: the show's only men of color are homosexuals. As a result, this season provides an interesting opportunity to investigate the political and ideological motivations behind MTV's representation of homosexuality and race on *The Real World*.

The differences in Karamo and Willie's sexual behavior and personality traits are presented as a heterogeneous representation of homosexuality, but as a homogenous representation of race. They are contrasted with the homogenous white male heterosexual behavior of the white and heterosexual men on the show: Landon and MJ. The white men on the show do not have as many variant behaviors as Karamo and Willie. Therefore, their actions are portrayed as normative, or the standard from which all other behaviors deviate. For example, Landon and MJ exhibit plain and standard "jock" behaviors. MTV.com's profile of Landon portrays him as a "sports fanatic," "a state champion in doubles tennis and ranked fifth in state in wrestling," noting that he was "on the water-skiing and wakeboarding teams."[3] MJ is described as a "good-looking, blond, hard-bodied Southern boy with a warm heart," and a "star football player ... [who] dreams of playing professional football" (MTV.com). White male viewers can easily and may eagerly wish to identify with them. As a result, the show has taken Karamo and Willie, men of color, and placed them in contrast to these figures who make white men feel privileged and the norm. By racializing the homosexual, heterosexual white men benefit from the show's and producers' prevention of erosion of the distinctions between white men and the raced and sexed other. Karamo and Willie serve as a tool to normalize the heterosexual white male prerogative.

The show's distinct mechanics, along with producers' editing and framing of footage from the show, privilege this point of view as well. For example, at the start of the season's first episode, MTV.com describes Karamo as a "buff guys' guy from Houston," while Willie is described as "gay and hop[ing] to find a hot, fantastic, fabulous, sexy relationship while in Philly." Willie's sexuality is made explicit from the start — off and on camera; Karamo's is not. He reveals his sexuality to viewers after the first night out with his roommates — all on camera via "the confessional."

A separate, sound-proofed room in the house, where the cast member sits in front of an unmanned camera, the confessional serves as a sort of diary session for the roommates where they can reflect on their feelings and vent their frustrations concerning their roommates and their personal lives. Only viewers, not cast members, are privy to this footage. These elements surround and explain the dramatic footage of the house and help viewers inspect the visual evidence provided by the cameras. As a curatorial strategy, the confessionals function much in the same way as Walter Benjamin's captions. Benjamin's prediction about increased camera access in the 1930's supports this statement:

> The camera will become smaller and smaller, more and more prepared to grasp fleeting, secret images whose shock will bring the mechanism of association in the viewer to a halt. At this point the captions must begin to function.... Will not captions become the essential component of pictures? [793].

Benjamin's observation on the relationship between the visual and the verbal is surprisingly well fitted to reality TV featuring authentic recordings of dramatic events. The visual evidence is not merely visual (794). The confessional, like voice-overs featured in news telecasts, helps viewers to focus their gaze as well as their understanding of the footage. Producers then edit this material into the show to serve as a framing for the events going on in the house; confessionals provide viewers with a context for the happenings of the show. This distinct mechanism of *The Real World* positions viewers as confidant and critic. Viewers' accessibility to these intimate confessional sessions encourages them to frame, but also evaluate, footage. Simple viewing involves viewers witnessing those on screen "being alternately kind, cruel, strong, sorry and sweet" (Chvasta and Fassett 215). Projecting themselves into the situations on screen, viewers are encouraged to decide whether they would behave similarly. Confessionals, however, persuade viewers to be more critical—encouraging them to decide if these behaviors are "kind, cruel, strong, sorry and sweet." Confessionals, then, create a televisual space where people are held accountable for their actions. Marcy R. Chvasta and Deannea L. Fassett argue that we, as viewers, "delight in their [cast members'] accountability; we demand it" (215). The confessional, then, serves as an apparatus to make the cast members transparent; making them confess who they are eradicates the space of their mystery so that the person becomes reified (objectified), made public (Jagodozinki 325). This collapse of the public/private space makes characters out of the real people on the show, fostering a "non-presence." "Real People" turn out to be "flat" having no depth (336).

I would like to argue that these non-diegetic elements (Chvasta and Fassett 214), or how the story is conveyed—e.g., the use of multiple cameras, the manipulations of lighting and sound—support or reinforce diegetic elements (214), what is being conveyed—narratives that privilege whiteness. The space between these diegetic and non-diegetic elements provides a comfortable place where viewers, in their roles as critics, can be less critical of compulsory whiteness. This is the viewing comfort zone, or Fetveit's aforementioned "safe environment," where one no longer needs to share physical room with the underprivileged (799).

Several examples, all revolving around cast members Karamo and Willie's sexual and racial orientation, illustrate maneuvers that encourage viewers, heterosexual or not, to accept versions of narratives privileging whiteness and to disregard narratives concerned with Karamo and Willie's perspective as men on the sexual color line. All of the episodes that I will analyze blend confessionals with actual footage of events from the show. For example, in the first episode of the season, Shavonda, in her first confessional, narrates that while at the bar in a shocking turn of events, "guys' guy" Karamo, the other African American on the show, "comes out" to her (*The Real World: Philadelphia* Episode 1). Her jaw drops. In the second episode, Willie tells Melanie that he thinks there is a possibility that Karamo is gay, but he is not sure. Karamo narrates from the confessional that he does not feel the need to come out to everyone just yet. In a telephone conversation to a friend from back home, Karamo expresses fear of coming out to MJ and Landon, the white males on the show, because they will turn on him if they discover he is gay. MJ, in his confessional, declares Willie "the gay roommate" and then narrates he is very intuitive and would be able to tell if he were living with someone who was gay. The second night out, Willie decides he wants "to go to a gay club" (*The Real World: Philadelphia* Episode 2), so the girls go with him, and MJ and Landon go to another club joined by Karamo. When MJ asks his companions if they would be comfortable going to a gay bar, Landon quickly replies no; Karamo replies that he has and reveals that he is, in fact, gay. MJ and Landon respond with no speech, only horrified looks of disbelief. MJ narrates that Karamo has "blown any stereotype I had out of the water. If Landon comes out, I'm going to lose my mind" (*The Real World: Philadelphia* Episode 2). Faced with the possibility of being the only heterosexual male on the show, MJ hints, albeit jokingly, at insanity — viewers, however, can sense MJ's honest anxiety at what he perceives as his roommates' dubious labels. After some time, however, the confessional along with the footage successfully work to expose each cast members' secrets and weds them to their race, gender, and sexuality. After this, MJ, along with the viewers can settle into a comfortable space where there are no more surprises.

More drama over Karamo's race and sexuality finds expression in episode five, which begins with Karamo in the confessional describing an upbringing that was filled "with strong anti-white prejudices," admitting to being a "borderline racist," stating that he typically does not have white friends, and reflecting that he knows his father might have influenced him in some ways that he is realizing now were not right. The episode ends with Karamo engaged in a confrontation with police at a bar where his microphone, which cast members are required to wear nearly all the time, is mistaken for a gun holster. Despite the fact that Karamo never explicitly uses racist language out right, viewers enter the arrest-scenario with Karamo's confession of borderline racism lingering in their minds. The episode revolves around a series of volatile conversations between Karamo and other various cast members focused on race. Confessionals from each conversant backdrop all of these conversations and provide insight and reactions to the subject matter of the conversations themselves. For instance, while playing pool, Landon tells Karamo that when he was younger he said the "N word on a school bus and learned really fast that I shouldn't be uttering words like that." Landon narrates, in the confessional, that he was brought up not to have prejudices against anyone — while Karamo narrates that Landon makes what he would consider offensive comments, and he lets them slide.

In another conversation, outside the confessional, Karamo opens up to Shavonda about being out of his comfort zone in Philadelphia and feeling like he is about to "shut down." While Karamo talks to his mother on the telephone, he relates that things are not going well and he needs to reactivate his mind before he goes crazy. Later that evening Karamo, MJ, and

Landon go to a bar. MJ tells a story about how he got hassled when he drove in the projects one time, and Karamo takes the opportunity to explain to Landon that he did not like to hear him use "the N word." Landon feels misunderstood by Karamo and says he has a lot of respect for Karamo but does not feel the same respect in return. Landon's explicit use of the word "nigger" leaves his degree of prejudice comfortably dubious. Karamo's unstable emotional state makes his justifiably angry response to Landon's use of the word "nigger" seem inappropriate. This applies as well to his angered and emotional outburst toward the police who nearly arrest him. Later that night, four police officers surround Karamo, and when he calls out to MJ he is not heard. The officers tell Karamo that they received an anonymous tip that he had a gun, and Karamo is furious. He raises his voice to the police officers while MJ, finally taking notice, tries to get him to calm down. Karamo feels that MJ is badgering him and implying that he is over-reacting. MJ narrates that he could not believe that Karamo got so upset and that he did not know if "it was because he's gay, black or what." Karamo is frustrated because incidents like this happen to him and his friends very frequently. After the officers conclude that Karamo's microphone was mistaken for a gun, the young people return home, where Karamo angrily tells his roommates of the incident and that this sort of thing happens to him all the time — more than twenty times. In what develops into a heated shouting match, Karamo asks MJ how many times this has happened to him, and he fails to provide an answer (*The Real World: Philadelphia* Episode 5).

This footage shows MJ attributing Karamo's "over-the-top" reaction first to his race, when he says in a reflective confessional, "I'm trying to convince him that they didn't do it because you're black," and then to his sexuality, when, in another confessional MJ says: "I don't know if it's because he's gay, black or what." This exchange runs parallel to MJ's angry and equally aggressive response to Karamo's questioning of "how many times?" MJ provides Karamo with no answer, and furthermore, neither MJ's race nor his sexuality are called into question to explain his behavior. These two factors testify to the show's unwavering commitment to privileging a white male sexual prerogative. This incident screams of racial profiling, something MJ and Landon seem to be completely unaware of, but with the aid of sly editing techniques, Karamo's frustration is written off as an over the top reaction. Worse, it is attributed to his sexual preference and race. The tropes of the frustrated homosexual and the angry black man create distinctions that would set any heterosexual and homosexual white male far apart from that which Karamo is constructed to embody. This works to create distance between white male viewers and Karamo. Such a stereotyping of Karamo's honest emotional response to the event speaks to the political power of sexual racism. The white male prerogative will not allow

Karamo, a black homosexual, a "macho" response to the incident with the police. By framing the incident first with Karamo's discussion of his racist upbringing and his disinclination to associating with "white friends," and then following the incident with MJ's confessionals reinforcing an unsympathetic viewer reception, producers posit Karamo's frustration at the run in with the police as an irrational response. The white male prerogative allows MJ's angry outburst to go unqualified. But it will not allow Karamo an equally charged response to the incident. His is discarded as "gay, black or what"— relegating his masculine and angry response to the margins of a white masculine status quo.

White male privilege dominates the relationships Karamo forges with other characters on the show as well — particularly with Landon and Shavonda. Karamo and Shavonda forge, in the show's earliest episodes, a strong friendship founded on a racial alliance. Shavonda, for example, is the first cast member to whom Karamo confesses his sexuality. As the season progresses, though, Landon and Shavonda engage in romance (*The Real World: Philadelphia* Episode 20). Landon and Shavonda's interracial romantic bond competes with Karamo and Shavonda's racial bond. Karamo sees this romance positioning Shavonda as an accomplice working to reinforce the privileging and dominance of the white heterosexual point of view. Karamo views Shavonda's sexual relationship with Landon as a pervasive assent to the prejudice of white male superiority guaranteeing superior status to the white males of the house, and inferior status to racial alliances. Women, as a result, are positioned as accomplices in this story of white privilege. An interracial romantic alliance trumps racial alliances where, previously, Landon and MJ's racial alliance trumped Karamo and Willie's sexual behavior.

Karamo and Willie, nonetheless, do engage in their own romantic adventures. The white male prerogative, however, hovers omnipresent to render a lasting verdict privileging white male heterosexuality and, most importantly in this case, homosexuality. For example, in episode eight Karamo tells Willie that he is sexually frustrated and that he needs attention "very, very, very soon." He turns his attention to Dorian, a homosexual African American male (not a cast member), who registered the cast members at a nearby gym. At a nightclub, Karamo runs into Dorian. Karamo is surprised because originally he did not think Dorian was gay. They dance seductively, and Willie is excited for Karamo's potential romance. Karamo, later that night in the confessional, claims to like Dorian because Dorian "doesn't act gay." Karamo has a first date with Dorian where they both talk about their coming out experiences, and Karamo explains that his family had a difficult time hearing and understanding that he was gay. As the date ends, Karamo seems shy and awkwardly shakes Dorian's hand. Returning home, Karamo states in a conversation with Willie's current love interest Daniel, a white male (not a cast member), that he "cannot be myself with the cameras on." Willie narrates that it appears Karamo is not that comfortable with his sexuality and therefore feels the need to hide it. Daniel has a really simplistic and rather unsympathetic response for Karamo's dilemma, "You have to deal with some shit," he says, "that's life." Karamo responds with a defiant stare into the camera, saying that "then I'm going to have to abstain for the next four months." He decides that it would be easier if he were not intimate with anyone for the duration of his stay at *The Real World* house. Pushed as he is to the margins of sexual representation, in this gaze Karamo exhibits a brief moment of agency.

This moment in episode eight illustrates Karamo's momentary return of the scrutiny of the cameras. As he defiantly returns the gaze of the camera, briefly, he usurps the camera's power.[4] In this moment, Karamo disrupts the invisibility of the viewer and the production team. His return gaze deconstructs the camera as objective viewer. Briefly, Karamo's return gaze pulls viewers into the on camera rubric. He unveils, through his role as a character in a contrived pop culture apparatus, the political strategy of the privileging of the white male prerogative. At this moment he no longer exists as a flat, depthless, character on screen; his return gaze gives him shape. By taking on the camera with his own eyes, he unmasks the constructed nature of the comfort zones of his viewers. His defiant act of agency demonstrates that reality television is merely a pretense at reality. He demonstrates that it is a construct.

Karamo's threat of inaction puts the fabric of the show's appeal in peril — his vow of abstinence would be cause to end the drama caught on tape. Inactive or dormant characters cannot function in the world of reality television. Karamo's threat of inaction is a refusal to participate in the drama of his own life put on screen — a representation constructed to privilege white male sexual politics. As resistant as this brief moment is, however, Karamo must ultimately surrender to the camera's gaze. He succumbs to his role as a player in "The Real World." Ultimately, he cannot escape the push of the white male prerogative; he is subsumed back into the straight white male story. He is forced back to the margins, and viewers settle back into their comfort zones quickly and eagerly, pushing this very "real" moment where their eyes met Karamo's to the back of their minds; he must submit to his role as racial and sexual Other. Karamo and Dorian go on a second date, and Karamo strives to be more himself and open up to his date. Karamo narrates that his conversation with Daniel inspired him to be more affectionate and be simply who he is. He does not want to worry about what his family or someone else may think of him. Karamo and Dorian conclude their second date affectionately on a couch at the back of the house, seemingly out of the camera's view (*The Real World: Philadelphia* Episode 8).

Episode eight also explores Karamo's own developing understanding of his homosexual desire. Karamo understands his attraction toward Dorian, a tall, muscular black male similar to himself, to be the result of what he thinks is Dorian's complex and contradictory rendering of homosexual desire. Karamo describes Dorian's behavior as "not gay," a reaction similar to MJ and Shavonda's reaction to Karamo's own sexuality on the season's first episode. As a result, Karamo and Dorian's homosexuality is presented as different from Willie's. Willie's behavior is quickly and unquestionably labeled "gay" by his roommates, while, conversely, Karamo and Dorian's homosexuality takes time become apparent. The show's heterogeneous representation of homosexuality expands as Daniel, a white homosexual male, enters the spectrum. Daniel and Willie meet earlier in episode four at a gay festival in the city. Willie, in the confessional, describes Daniel as a guy he used to "kiss, hug, and talk with" (*The Real World: Philadelphia* Episode 4). After this coincidental reunion, Daniel and Willie come back to the house where they "snuggle in bed together" (*The Real World: Philadelphia* Episode 4). A night later, Willie and Daniel are shown in the shower making out and then naked in bed together. Shavonda, Landon, and MJ catch glimpses of these activities from their adjacent bedrooms. Unlike Karamo and Dorian's romantic liaisons, which take place at the back of the house seemingly far from the cameras' lenses, Willie and Daniel's romantic encounters are explicit and readily available to the camera's and roommates' views.

What results is a complicated representation of male homosexual desire. Production mechanisms position interracial homosexual desire between a Puerto Rican American male and a white male as readily available to the cameras—there are no obstructions to scenes of intimacy between Daniel and Willie. Homosexual desire between two black men, as we experience footage of intimacy between Dorian and Karamo, is something to be hidden from the cameras, and furthermore, its dynamics are left ill defined. The framing of this footage is a purposeful move deployed to suggest a particular kind of sexist and racist politics— specifically, a systemic white male form of identity politics based on the anxiety caused by sexual and racial others. This leaves one to conclude that Daniel's presence as a white homosexual male lends legitimacy to his relationship with Willie, a man of color. Daniel's race trumps his sexual relationship with Willie. This racial eclipse posits Willie as sexual caricature, so much so that Willie tells cast mate Mel that he thinks MJ and Landon think of him as a character, not as a person (*The Real World: Philadelphia* Episode 26). What results is a twisting of a typically masculine space in representation. As feminist film-critic Laura Mulvey observes, the male is generally the one that holds the power in the narrative of the film; he, typically, is the active subject advancing the story, making things happen.[5] Mulvey suggests that women serve as the signifier for the male other, bound by a symbolic order in which a man can live out his fantasies and obsessions through linguistic command by imposing them on the image of woman still tied to her place as bearer of meaning, not maker of meaning (62).

The Real World: Philadelphia, I would argue, positions men of color within interracial homosexual relationships, as bearers not makers of meaning. Karamo, Dorian, and Willie's imagined or constructed sexual lack must be circumvented. Patriarchy demands that reality television provide a narrative and a structured representation that preserves its ideology of whiteness. The image of homosexual men, like Mulvey's women, is stolen and used for this end. Therefore, Willie cannot transcend Daniel's white presence, and he is made into a caricature. This representation positions white males as makers of meaning — heterosexual or not. Karamo and Dorian's sexual presence is something to be overcome. Producers communicate this desire through filming techniques. Producers film Karamo and Dorian's sexual intimacy behind curtains, through whispers, and around various obstructions. Willie and Daniel, in intimate settings or not, receive ample and unobstructed filming. The white male prerogative, here a homosexual prerogative, of a rather insidious nature, pushes Karamo and Dorian's liaisons, and even worse, Willie's very presence within a relationship, to the margins. This marginalization names the condition of homosexual men of color within a panicked logic of white male sexual dominion.

As this study has shown, the cultural narrative put forth by the fifteenth season of *The Real World* constructs a story that privileges a white male heterosexual (and homosexual) prerogative. This story begins with its characters—four white characters, two African American, and one Puerto Rican American. The fact that the only homosexual cast members are men of color puts Karamo and Willie on the margins of this cultural narrative. Despite brief moments of agency, Karamo and Willie ultimately must surrender to the power and authority of this white male story. Karamo and Willie function as the vehicles by which white male viewers construct comfort zones where the most problematic aspects of their realities, the fact that they live in a society where raced and homosexual male bodies intersect beyond their control, find erasure. Viewers can disregard the importance of angry gay black men because that anger and sexual presence is framed between the politics of heterosexual white men. Viewers can disregard Karamo's anger toward Shavonda and Landon because their sexual relationship and interracial bond dominates any friendship or alliance Karamo and Shavonda, both African Americans, had at the beginning of the show. Viewers can disregard the reality of Willie's relationship with Daniel because Daniel is white, and consequently, his presence as a white homosexual male obscures the fact that Willie is a man of color. Daniel's race trumps his sexual relationship with Willie. Daniel's white body pushes Willie's raced body further into the margins. In a rather insidious way, the white male prerogative, heterosexual or not, works to push homosexual men of color, in any relationship they possess, be it friendship or romance, to the margins. All of these examples, taken from various episodes of *The Real World: Philadelphia*, illustrate how the homosexual men of color on the show are represented though filmic mechanisms, such as the confessional, working to reinforce a "tuning out" to the reality of racial and sexual diversity and racial and sexual oppression.

In only the last few years, reality television has become television's most popular form of entertainment. Mention the genre in conversation, and one is sure to get a slew of references to highway hijackings, islands, bachelors, and big brothers— too many references to count or to tune in to for that matter. The popularity of these television hybrids is worthy of investigation in light of what they claim to represent — the unfolding of the authentic human condition. Viewers are encouraged to take these representations of the human drama, despite their dubious authenticity, and from them construct their own identities both as individuals and collectively as a society. Viewers of and cast members on *The Real World: Philadelphia* engage in an exchange of cultural meanings through the conveyance of authentic footage taken from "real" people's lives to form a cultural narrative that privileges white heterosexual and homosexual men at the expense of homosexual men of color. Thus, while MTV's cast members may be exploring "what happens when people stop being polite and start getting real," viewers are not even coming close.

Works Cited

Baker, Sean. "From *Dragnet* to *Survivor*: Historical and Cultural Perspectives on Reality Television." Smith and Wood 57–70.

Chvasta, Marcy R. and Deannea L. Fassett. "Traveling the Terrain of Screened Realities: Our Reality, Our Television." Smith and Wood 213–224.

Fetveit, Arild. "Reality TV in the Digital Era: A Paradox in Visual Culture?" *Media, Culture & Society* 21 (1999): 787–804.

Gilman Srebnick, Amy. "Book Review: Kevin J. Mumford. *Interzones: Black/White Sex Districts in Chicago and New York in the Early Twentieth Century.*" *The American Historical Review* 104.4 (1999): 1328.

Goddard, Ellis. "Reel Life: The Social Geometry of Reality Shows." Smith and Wood 73–96.

Jangodozinki, Jan. "The Perversity of (Real)ity TV: A Symptom of Our Times." *JPCS: Journal for the Psychoanalysis of Culture & Society* 9.2 (Fall 2003): 320–329.

Johnson, Elizabeth A. *She Who Is: The Mystery of God in Feminist Theological Discourse*. New York: Crossroad Publishing Company, 1999.

"Meet the Cast: Landon." *MTV Shows: Real World Main*. 2004. 22 April 2004. <www.mtv.com/onair/dyn/realworldseason15/personality.jhtml?personalityId=1129>

"Meet the Cast: MJ." *MTV Shows: Real World Main*. 2004. 22 April 2004. <www.mtv.com/onair/dyn/realworld-season15/personality.jhtml?personalityId=1131>

"Meet the Cast: Norman." *MTV Shows: Real World Main*. 1992. 22 April 2005. <www.mtv.com/onair/dyn/realworld-season1/personality.jhtml?personalityId=1026>

Mulvey, Laura. "Visual Pleasure and Narrative Cinema." Penley 56–68.

Mumford, Kevin J. *Interzones: Black/White Sex Districts in Chicago and New York in the Early Twentieth Century*. New York: Columbia UP, 1997.

Penley, Constance ed. *Feminism and Film Theory*. New York: Routlege, 1988.

"Real World Main." *MTV Shows*. 2004. 14 November 2004. <www.mtv.com/onair/realworld/>

Rony, Fatimah Tobing. *The Third Eye: Race, Cinema, and Ethnographic Spectacle*. 3rd ed. Durham, NC: Duke UP, 2001.

Smith, Matthew J. and Andrew F. Woods, eds. *Survivor Lessons: Essays on Communication and Reality Television*. Jefferson, NC: McFarland & Company, 2003.

THE REAL WORLD: PHILADELPHIA, EPISODIC REFERENCES

"Welcome to Philly!" Episode 1. *The Real World: Philadelphia*. Prod. Mary Ellis Bunim and Jonathan Murray. MTV, New York. 31 August 2004.

"'Out' In Philadelphia." Episode 2. *The Real World: Philadelphia*. 7 September 2004.

"Boys Will Be Boys." Episode 4. *The Real World: Philadelphia*. 21 September 2004.

"Gunning for Karamo." Episode 5. *The Real World: Philadelphia*. 28 September 2004.

"The Roomies Have Soul." Episode 6. *The Real World: Philadelphia*. 5 October 2004.

"Frustrations." Episode 8. *The Real World: Philadelphia*. 19 October 2004.

"Romantic Getaway." Episode 20. *The Real World: Philadelphia*. 25 January 2005.

"Losing You." Episode 26. *The Real World: Philadelphia*. 8 March 2005.

Notes

1. *The Real World: Philadelphia* [television broadcast], 31 August 2004, New York: MTV. This phrase accompanies the beginning of each episode of *The Real World*; it is voiced-over a montage of photographs and images blending the seven cast members with the host city for each season.

2. Mumford explored this concept first in an article, "'Homosex Changes' Race, Cultural Geography, and the Emergence of the Gay," *American Quarterly*, 48.3, 1996: 395–414, and then in his book, *Interzones: Black/White Sex Districts in Chicago and New York in the Early Twentieth Century*, 1997.

3. MTV.com provides short biographies and interviews of every cast member for the show's 15 seasons. See: www.MTV.com/onain/realworld-season15/meet_cast.jhtml.

4. This brief power play is a concept explored further in Fatimah Tobing Rony's *The Third Eye: Race, Cinema, and Ethnographic Spectacle*, Durham, NC: Duke University Press, 3rd ed., 2001, 41.

5. Laura Mulvey's work references psychoanalytic theory as it applies to cinema and film. I am carrying it over to analyze the footage and television episodes of *The Real World: Philadelphia*.

12

Racism and Reality TV: The Case of MTV's Road Rules

MARK ANDREJEVIC AND DEAN COLBY

> The idea from the very beginning was to put a diverse group of people from different backgrounds together, whether it's different racial or economic backgrounds or different sexual orientations. We're sort of trying to put together a little global village. [Jon Murray, co-producer of *Road Rules*, personal interview, November 19, 1999].

> There was so much that was real that was not real at all [Wallace Stevens, *The Solitude of Cataracts* 366].

Reality TV producers have made much of the element of social experimentation associated with the genre — a genre that has allowed entertainment producers to pick up where university ethics committees forced social psychologists to leave off after the notorious experiments of the '50s and '60s. Many formats, including *Road Rules*— a spinoff of the popular MTV show *The Real World* and the focus of this essay — lay claim to an element of social experimentation, purporting to create contrived situations in order to gauge the response of those "real" people who agree to submit themselves to the whims of their producer taskmasters. It is worth pointing out that this appeal to the authenticity of the experiment is not necessarily diminished by the recognition that reality TV is not *really* real — a truism echoed by fans and critics alike. Neither, of course, is the controlled setting of a laboratory experiment, and yet it is this very element of contrivance — the fact that circumstances can be controlled and closely monitored — that paradoxically underwrites the evidentiary quality of the experiment. Reality TV takes advantage of a certain slippage between the methodology of natural sciences and social sciences that allows contrivance to serve as a means of isolating elements of so-called reality. The equation is by no means unique to the current generation of reality TV programming: Stanley Milgram, whose famous obedience experiments should be counted among the spiritual ancestors of the current generation of reality TV, once wrote commentary for a collection of episodes of *Candid Camera* designed to serve as part of an instructional curriculum for social psychology. Moreover, in referring to his own work, Milgram once observed that "an experiment in social psychology smacks ... of dramaturgy or theater" (Blass, 2004; 263–4).

By the same token, reality TV as an entertainment genre smacks of experimentation, as suggested by MTV's tagline for *The Real World*, an invitation to "find out what happens when people stop being polite and start getting real" (MTV.com). Human relationships of all kinds are the raw material for the producers' explorations, which have touched upon — and domesticated — potentially charged issues including race relations, psychological disorders, substance abuse, and sexual identity. Jon Murray, co-producer of both *The Real World* and *Road Rules*, has described the shows as attempts to make individuals from different backgrounds confront such issues in a domestic setting — one in which they cannot dodge confrontation because of their close quarters confinement with those whom they might otherwise choose to avoid, ignore, or malign. The advantage of the contrived environments is that they render the drama of societal conflict in intimate personalized terms. The petri dish of *The Real World* apartment or the *Road Rules* Winnebago magnifies personal relationships for close inspection — and producer probing. At the same time, it decontextualizes social issues, shrinking them down to fit the dimensions of personal relations between seven individuals. The result is what Janice Peck describes as the triumph of a therapeutic ethos that manages social conflict and contradiction by translating it into the realm of the individual psyche and providing a therapeutic solution.

In fact, the decontextualization of social issues in reality TV portrayals has been noted by several scholars, including Peck, Andrejevic, Brenton and Cohen, and Andersen, but there has been, as of yet, little in the way of scholarship devoted to its impact on the portrayal of race in entertainment formats. This essay, based on the consideration of one season of the show *Road Rules*,[1] attempts a preliminary consideration of the way in which the explicit attempt of producers to engage with issues of race is delimited by the microcosmic character of the show. In abstracting away from the a broader social context in order to show how individuals who might never have chosen to interact with one another negotiate their differences, the genre does the ideological work of reducing social issues— requiring collective action — to individual character traits and thereby dismissing issues of race even as it invokes them in the name of socially engaged programming — and, of course, entertainment. As a genre directly invoking issues of race, reality TV offers the promise of access to the means of signification to selected members of the audience — including minorities — with the implicit suggestion they might be able to play some shared role in refashioning the mediated portrayals that have been foisted on them "from above" by a centralized, top-down, mass medium. Rather than passively watching themselves being represented, members of the audience — the non-media "real" world — might be provided with the opportunity to take a part in representing themselves.

This article attempts to trace the limitations of the participatory promise, highlighting the ways in which self-representation is structured by the conventions of the reality TV microcosm, and how the use of the genre can successfully manage the popular legitimation of elite power by disabling the political force of dissenting race representations. In so doing, the article traces the intersection of three strategies of decontextualization: the individualization of societal tensions, the abstraction of the social "experiment," and the equation of democratic representation with self-promotion (the portrayal of the market as the model for democratization of the media). We do not attempt a comprehensive overview of the portrayal of race in either MTV's reality formats or the genre as a whole. By focusing in some detail on one season of a particular format we seek to highlight one aspect of the logic of the portrayal of race underwritten by the promise of access to reality via the contrivance of reality TV — an aspect that we hope might be of use in shedding some light on the ways in which reality shows decontextualize and individualize social issues. Specifically, we focus on the deployment of a particular stereotype: that of the tough, mouthy, ghetto-girl played by a cast-member named Gladys on *Road Rules* and the way in which this portrayal served both as the niche that helped earn her a place on the show (and the opportunity of access to the media world), and as an individual, *real* "character trait" that eventually compelled her ratings-grabbing banishment from the show.

Metonymic Realism, Race, and Reality TV

Most participants and audiences know reality TV is contrived (Kilborn). This savviness, though, is exploited by reality programming. The seduction of reality TV also includes the creation of a cultural space in which the practices of ceaseless self-referencing can occur. Reality television is what we shall call metonymic realism. By this is meant a mode of producing the real that succeeds by simply permitting participants the opportunity to reproduce identities comporting to the logic and rules sanctioned by the show's producers and director. The inner sanctum of the reality created in this way selectively excludes a social totality riddled with systemic coercion and institutionally protected forms of domination. The exclusive bubble of the of reality programming's reality offers to participants and audiences a kind of utopian consumerism in which the contrivance of the real persistently refers to that which is immediately demanded. That many participants and audiences are aware of such contrivances does not diminish the ideological force the genre has in vindicating and reproducing the notion of consumerism as the nexus of human freedom.

As co-producer Jon Murray suggests in the quote that opened this essay, he is not just interested in documenting a slice of real life, but also in creating an artificial microcosm in which people who would not otherwise be likely to encounter one another are forced to live side-by-side and to get to know each other as individuals. His stated hope is these intimate encounters will force cast members to confront their own prejudices and preconceptions, thereby helping to foster broader awareness and discussion among the show's fans (personal interview, Jan. 17, 2000). He is particularly — and perhaps justifiably — proud of the role *The Real World* played in promoting AIDS awareness thanks to the high-profile struggle of cast member Pedro Zamora with the illness. Media critic Josh Gamson has praised *The Real World* for portraying not just the reality of Zamora's life with AIDS and his eventual death, but for providing a multi-dimensional and complex depiction of Zamora that challenges the two-dimensional stereotypes of homosexuals. In some rare ways perhaps, as in the case of Zamora, the reality TV genre opens up a space in which strategic construction of a kind of "counterpublic" can occur within the commercial management of popular culture (Muñoz); the tools of cultural reproduction can be fleetingly used by marginalized persons to expose the oppression of these persons to the wider public.

Yet, when it comes to the portrayal of Black cast members, or race relations per se, viewers and media critics alike have noted that *The Real World* and *Road Rules* have been less successful in challenging mainstream media stereotypes. On the contrary, the "reality" on offer has tended to reinforce a litany of media caricatures. As Darling notes in his discussion of *The Real World*: "it's bothersome to see black men once again straitjacketed as either nitroglycerin explosive, fat-cat lazy, mack daddy randy or some combination of the three" (1). Certainly the portrayal of the Black cast members of the first several seasons of the series bear out Darling's observations: Kevin, the only Black cast member on the first season, was accused of throwing a candlestick at a White housemate and fell neatly into the "nitroglycerin explosive" category; David, in season two, was accused of being sexually aggressive and threatening and was the first person to be kicked off the show. Syrus, who had an affair with the single mother of a child in the day care center where he worked during the Boston season and Teck, the womanizer from the Hawaii season, both fall into the "mack daddy randy" category; and Stephen from the Seattle season was required to take anger management classes after slapping a housemate with whom he had been feuding.

With respect to the portrayal of Black women on reality TV, the stereotype gaining the most media currency seems to be that of the angry Black woman (e.g. Jones; Wiltz). Reality TV shows like *The Apprentice*, featuring the manipulative Omarosa Manigault-Stallworth, and *Survivor: Allstars* with Alicia Calaway exploit the stereotype — one that harkens back to the role of "Sapphire" on *Amos 'n Andy*. As Hill Collins says, the "controlling images" (69) of Black women most often serve the purpose of reducing the particular assertiveness of these women to the nonpolitical objectification of the Black woman as a natural harpy and whore, emasculating welfare queen, or subordinate and sexless mammy. These images obviate the power of self-definition of Black women and continually posit them as the Other who provide the point of reference needed for the self-definition of Whites.

This is not to say that the White characters have not fallen into their own set of stereotypes. However, the caricatures seem more malleable — the White stereotypes serving up mostly the correction to what opposes Whiteness. Here, reality TV is especially skillful in, as Fiske puts it, "exnominating" whiteness (42). Whiteness becomes a Pascalian point in culture that evades a fixed nomenclature; Whiteness *is* only by what it recuperates as the least objectionable alternative to the baleful Other. In this sense, the "sign of blackness" (Gray 14) serves to clarify what Whiteness ought to be. Black female stereotypes, like the hypersexualized "she-devil," have the effect of what Wyatt refers to as "stealing women." While Black women are obsessively signified by popular culture in this way, and indeed Black women often regard these stereotypes as part of a Black woman's nature, Whiteness — in this case, what White women *are not* — is conveniently and always figured by fixing, by reifying, by *stealing* Blackness.

Admittedly, the manipulation of racial stereotypes of any kind is never fully predictable. This is the case when reality TV, perhaps like traditional television programming, offers a "gap" (Smith-Shomade 23) in which women of color, for example, can more subjectively determine the inevitable racial representation — in this sense, reality TV could do for racial signification, what *The Real World* did for the humane presentation of the stigmatization of AIDS. The cultural hegemony of elites, as Williams said, is never complete (125). One should not dismiss any mode of cultural transmission as wholly impenetrable to the struggle of representations of race.

Yet in its participatory promise and its appeal to the evidentiary character of the contrived experiment, reality TV sets itself apart from fictional (and even news) formats as a mode of conveying racial stereotypes. The contribution to the critical theory of race offered by this article is to explore how and why reality TV can be a quite effective way to close off access to racial signification — to preemptively seal off the "gap" it ostensibly opens, indeed, to exploit the promise of the gap to encourage the reproduction rather than the subversion of racial stereotypes.

In the World of Road Rules

The *Road Rules* 1999 season, analyzed here through interviews with the cast members and producer and through analysis of the show's content, featured six young adults in a trip through Mexico. The cast included Sarah, a woman of partly Mexican-American descent; Josh, a White, self-professed pacifist who was described by others as coming from a moneyed family; Holly, a White whose background is, by her own admission, fairly middle-class and "normal"; Abe, also White, whose background was described as lower-class and who reportedly made a living as a computer hacker; Brian, another White who was from an upper middle-class New Jersey family; and, Gladys, from as the show put it, "the projects of Cambridge [Massachusetts]."

The focus of this article is upon the portrayal of Gladys, the African American woman who was expelled from this 1999 "cultural edition" of *Road Rules*. The form of reality manufactured by the show's producers exhibits a narrow range of racial stereotypes that confirm the status quo of social relations. This representation of race is ironic given the ostensible aim of *Road Rules* to challenge bigotry by encouraging cast members to learn how to live in close quarters with people from a variety of backgrounds. By examining how Gladys is invited to perform a certain racial stereotype, this article exposes what has become a routine of race representation in reality programming. Rather than exploring the ways stereotypes underwrite dominant social relations (e.g. Seiter) — reality television instead reproduces racial stereotypes in order to induce a familiar catharsis and resolution. The catharsis comes in the form of the dramatic titillation provided by the deployment of recognizable stereotypes, in this case, the portrayal of Gladys as an angry black woman. The show's directed thaumaturgy, the solutions the show provides, suggests that racism is a purely personal problem. Gladys' self-discovery, in this sense, only points in one direction, and that is away from *any* representation that means to expose the social dimensions of race and racism.

Gladys was portrayed from the start as the tough, inner-city Black woman who would defend herself when challenged — even if that meant getting physical. Indeed, she said that it had been made clear to her during the course of her interviews with the producers that her tough, "don't-mess-with-me" attitude helped make her a desirable candidate for the show (personal interview). The stereotype has long functioned as a means of drawing White viewers, especially to Black comedy shows (Bogle 379), by affirming the Black woman as harridan and revealer of the presumed fecklessness of Black males. *Road Rules* selectively exploits this stereotype, but offers a form of reconciliation for Gladys and the others by promising to improve the lives of the show's participants. Gladys was not only being offered an economic opportunity — a ticket out of the ghetto, as it were — but a personal one: a challenge to transcend her background as she learned how to live with a group of people from different ethnic and socio-economic backgrounds in very close quarters (as if, of course, she was the one who needed to do the transcending). Freed from the constraints of the ghetto, Gladys was invited to express to the camera and to her traveling partners, who she *really* was. The fact this version turned out to be little more than the two-dimensional stereotype such an experience was purportedly calculated to transcend highlights the fundamentally conservative nature of the project itself.

It is important to note that auditioning for a reality TV show is, of course, a performance in itself: an invitation to gain access to the media world by enacting a version of oneself that fits the emerging conventions of unscripted reality feted by the producers. The coordinates of these conventions were well known by the target audience and talent pool for MTV's reality shows by the time the1999 season of *Road Rules* was taping.

Of all of the cast members, it was perhaps Gladys who had the clearest idea of what was expected from her. She said that during the course of her casting interviews it became clear to her that the producers liked the fact that she came across as an outspoken, strong-willed, inner-city Black woman. Bunim and Murray say they typically try to bring in people from a range of backgrounds and that they cast for potential conflicts (see Cerone), and it was clear to Gladys that her street credentials fit the bill. As she tells the story, when she first arrived on the set for the show, one of the crew members told her they had been forewarned about her by the producers: "'They tell us each about you guys, and you were the ghetto-girl that comes from the projects that doesn't take any shit.' That's how they summed me up" (personal interview, October 15, 2000).

Whether or not this was the sum total of Gladys' significance to the producers, it is clear that her background and her street savvy figured heavily in creating the diversity that is part of the Bunim-Murray casting formula. As co-producer Jon Murray suggests, what makes the show an interesting social experiment is the way *Road Rules* (and reality programming generally) forces those who would not be likely to choose one another as roommates to live and work together. Breaking barriers, for Murray, means abstracting from the social relations that foster them and forcing everyone to "start over" at the same level, thus creating an MTV approximation of the liberal ideal of "fair equality of opportunity." To highlight this fresh start, the beginning of every season of *Road Rules* depicts the (temporary) surrender of assets: all the cast members have to relinquish their wallets and credit cards for the duration of the show. They leave behind their family members and all enter the Winnebago that will serve as their home for the next several weeks as a group of strangers— equal in their anonymity — who need to learn how to get along with one another — or so the formula goes. The microcosm is small enough that prejudices are supposed to give way to individual experience. Cast members may, for example have preconceptions based on race, class, and sexual orientation, but, Murray argues, the process of having to live and work together in close quarters forces them to push beyond their own preconceptions:

> This show is about breaking down those barriers. And when you do that there are misconceptions that occur and arguments that result. But I think that overall at the end, people learn a lot about each other. And hopefully, maybe this is my bleeding heart liberal sentimentality, I think that in the end they find that they have something in common.... Our message about race fits into this along these lines [personal interview, November 19, 1999].

Or, of course, they find that they do not get along — and take to fighting, as happened midway through the seventh season, providing an opportunity to tease out some of the implications of the "message about race" and the search for commonality. The season's main event was an altercation between Gladys and Abe. Over the course of the group's travels, the two, who had originally been very friendly with one another — a friendship bordering on romantic interest —found themselves pitted in an escalating conflict that culminated when Gladys attacked Abe after he called her a "bitch." Gladys, who had been engaging in intermittent flirtation with Abe, was apparently mad at him for his casual romantic encounter with a female cast member from a previous season, the cast of which had visited the *Road Rules* set for a series of competitions. After calling him a slob and criticizing both Abe and his date for not having any class, Gladys was told to shut up and was insulted by Abe, who called her a "psycho bitch," thereby triggering the physical attack. The encounter was a brief one, but Gladys landed a couple of blows before the two were separated, and Abe, who claimed he was "emotionally scarred for life," vowed to ensure she was kicked off the show. When Abe threatened legal action, the show's producers decided to remove Gladys. This bit of theater resulted in the highest ratings ever for an episode of *Road Rules* (Nielsen Media Research, personal communication, June 3, 1999).

Gladys was portrayed as the one who started the fight by provoking a relatively calm Abe, who fought back by using an insult, "psycho bitch," that he knew from past discussions with Gladys would be the most effective way to goad and upset Gladys. As she put it after the fight, "I think the most degrading thing you can call someone is a bitch. I don't like it at all, I told everyone, you don't mess around with me and you don't call me that word. My name is Gladys, use that. If you don't want to use my name, walk out."

Interestingly, Abe attributed the experience to Gladys's openness: her drive to say what she thought and how she felt regardless of the impact she has on others. The fight started, in short, because she was being real: herself. As Abe put it, "I think she's the most incredible person I've met in terms of being whole and being right there and being completely who she is." By extension, of course, her physical assault on Abe remained consistent with her irrepressible, uncensored character. If she felt attacked, she would fight back — this was the persona she had projected on the show and the one for which she had been selected. As she put it in her final episode: "I have no problem defending myself when people disrespect me and if they do I'm going to fight 'em to the end. I fought Abe to the end and today is the end for me."

This fatalism was echoed by the other cast members who rehearsed their own understanding of the role for which both she and they understood she had been cast. In a conversation with Abe after the fight, Brian, another cast member, reinforced the image of Gladys as the scrappy ghetto-girl who is as quick with her fists as with her mouth. "You know she's not going to calm down.... It's not her. She's all about speaking her opinion." This, of course, was Gladys' character. She always posed the threat of violence. As she knows and the others know, that was always expected of her. Following the fight, Gladys referred back to the image of herself with which she had been confronted during the first day of taping, telling the others that "if they want to see me go ghetto, I'll go ghetto." In the end, the cast agrees with Abe that such conduct is impermissible and the "threat of violence" not worth living with. Gladys chose to hit Abe, "and that's all there is to it," says Josh.

The dimension of race — as important as it had been in the various subtexts that circulated around Gladys, including her rough childhood "in the projects" and her ghetto-girl toughness— never surfaced in the discussion of the fight and was discounted by the producers who had cast her as the one Black cast member. As co-producer Jon Murray put it more than a year after the fact, "I honestly don't think that race had anything to do with her confrontation with Abe. Again, it's been awhile. But, I don't remember anyone bringing up the issue of race" (personal interview, November 19, 1999). Murray's recollection is accurate. The conflict between Gladys and Abe did not explicitly touch on race issues. Race was merely part of the repressed background: a quality that helped associate Gladys with a familiar constellation of racialized associations and images, but that was barred from entry into the purely personal conflict between two individuals transported into the microcosm of the Winnebago. The show exploited Gladys to portray the racial stereotypes it needed to add to its arsenal of dramatic conflict, but in no way could it allow Gladys to claim her status as Black "ghetto-girl" as a difference which acknowledges political and economic oppression. The angry girl stereotype can either function as an expression of the structural delimitation of life, or can serve to prove, however perniciously, that race representations are merely the purveyors of style.

One might understand this paradox in another way. The ambition of dissenting representations is to betray some quality of life that is painfully experienced as a difference that cannot be chosen. This difference is real and crucial, and what has been called "outlaw culture" (manifested in the cultural dissonance of the "ghetto-girl") is needed to affirm African-American identity and subvert norms and representations harmful to politically alienated communities (e.g. Evans). However, the "ghetto-girl" pose, which could serve the function of counterhegemony by revealing a sense of dissatisfaction with the social relations that reproduce poverty and cultural marginalization, is evacuated by the *Road Rules* producers. Ultimately the show's framing of Gladys' difference intends reinforcement of an unquestioned assumption about racism. The assumption is all racism is the result of primarily individual irrationality and not the systematic, structural marginalization of peoples. The individualization of racism is "inferentially racist" because it ignores the potential for race representation to express the fact that persons, because of their race, are often denied material opportunities that include access to the means to represent this fact. (Hall).

Road Rules' inferential racism does not permit the angry girl affect to refer to racially motivated economic exclusion. The result is deeply antagonistic because, firstly, Gladys is made solely responsible for presumably choosing to be the angry Black woman. But this antagonism does not end with Gladys. Because the producers of the show impute this stereotype to Blacks per se — after all, Gladys was expected to perform the stereotype because she was "from the ghetto" — the presence of race representations that seem common to Blacks "from the ghetto" must be the demonstration of a kind of collective delusion in Black communities. Such is the pervasiveness of the inferential racism on *Road Rules.*

Getting the Message

If, as Murray suggested, the show's message about race is that, by abstracting individuals from their social contexts, their common humanity can be allowed to come to the fore and to unite them, the Gladys incident has the disturbing result of incarnating and essentializing the stereotype she was invited to adopt in order to transcend. The Murray message, as it were, is that the abstract character of social relations ought to get the blame for social conflicts based on race, gender, class, and sexual preference. Consequently, social relations themselves must be backgrounded if our common humanity is to come to the fore. In this respect, reality TV replicates what Peck describes as the "repression of the social" in the therapeutic discourse of popular television — a discourse repeatedly invoked in reality shows, which invariably stress the forms of personal growth and therapeutic learning "about oneself" associated with even the most traumatic and contrived aspects of life lived in the glare of the spotlight. Even after being told she would have to leave, Gladys spoke fondly of the benefits she had received from the experience of being on the show: "I feel that I've grown stronger on this trip.... I'm just happy that I met the people that I met and I'm happy that I spent three wonderful weeks with everyone in Mexico" (personal interview, October 15, 2000).

Part of being on reality TV is, on the therapeutic account, learning the truth of who one is— and part of getting at that truth is abstracting oneself out of one's context and history, in order to isolate one's essence. It is this self that becomes the focus of problems to be worked on. As Peck puts it, "Therapeutic discourse proposes that we change ourselves without conceding that our identities and actions are determined by social conditions that will not change just because we interpret and handle them differently on an individual basis" (80).

The paradoxical result is that our common humanity takes on the character of an abstraction: it is what would allow us all to get along if only we did not live in society. This is, perhaps, an appealing promise insofar as it mobilizes the themes of the critique of mass society: social relations have themselves become so abstracted that we need to abstract away from them in order to get to know one another as individuals in all our particularity. The danger of this solution, of course, is that it fails to recognize how an individual removed from social context loses also the character of his or her particularity. The absolute individual, like a non-dimensional point in space, remains at the level of pure abstraction. Gladys is not who she is despite her history — her individuality incorporates this history.

The further implication of this approach is a hallmark of the liberal tradition in both communication and politics: conflict is the result of a mutual misunderstanding. Once the world is shrunk to the size of a Winnebago, this formulation has its element of truth. However, the attempt to generalize back to the real world, as it were, is flawed to the extent that social antagonisms result not always from misunderstandings, but from persistent conflicts between social groups and classes, not to mention the way these conflicts are represented often in ways that militate favorably to the status quo of power. While it may be true the *Road Rules* cast shares common interests and personal experiences that favor the attempt to move beyond stereotyped preconceptions and to forge personal bonds, it is not necessarily the case that conflict is always the result of mutual misunderstanding or of hackneyed stereotypes. Indeed, such conflict is often between groups of people who understand each other and their competing interests only too well. Interestingly, the assertion of an abstract, shared, common humanity fails to address these conflicts, which is not to give up on the notion of common human interests, but to suggest these are best addressed by engaging with history and social relations rather than suppressing them. A history of social conflict cannot be erased by ignoring it, for it gains its reality precisely through the individuals who live out this conflict.

The ostensible goal of the Bunim-Murray casting formula is to encourage cast members to transcend the stereotyping this kind of realism imposes on them. The gay character, the inner city Black woman, the sheltered suburbanite, and the spoiled rich kid are supposed to serve as starting points— caricatures to be revealed as such when viewers get to know the cast members better and see them as "real people." The predicament of Gladys highlights the incoherence of the *Road Rules* version of individualism. She has been offered the MTV equivalent of the American dream: a ticket to the lottery of celebrity. Indeed, MTV bolsters its own liberal credentials with the assertion that it offers these tickets on an equal opportunity basis: anyone, regardless of background, ethnicity, etc. is eligible for a spot on TV (assuming, of course, they are the right age and have the right image). However, it is not at all accurate to suggest Gladys was chosen *despite* her inner city background. Rather, as became clear from her perception of the casting process and the reactions of the production crew, she was chosen in large part *because* of the fact she was a Black woman who grew up in the projects. So her big break was predicated on her ability to play the role of an angry Black woman from the inner city.

In terms of MTV logic, there is nothing surprising about this paradoxical formulation, which has made millionaires out of many a rap star. To some extent, African Americans accrue some cultural power by reproducing caricatures that are popularly perceived to be counterhegemonic. But reality TV dissembles the discursive production of reality, conceals the deeply social struggle for signification, by limiting the potential for "outlaw culture" or, as Fiske puts it, by silencing the revolt of "counterknowl-edge" and "counterhistories" against the "nature" of individualism (192–93). This "silence" occurs because the stereotypes intended as counterknowl-edge become, as Boyd puts it, racial "distractions" (37); the attempts to confront power really only further adumbrate class conflict and the usual competition for meaning. In the register of reality TV, this irony takes on the added complication of the fact that the entire point of the show is to eradicate the gap between the image and the reality. According to the show's premise, Gladys was not expected to "play the role" of the ghetto-girl, but to live it — and to work on herself in the process. But this requirement for-feits the energy of the "ghetto-girl" as a means of protest because, when trapped in the microcosm of reality in *Road Rules,* the social relations that are the object of such angry Black girl representations *do not exist.*

Explained in a slightly different way, reality TV does not attempt what Harper distinguishes as "mimetic" or "simulacral" realism (70). Simulacral realism on television attempts to provide race representations, in the form of positive role models like Bill Cosby, which can then be emulated by view-ers. Mimetic realism attempts the difficult task of reflecting social reality for the purpose of generalizing a "Black experience" (71). Reality television does something else: metonymic realism. The subject of reality, in this case Gladys, can only regard her own ideas about herself as the only reality. This reality neither refers to an experience of life often beyond one's control, nor does the reality TV *reality* establish a model for social relations beyond the show's existence. The show only refers to itself, and in this way the dis-tance between appearance and reality, between race reference and experi-ence, vanishes. We are faced with what Theodor Adorno, in his critique of positivist social science, described as "a simple circle." The "essential" Gladys, abstracted from the social context that helped define her according to the stereotype of the angry Black woman, outspoken and occasionally violent, turns out to be the same as her caricature. Reality TV follows through on its promise to slip behind the unessential appearance and deliver the essential reality *by demonstrating that the appearance itself is the reality.*

Conclusion: The Ideology of Reality

The double-bind in which Gladys was caught is only partially cap-tured by Josh's claim that "the reason she needed the show most is the same reason she had to leave." The flip side of this formulation fills out the par-adox of her position: the reason she had to leave was the reason for her being recruited to the show in the first place. If Gladys' ticket out of the ghetto was premised not merely on the understanding that she would play the role of the angry Black woman from the inner city, but as she put it, on the expectation that she might at any time "go ghetto," the reality formula superseded the reality it displaced. In a complementary double gesture, the show backgrounded the social relations of the inner city, and replaced these with the social relations of prime-time television production. Gladys is simultaneously offered a trip out of the inner city and invited to bring the inner city into the *Road Rules* microcosm.

Reality programming in this sense goes much further than drama by extirpating from the viewer's mind (at least this is the promise) the more transparent deception of artifice. As it turns out for Gladys, the producers of the show wanted the inner-city "reality" to prove the corrective artifice of the social relations in the Winnebago. Gladys early on was aware of the sacrifice she needed to perform: "I don't know if they [the producers] thought that it was going to that point that I was going to fight Abe or not or whether I was just going to walk away like I had been walking away, but I think they wanted it to go that far, but they didn't expect it to be that soon" (personal interview, October 15, 2000). Because this sacrifice is embedded in so much reality, it actually appears the "ghetto-girl" was nothing more than an arbitrary pose and that the history of the social relations that produced the attitude as a potential means of confronting power was equally unreal.

But none of the cast or even the producers understands this contradiction. For co-producer Jon Murray, *Road Rules* is all about removing barriers that separate races. Like pushing the tables together in a segregated school lunchroom, we need to throw people together so they can confront and overcome not only their differences of race but also the distance that separates them economically. That Gladys chose to settle her differences with her fists is something Murray is willing to acknowledge as a difference associated with Gladys' upbringing on the "streets of Boston." Gladys' trajectory along the "story-arc" of the show's narrative was anticipated as potentially volatile, but her reaction "at that level" of violence was impermissible. Whatever residual behavior remained that was "ghetto" was intolerable in Gladys' new economic parity with the others (personal interview, October 15, 2000).

As a documentary, *Road Rules* documents the facts of Gladys' life. On the other hand, the facts are removed from history by the show's seemingly unambiguous creation of a televisual reality that permits a person like Gladys to become someone other than herself, someone other than the combined historical facts of her life. The attempt, however, to nurture this transformation in the reality TV lab backgrounds the determinations within which it takes place: the conditions of production of reality TV itself. The result of such an attempt to transcend historical determination by ignoring it is the perpetual return of the stereotype in the register of reality itself: Gladys is not transformed, but rather her behavior, which is no longer discerned within a web of social relations, becomes the expression of the kernel of her individual essence.

Paradoxically, as the one Black cast member — chosen in part because of her Blackness— this kernel comes to stand for her essence not as the historically particular Gladys (for she has been deprived of this particularity), but as the abstracted Gladys: the character of the ghetto-girl divorced from the critical, counterhegemonic substance of that pose. In complementary fashion, the image of the ghetto-girl is itself de-historicized, and thus turned back into a general category: the non-dimensional point of racially-coded inner-city anger, removed from history, becomes an abstract personality trait.

The strategy is so successful that we are left wondering with the cast whether Gladys' reality as "ghetto-girl" was no more than a delusion, a fabrication of her own hysteria. This is supported by the views of the cast members. As Holly put it, answering whether Gladys was supposed to fulfill this role:

> I think that may be the stereotype. But that's what Gladys is like. That's what they liked about it. She's this spunky, no-holds-barred girl and ... that's why they wanted her on the show because of that aspect of her personality, not because she was the Black, angry girl [personal interview, November 17, 1999].

This is why Gladys' experience as a "ghetto-girl" is so lackluster when contrasted with the *Road Rules'* reality. Indeed, the producers have made it very clear that the farthest thing from their mind is any attempt to "do reality" in the ghetto. "That's not what our viewers want," says Murray (personal interview, November 19, 1999). The ghetto, despite its MTV romanticization and the popularity of its style, music, and attitude in middle America, does not represent the fantasy escape of the type of reality that Bunim-Murray productions strive for. Part of the appeal of the show, according to Murray, is the glamorous element: the fact that a group of young adults lives in an environment that they would otherwise be unlikely to afford. The result of this fantasy version of reality is the resultant unreality of the cast members' prior history.

Gladys is required to impossibly embody racist stereotypes of Blackness— with all the baggage of violent problem-resolution thought to be intrinsic to African American culture — and she must transcend these stereotypes as a responsible individual who knows these stereotypes are wrong. She must live a lie. She must displace her oppressor with her ego, and the conflict of the dialectic of the slave and master is cruelly sequestered in her own defective "individuality." Such is the perverse stoicism required of Gladys. And certainly, this perversion seems to confirm simultaneously the legitimacy of what oppressors *do*. In this "simple circle," this metonymic reality, Gladys confirms that being "ghetto" is no justification for acting Black. She ought to simply choose to do what White people do within this reality: Choose to be White.

Works Cited

Andersen, Robin. *Consumer Culture and TV Programming*. Boulder, CO : Westview Press, 1995.

Adorno, Theodor. "Sociology and Empirical Research." *The Adorno Reader*. Ed. Brian O'Connor. Oxford: Blackwell, 2000. 174–192.

Andrejevic, Mark. *Reality TV: The Work of Being Watched*. Boulder, CO: Rowman and Littlefield, 2004.

Bogle, Donald. *Prime Time Blues: African Americans on Network Television*. New York: Farrar, Straus and Giroux, 2001.

Boyd, Todd. *Am I Black Enough For You?: Popular Culture From the 'Hood and Beyond*. Bloomington: Indiana University Press, 1997.

Brenton, Sam and Reuben Cohen. *Shooting People : Adventures in Reality TV*. London; New York : Verso, 2003.

Cerone, Daniel. "MTV's Sort-of Real 'World.'" *Los Angeles Times* 28 May 1992: 1F.

Darling, Cary. "Reality TV Just Enhances Stereotypes." *Milwaukee Journal Sentinel* 2 Aug. 2000: 1E.

Evans, Monica. J. "Stealing Away: Black women, Outlaw Culture, and the Rhetoric of Rights." *Critical Race Theory: The Cutting Edge*. Eds. Richard Delgado and Jean Stefancic. Philadelphia: Temple University Press, 2000. 500–13.

Fiske, John. *Media matters: Race and Gender in U.S. Politics*. Rev. ed. Minneapolis: University of Minnesota Press, 1996.

Gamson, Joshua. "Do Ask, Do Tell." *The American Prospect* Fall 1998: 44–52.

Gladys. Telephone interview. 15 Oct. 1999.

Gray, Herman. *Watching race: Television and the struggle for "Blackness."* Minneapolis: University of Minnesota Press, 1995.

Hall, Stuart. "The Whites of Their Eyes: Racist Ideologies and the Media." *Silver Linings*. Eds. George. Bridges and Rosalind Hunt. London: Lawrence & Wishart, 1981. 7–23.

Harper, Brian. "Extra-Special Effects: Televisual Representation and the Claims of the "Black Experience." *Living Color: Race and Television in the United States*. Ed. Sasha. Torres. Durham. Duke University Press, 1998. 62–82.

Hill Collins, Patricia. *Black Feminist Thought: Knowledge, Consciousness, and the Politics of Empowerment*. New York: Routledge, 2000.

Holly. Telephone interview. 17 Nov. 1999.

Jones, Vanessa E. "The Angry Black Woman." *Boston Globe* 20 Apr. 2004: F1.

Josh. Telephone interview. 20 Nov. 1999.

Kilborn, Richard. *Staging the Real: Factual TV Programming in the Age of Big Brother*. Manchester: Manchester University Press, 2003.

Muñoz,, José Esteban. "Pedro Zamora's *Real World* of Counterpublicity: Performing an Ethics of the Self." *Living Color: Race and Television in the United States*. Ed. Sasha. Torres. Durham. Duke University Press, 1998. 192–218.

Murray, Jon, Telephone interview. 19 Nov. 1999.

Nielsen Media Research. E-mail contact. 3 June 2000.

Peck, Janice. "Talk About Racism: Framing a Popular Discourse of Race on Oprah Winfrey." *Cultural Critique* 27 (Spring 1994): 89–126.

Sarah. Telephone interview. 17 Jan. 2000.

Seiter, Ellen. "Stereotypes and the Media: A Re-evaluation." *Journal of Communication* 36 (1986): 16–26.

Smith-Shomade, Beretta. *Shaded Lives: African-American Women and Television*. New Brunswick: Rutgers University Press, 2002.

Stevens, Wallace. "The Solitude of Cataracts." *Collected Poetry and Prose*. Eds. Frank Kermode and Joan Richardson. New York: The Library of America. 1997.

Volosinov, V. N. *Marxism & The Philosophy of Language*. New York: Seminar Press, 1973.

Williams, Raymond. *Marxism and Literature*. London: Oxford University Press, 1977.

Wiltz, Teresa. "The Evil Sista of Reality Television." *Washington Post* 25 Feb. 2004: C01.

Wyatt, Gail E. *Stolen Women: Reclaiming Our Sexuality, Taking Back Our Lives*. New York: John Wiley & Sons, 1997.

Notes

1. *Road Rules* is produced by Bunim/Murray Productions. The show premiered in 1994 on MTV and is now in its eleventh season. Though the American reality genre has an old pedigree, perhaps most fully initiated by the 1973 PBS multi-episode *An American Family,* Bunim-Murray's early 1990 contributions to the genre set the stage for the explosion of reality television programming. *Road Rules* combines the road-trip with the game show. Several young adults are chosen from massive single-day auditions usually held throughout the year in various college towns. The early twenty-something adults are provided with a large recreational van and a specific allotment of money and a trip itinerary that includes numerous competitive challenges usually oriented to athletic pursuits. The group's interaction is filmed by an accompanying camera crew. The 1999 season chosen here for analysis is *Road Rules: Latin America,* a "Cultural Edition" of the show, referring to the attempt by producers to extend the seventh season's milieu to include the cast's exposure to a foreign country. The 15-episodes of the show followed the six member cast's trip through the American Southwest, Mexico and Belize. After completing various competitive "missions," the group vied against one another in a mock paramilitary exercise on an island near Panama. The winner of the contest received a new automobile.

13

The Amazing "Race":
Discovering a True American
Jordan Harvey

Teetering on the edge of cancellation, CBS' *The Amazing Race* finally emerged in its fifth season, assisted by an EMMY award. CBS relegated earlier seasons to the menial sections of TV's schedule, namely summer and winter. Now, after back-to-back EMMY awards, *The Amazing Race* has solidified its spot in CBS' primetime fall and spring lineups. Its unique concept of sending American teams of two on a race around the world conjures up images of a Jules Verne escapade. Millions of viewers regard the show's picturesque locations as incomparable and its grueling system of travel and challenges as strenuous and burdensome to even the firmest of relationships.

The idea of "nation" is a hallmark of the series. During each leg of the race, contestants must traverse from continent to continent and accomplish "detours" and "road blocks" in which they perform a task symbolic of the culture/nation they currently inhabit. For example, in season seven the contestants performed a "detour" in Cuzco, Peru in which they chose either to rope two llamas into a pen or carry alfalfa in a basket on their backs to a nearby store while wearing a colorful Indian poncho. The next episode found the contestants performing a "road block" in Santiago, Chile in which one member had to shine shoes supervised by a shoe shine tradesman for one Peruvian sole per client (about $0.30 USD).[1] At each "pit stop" host Phil Keoghan along with a representative from each country (usually dressed in symbolic garb) eagerly await the arrival of each team. The last team to arrive at each "pit stop" receives the unfortunate news that they have been eliminated from the race and a chance for one million dollars. Eventually, the team "that best blends speed with brains, tenacity and a decent sense of direction" is deemed the winner of *The Amazing Race* (Bianco 1D). Along the way, viewers vicariously encounter many different nations and cultures.

How does the show treat these other nations? Quite often, race sites trivialize foreign cultures by focusing on their food, alcohol of choice, or methods of labor, thus forcing an ideal of otherness upon them. This paper will primarily focus on the most recent seasons (four through seven) of *The Amazing Race*.[2] Transitioning from the placement of other cultures into workable categories of otherness, we will then discuss the creation of a national American identity.

I believe that *The Amazing Race* offers audience members a template with which to formulate and reinforce a dominant ideal of true Americanism, while simultaneously discounting African Americans, gays, and women as prototypical Americans. Before delving into the construction of American culture, I first need to discuss the work of Stuart Hall, Edward Said and others through their discussions on marginalization and the discourses of colonialism. By studying how *The Amazing Race* depicts other cultures and nations through the models set forth by the aforementioned theorists, we can then utilize Michele Hilmes and Rick Altman's work to reveal the relationships and hierarchies created among Americans resulting in the production of an exclusionary culture.

The Creation of Otherness: Orientalism *and* The Amazing Race *Abroad*

Placing Americans in other nations revitalizes old power relations. Who has the power to control the representations of other nations on *The Amazing Race*? Ultimately, the producers on the show as well as the contestants control how a foreign nation is represented through actions, words, and editing choices. Contestants are often put into third world countries markedly different from America's "land of opportunity." As a result, contestants frequently remark on the impoverished people with a tone of superiority and disgust. The foreigners are characterized as sexually perverse and culturally unstable. Through casting choices, producers are able to secure the personalities needed to propagate and maintain the slanted power relationships. Assisted by contestant actions and words, producers edit the show in order to impart the notion of America's western ideals as culturally and economically superior.

By providing contestants with "the real universal language ... a flash of some cash," producers are able to maintain economic control through the use of the American dollar, which is predominately worth a considerable amount more than the currency in most nations *The Amazing Race* visits (Behr 15). Equipped with monetary power, contestants are often susceptible to the deceitfulness of foreigners, as we will see later. As a result, producers garner additional footage to help shape a nation's representation through the contestants' constructed power relationships. In thinking about this issue, it helps to use Edward Said's notion of Orientalism to understand how dominant nations gain the ability to control the representations of "lesser" nations.

Europe's prolonged dominance over the Orient involved organizing a wide range of distinct groups into one cultural entity, thus removing it from the realm of mystery. Prior to the 18th century, the Orient often remained off-limits to westerners, and imaginations ran wild as to the inner workings of the east. The European culture considered itself supreme due to its highly advanced Roman and Greek lineage, but it soon began to question its own magnitude. Was the eastern culture better than the west? Were they a more civilized and advanced group of people? Europe certainly felt threatened by the unknown. Yet, as Europe broke through the mythical aspects of the east both economically and militarily during the 19th century, the natural need to define Orientals and place them into a cultural box arose. Fear subsided from the west, but Europe needed to redefine its position atop the cultural hierarchy.

Said's work on Orientalism contends that the European culture was able to enhance its ability to control, as well as dramatically improve and legitimize itself, by distancing itself from any similarities within the Oriental culture and perpetuating stereotypes of "backwardness" onto non-Europeans (3). This method of cultural legitimization thrives under the assumption that the others must be controlled and tutored by their natural superiors, Europeans. Through this rationale, European elitists branded the others as uncivilized and mentally incapable of determining the correct principles with which to construct their own culture. The combination of technological, religious, educational, and cultural inferiority placed upon non-Europeans allowed westerners to position themselves favorably. After solidifying its rightful place atop the cultural hierarchy by breaking down the preexisting culture, the western world felt compelled to construct an "appropriate" culture for the miscreants. Unfortunately for the others, the newly created culture served only as a tool for increased hegemony by the western world.

Europe began its assault on the character of the others in order not only to hasten the marginalization of non-Europeans, but also to begin the process of cultural assimilation. The realization of hegemonic control by western culture relied on framing the others with sweeping generalizations about their inherent lack of morality. Sexual perversion was one of the most effective stereotypes in creating the idea of otherness. Devout Europeans feared the licentiousness of the others and perceived all non-European males as disruptive and dangerous to the purity of European morals. These stereotypes allowed Europeans the leverage to quickly dissolve old cultural values and deliver a westernized, materialistic culture to the others, a culture that was often in conflict with their prior religious and social norms. Through these mechanisms, the hegemonic powers initiate cultural assimilation and disrupt the ability for any smaller cultural entity to externally distinguish itself from the new blanket culture.

By basing each new group on a "fixed transcultural or transcendental racial category," the dominant culture excludes the constructed group from attaining any rights in the natural framework of life (Hall, "New" 165–69). The Orient was home to dozens and dozens of individualized sects of people, each with a different set of beliefs. However, distinction amongst inferior cultures is eradicated through the creation of the colonial subject, a subject disarmed of individuality. The subject is immediately transformed into a stereotype, a uniformed being unworthy of respect. Thus said, the colonial subject is controlled most effectively through "an articulation of difference through racial and sexual discourses" (Bhabha 88). Identifying a group of people as black or Oriental is a blanket for groups with differing backgrounds, traditions, and customs.

Stuart Hall comments on the hegemonic ploy of presenting a solitary identity across ethnic and cultural differences. The important issue lies in discovering what these unifying classifications signify. Ultimately, the failure to recognize the experiences of multiple identities represents a clearly contrived political and cultural formation of a new group. This form of cultural imperialism by whites induces the feeling of colonized subjects as "somewhere else" and unable to effectively speak from a position of power. The result of this cycle is the characterization of others as problematic both politically and culturally (Hall, "Minimal" 115–19). Playing upon those characterizations of inferior races often allows the hegemonic groups freedom to create popular culture from the discourses of race.

Producers on *The Amazing Race* play with the discourses of race by pointing out and exploiting foreign countries' otherness in an attempt to make them seem "backwards." Host Phil Keoghan believes that "this show opens people's eyes to the rest of the world, different cultures and different ways of thinking" (qtd. in Keveney 4). Yet, the producers of *The Amazing Race* dictate what we are to think of these differences. By filming the stereotypes believed of a certain society, the show reinforces such stereotypes among its viewers. Whether it is "washing" dirty garments in murky water in India or trying to control a water buffalo with rudimentary tools in Manila, viewers see primitive practices unusual to our capitalistic society.

Casting on *The Amazing Race*— the contestants are often superficial white actors and models— helps facilitate the construction of Orientalism and further enhances the poignancy of the editing practices. In season four, the teams arrive in Mumbai and gaze upon the vast poverty dominating the city streets. Reichen and Chip (Season Four's winners) ponder how the city got so grotesque and ask, "What happened?" Kelly states, "This is my worst nightmare," in reaction to the crowdedness and stench of the area, while her mate Jon says, "Welcome to Bombay." The teams return to India in season five as well. Colin (2nd place Season Five), a competitive young man, sarcastically notes with an impish grin, "Calcutta is just a beautiful city; it really gives you a good look at the human culture." His female partner Christie looks at him in disbelief because she knows he is uttering a gross misstatement.[3] The American contestants witness Indian children rummaging through filthy streets alongside pigs and dogs without any regard for sanitation or safety. Traffic lines are non-existent as pedestrians, cabs, elephants, bicycles, and rickshaws dangerously converge in the small streets. Basically, contestants witness a culture that deemphasizes American values such as education, safety, health, and general order.

In ways that reflect Said's theories, producers utilize specific editing techniques and subtitles to portray the others encountered by the contestants as sexually perverse. The most lasting images from India concern their mass transit rail lines. Passengers must force their way onto the train in a rather furious manner, while others simply disregard safety by hanging off the sides. Contestants comment on the retched smell emanating from the dozens of men air-packed into the cars. To make matters worse, attractive women are fondled and groped in a most inhumane manner. Camera shots capture the perverted and morally lifeless faces of these men as they dehumanize the women aboard. In season four, the female team of Tian and Jaree are depicted in slow motion writhing in pain from multiple pinches on the "boobs" and "ass."[4] The use of slow motion provides a sense of trauma to the scene, as if to emblazon the images of sexual indecency in our minds. Juxtaposed to these slow motion images are quick cuts to multiple Indian men on the train devilishly smiling at the violations occurring onboard. Thus, the producers have effectively lumped all of the Indian men into the category of sexual impropriator. Since we cannot identify a single culprit, we are to assume that all Indian men condone the devious practice.

Producers on *The Amazing Race* claim to be docile and objective towards other cultures, but contrasting their words are the visuals from India and other places.[5] For example, India's industry is depicted as archaic and its cities as filthy and chaotic. Contestants on season five must make mud bricks one by one at a brick factory. Unlike America's assembly line style of making colorful and long-lasting bricks, India still relies on a tedious, six thousand year old method to produce a structurally and aesthetically disappointing product. The time commitment put into making just a small batch of bricks is unbelievable to the contestants. The show also criticizes the lack of basic hygiene in the locales visited. Each team comments on what they see, most likely prompted by questions from the cameramen, and their responses typify the results of a construction of otherness. Phrases such as "these people" are often uttered upon gazing at pigs scrounging through the dirty "residential" streets of India. Tirades at incompetent cab drivers in Egypt and China are much more commonplace than European criticism.

The Amazing Race follows the models of cultural imperialism illustrated by Said and others in its depiction of non-western cultures. By putting cultures into categories of otherness, the show lauds the power and supremacy of western ideals. The depiction of other nations allows America to assert its own values. Clearly, America does not praise the values of economically inferior countries. Rather, the rejection of otherness puts forth an idealistically imagined community for America to build upon.

America's Construction of a Homogenized Culture

America's history as the great melting pot, however, does not translate here into equal respect for the diverse gathering of American contestants, reflecting our history of exclusion. Our process of cultural consolidation involved the inclusion and exclusion of certain racial groups. European whiteness served as the foundation for our cultural existence, while other groups were cast out into the cultural borderlands. The vast number of non-European races and ethnicities that helped push this nation into prominence never reaped the benefits. America still functions under the veil of equality; in reality and on reality TV, however, white males are the great benefactors of wealth and privilege. It seems our melting pot served only to homogenize whiteness, while ridiculing and oppressing others. The characterizations of *The Amazing Race*'s participants portray America's true *raison d'être*. Highly competitive teams predominately consist of young, strong, heterosexual whites. The producers of the show also provide several token teams: the older couple, gays, females, and black team. However, these teams generally do not make it into the final groups vying for the one million dollar prize. Before delving into the portrayal of these teams on *The Amazing Race*, we must first look at the reality genre in itself and its inherent meanings to our society.

Rick Altman theorizes that genres function like nations in their comparable abilities to tie social groups together through certain textual choices. The reality TV genre unifies our factions into a "single social fabric." Regardless of our race, gender, or sexual preference, we all read reality TV's texts and are bound together invisibly by them. However, genres, like nations, emanate from a symbolic center and do not allow the periphery to contribute. The creators of reality TV shows constitute the center and broadcast out to the periphery certain messages about how we should think of different races, genders, and sexual preferences. Similarly, the construction of a nation through the influence of its genres does not allow the collective minorities (blacks, women, and gays) a culturally nationalistic representation. Thus, America through texts such as *The Amazing Race* produces a template for nation building and the construction of an ideal cultural identity.

An important corollary to the idea of reality TV as nation/genre is Benedict Anderson's notion of the *imagined community*: individually shared experiences that lead us to conceive the other members of a much more expansive community (Altman 195–206). Alone, we are unable to view the entire population of America, but the media helps us to imagine our nation. Reality TV, and *The Amazing Race* in particular, operate on a set schedule of consumption by multiple factions within the broader American community. Therefore, the continual flow of ideas through the texts forces us to imagine the others within our own culture. Although we may not cognizably recognize the messages concealed throughout reality TV's texts, the constant visual cues and content provide us with a formula for defining Americanism.

This phenomenon of picturing the other members within America's community, however, goes far beyond visual cues. As Michele Hilmes points out in her study of Chicago radio in the 1920s, imagining race in a community is a complicated and often exclusionary practice. The inherent dichotomy of radio, in terms of racial access, allowed a stage for African Americans, but strict limitations were forced upon those few fortunate ones allowed to address the largely white audience (Hilmes 76). Therefore, what the audience received was merely a reinforcement of a dominant ideology, masking itself as all-inclusive. African Americans were never to be included in the programming from a production standpoint; nobody wanted to hear about the tragedies of African American history or soak up the intricacies of African society. Simply put, America enjoyed the black caricature, not the black culture.

The minstrel shows of the mid to late 19th century offer another example of an early American pop-cultural phenomenon built upon racial discourses. Michael Rogin's work on this form of vaudevillian performance exemplifies the power of hegemonic groups. By preventing any blacks from issuing their own characterizations, as well as through the degrading act of applying blackface in bestial and delusory designs, whites were able to take racial subordination to a new level (Rogin 35–44). The liberal fantasy of equality figuratively called for in the Declaration of Independence was mocked by applying black paint to a white face. Since America's history with Africa is centered on the slave trade and quasi-colonization, I believe it is fair to call African Americans colonized subjects. Their ethnic traits did not undergo a process of normalization by the dominant institutions, but instead remained strange and "ignorant." Those that were popular, such as jazz on the radio, were normalized through the secondhand ownership of whites. Thus, even with radio's ability to be racially invisible both literally and figuratively, it still relied on formulating identity by dismissing the nonwhite (Hilmes 96).

The Amazing Race also constructs troubling representations of African Americans and their place in America. On the surface, *The Amazing Race* welcomes the inclusion of African American teams, which have appeared, sometimes multiple teams, on each season. However, blacks are unable to choose their preferred mode of representation within the framework of American culture; they merely fall into the dominant characterizations forced upon them.[6] Our texts on black history tend to portray a "mass black constituency" as the only source of African culture (Baker, Jr. 9–10). Lumped all together, blacks are presented in this manner so as not to offend the largely white audience. For example, the diversity amongst the black experience in Africa is neglected in order to show Africa as the great homeland. Over the last few seasons, *The Amazing Race* has become extremely formulaic in its treatment of blacks in Africa. Only the black teams receive extended airtime to reflect on what they experience in Africa. Filled with emotion, the black teams are proud of their heritage and the African heartland. Interestingly, only once have we learned where the black teams' genealogy originates from within Africa. Amazingly, in a continent that spans over eleven million square miles, everyone is from the same place. Yet, in America (1/4 as large), we would never think of bringing a Seminole Indian home to Washington State.

We do not see white participants commenting on their homelands; we merely assume that their respective homeland is America. Black contestants, however, all become "African." On season five, the teams travel to Tanzania where Kim, teamed with her husband Chip as a black duo, states, "I've always wanted to come to Africa, ever since I was a little girl learning about my history, my heritage." The producers of the show provide the audience with a virtual wonderland for the black duo. During one of the "detours," the couple must deliver rocking chairs to an address in town. After delivering the chairs to an older black couple, Chip and Kim receive an amazing amount of respect, almost familial. They are asked to take a rest in the chairs and offered food. Chip declares, "Everywhere we look people look like we do, we are not used to this." Clearly, Africa is a homecoming of sorts for Chip and Kim.

Capitulating to expectations, black teams refuse to acknowledge their diversity. Instead, they opt to accept their "Africanization." This practice may occur for a number of reasons. For one, America's recognition of multiple cultures within Africa is nonexistent. Therefore, most African American teams may not know where their family derived from, due to a lack of historical sources. They may simply consider Africa as the all-encompassing homeland. Also, we cannot forget the possibility that the producers do not present footage of African diversity to the largely white audience. Host Phil Keoghan's summary of one African episode reinforced the restriction of African diversity with the line, "Chip and Kim felt right at home [in Africa]."

Unfortunately, the white teams do not have the same jovial experience in Africa. The white teams in Africa are frightened by black bodies and frustrated with the deceitfulness of the African people. While Chip and Kim return to their homeland, Christian models Brandon and Nicole and twins Kami and Karli pay $100 per team for a bus trip that others receive for a considerable amount less. Brandon called one of the money collectors "shady," and Nicole, quite frustrated after being confronted by the collector, eventually threw the money on the ground upon arrival at the destination.[7] In another encounter, Colin says "very bad" to the cab driver who drove with a donut as a tire and then proceeded to get a flat. Shaking his finger from side to side as if scolding a child, Colin fits right into the role of master. An irate Colin refused to pay the driver the $100 cab ride fee upon arrival, sparking an incident with the local police and possible jail time. Brandon and Nicole also were angered about the $100 cab ride and felt they were getting ripped off because they were American; meanwhile, Chip gave his cab driver a $20 tip on top of the $100 fare.[8]

Season six presents similar circumstances as the groups arrive in Senegal. Driving through town, white model Kendra comments, "We're in ghetto Africa." In addition, Kendra and her boyfriend Freddy fight with the cab driver who wanted more money for a cab trip. Kendra states, "Ten dollars here, five dollars here. They want to rip us off all the time." But not to be out done by her previous statements, Kendra also says when riding through town, "This country is wretched and disgusting. And they just keep breeding and breeding in this poverty. I just can't take it." The "they" is a powerful statement in terms of its negative connotations and placement of Africans in the category of otherness, but using the word "breeding" equates the African people to animals.

Although Africa is depicted as very dangerous for the whites, once again the black team gets emotional. The teams begin the next leg of the race with a trip to the Slave House, a place where slaves boarded ships through the "Door of No Return" to voyage to the New World. Each team placed a rose on the archway in remembrance. Yet, it is the black father and daughter team of Gus and Hera who steal the scene. Gus begins to cry and states that he did not cry at either of his parent's funerals, but when he "went through those doors, [he] saw himself" and then felt the connection between his inner self and his historical slave beginnings.[9]

Season seven includes more examples of degrading remarks about Africans and once again positions the black duo of Uchenna and Joyce back in their natural homeland. The two episodes shot in Africa both include moments of displacing the black team from an American heritage. While in South Africa, Joyce is very emotional when asked about her experience at an orphanage. Her husband Uchenna states, "South Africa is the motherland" and says, "This has been the most special moment of the race." The next episode includes a trip to Botswana and a "detour" that includes either carrying baskets on your head or milking a goat. The white contestants Kelly, Boston Rob, Lynn, and Alex all fail at carrying the baskets on their heads. However, Uchenna and Joyce accomplish the task with ease. Lynn and Alex say, "They were born to do this" in reaction to the black team's rapid completion of the task. Uchenna buys into the statement by stating, "My African roots are kicking in."

During this episode, we finally learn about a black person's lineage; Uchenna's father is a native Nigerian. Even though Botswana in southern Africa is thousands of miles from the western African country of Nigeria, however, Uchenna proudly states, "There is nothing like ... [putting] your feet on soil that your ancestors are actually from."[10] The producers as well as the black contestants fully accept that their homeland is in Africa when they arrive anywhere on the continent. Uchenna and the other black participants fail to preach their own cultural diversity. They simply lump themselves with all the other Africanized groups. Clearly, black teams are placed into their own separate, but all-encompassing category outside of the American culture.

However, if African American teams are not part of America's cultural fabric, how do we explain the winners of season five, black married couple Chip and Kim? Despite their achievement, Chip and Kim were often characterized as sneaky and untrustworthy as the race neared its conclusion. Before the final few episodes, it seemed as if Chip strove to be liked by the white teams. He helped Brandon with a difficult task in Egypt, one that required brute strength. However, as the contest neared its conclusion, there came a sudden reversal of respect from the other teams. In Manila,

Chip and Kim "yielded" Colin and Christie (this is where a team must wait one hour before continuing with the task). This was the only time the "yield" was used on the entire race by any team. Once Colin and Christie did wait out the clock and finished their task, Christie distraughtly pleaded with her driver to hurry to the next destination because Chip and Kim "played unfair." Also on this leg of the race, Chip and Kim betrayed the Christian couple Brandon and Nicole. While searching for the correct clue box on one of three islands, Chip lies to Brandon when both teams arrive at one of the islands. Brandon waited in the boat while Chip went to the clue box, which contained the next clue, but Chip told him it was the wrong island. Earlier Brandon claimed to trust Chip, but now the "true" side of Chip and Kim's Compton roots emerges. The very next challenge forced the players to scuba dive for a large clamshell holding the subsequent clue. When it appeared that Nicole was in danger of drowning, Chip comes to offer help, but Brandon says, "Beat it," fearing Chip will steal the clue from the helpless Nicole.[11]

If black teams are depicted as untrustworthy and un-American, all female teams do not fare much better. Thus far, the best an all-female duo has placed is fourth, a feat accomplished twice. The physical toll of the race's travel schedule is enough to handicap women physically without the addition of multiple tasks. Ultimately, the message portrayed is that women are in need of a man both for protection and to complete physical tasks in life and on *The Amazing Race*. Males on the show are physically and mentally superior to their female counterparts. In a race where sleep deprivation, unusual eating schedules, constant physical and mental stress, and emotional struggles persist, someone needs to be the rock on which the team can count. Unfortunately, the women in the most recent seasons are depicted as emotionally unstable under pressure and continually suffer breakdowns. The competitiveness to win pushes men to compete harder, but the women often end up crying in the face of adversity.

In season six, in particular, the representations of women include numerous moments of emotional stress, instability, and physical weakness. Season six is the first season in which no group member could complete more than six "road blocks" on the entire race. Clearly, the producers changed the rules of the game in response to the males on the previous five seasons completing most of the demanding challenges. Now, the women were forced to complete tasks that previously fell under the man's domain. Tears and hysteria seem to be the reaction of choice for the women on this race. Victoria, always pushed by her demanding husband Jonathon, has frequent struggles that result in a total loss of control. She gets hay fever and complains of her inability to breathe while rolling out hay bales. Jonathon states, "That's why women don't rule the world" in response to her weaknesses.[12] In addition, she sobs hysterically when Jonathon pushes and yells at her for picking up his bag when he purposely dropped it during a frantic sprint to the "pit stop." Victoria's obstreperous reaction to Jonathon caused host Phil Keoghan to intervene in an attempt to calm the situation. Aaron's partner Hayden is also a troublesome female. Her incessant panic about completing tasks as soon as possible culminates with her breaking a key while searching for the right padlock amongst over a thousand possibilities during a "roadblock." Eventually, the team quits the challenge and is eliminated. When women do complete difficult tasks, they are applauded and congratulated for doing something out of the ordinary. For example, most viewers were surprised to see the bowling moms of season five make it to the final four. Most of the confessional time concerning the two women dealt with their own surprise that two homemakers were getting along in the world.

Regardless of inherent weaknesses or strengths, women generally are portrayed as helpless during the race without the aid of a strong man. On *The Amazing Race*, female displacement from American culture centers on the inability of "women" to remain calm under pressure. From the audience's perspective, the best combination for success begins with two white heterosexual males, followed closely by a team combining a strong male and a subservient female. Usually characterized as strong, fast, and smart, these two combinations appear to be racing against themselves, as there are usually multiple teams fitting into these categories as the race nears its conclusion.

Homosexuals appearing on *The Amazing Race*, on the other hand, are also discounted because of social stereotypes. Generally, homosexual characters are depicted as moody, vitriolic, un-athletic, and vain. In an issue of the *Advocate*, the seven gay contestants from the first three seasons of the show were asked to provide some gay travel advice. The most common responses were to carry hair clippers (not just for the head), hair dyes, moisturizers, lotions, hand sanitizers, and face wipes on any trip (Allen 32). This sort of representation continues with the later seasons. Season seven brings us three gay participants, two males partnered together (Alex and Lynn) and Patrick, who is teamed with his mother Susan. Patrick is physically weak and has a very poor attitude throughout his quick stint on the race. Susan gets frustrated with her son's pessimistic attitude and poutiness when things are not running smoothly. He does not take advice from his mother very well, even though she has accepted his homosexuality and wishes he could find a partner. Instead of a positive portrayal of a homosexual, the audience sees Patrick as a whiny quitter who is angry at a culture that does not accept him.

Lynn and Alex are quite different from Patrick, although they also fulfill a common stereotype about gays. One might describe Lynn and Alex as the "flaming" homosexual types. At a market in Santiago, they are given a fish that is slightly less than the required three pounds. After discovering their error, the irascible couple confronts the fishmonger they purchased the fish from, demanding they get their money back for his faulty scale. As they cause a scene, other natives surround the pair and start to voice their disapproval for the ill treatment of one of their own. The only thing Lynn and Alex can say in response is, "Bitches." This phrase is uttered numerous times by the competitive duo. At another point during the race, the pair is in last when Lynn playfully states, "We're good at pulling up the rear." Everything from the high-pitched tone of their voices to their "girly" jogging style to Lynn's desire for eye cream reinforces common perceptions about homosexuality.

In spite of the stereotyped depiction of homosexuals on this show, in season four the gay married couple, Reichen and Chip, wins *The Amazing Race*, assumingly disproving the hegemonic rules about homosexuality. Unlike previous and subsequent gay participants, Reichen and Chip possess attributes that are seemingly heterosexual. Neither of the two well-built men is depicted as "feminine" in any way. Instead, these young and athletic homosexuals are incredibly analytical and full of magnanimity when it comes to running the race. In essence, Reichen and Chip embody the characteristics of the prototypical heterosexual teams while distancing themselves from the hegemonic perceptions of homosexuality. Unlike other gay teams, these two figures are not shown in petty squabbles with other participants or complaining about their need for revitalizing moisturizers. Both are determined to win the million dollar prize, which they achieve. One team calls Reichen and Chip, "Chip and Dale," in reference to their good looks and well-toned bodies. If one were catching the show for the first time, the viewer might assume the two were friends instead of married to each other. The show downplays the relationship between the two men, instead choosing to portray the participants as methodical and physically superior. These two men exemplify what the American culture attempts to be, except for the fact that they are gay, so their homosexuality is simply downplayed.

Conclusion

Premiering just days before September 11th, the first season of *The Amazing Race* almost never aired. Low-ratings and the fear of presenting an adventure show largely reliant on international air travel seemed insensitive and dangerous after the terrorist attacks. The fast paced nature of the show involves buying one-way tickets and sprinting through terminals to get outside of airports and into cabs, activities that are considered threatening in America's post-9/11 mindset. In a time when America was redefining its heroes, *The Amazing Race* served as a form of escapism to many. Yet, buried within the show's premise lay the foundations for strengthening the ideals of American culture and the ability to displace many entities from within our cultural framework.

The Amazing Race is the quintessential 9/11 series: it uses the world as a stage to define who counts as an American. By traveling from country to country, the show is able to showcase the "backwardness" of several other cultures. Magnifying the oddities of these respective cultures allows America to set itself apart from the non-western world, a practice also implemented within the discourses of the Bush presidency. Thus, by reenacting the popular dress styles, labor methods, gender roles, and cuisines from these countries, *The Amazing Race* is able to place foreign cultures into the realm of otherness. Some cultures are not even visited due to safety concerns and are placed into a deeper category of otherness simply through their invisibility (Keveney 4). This method of Orientalism ushers America into the role of hegemonic power.

Not only does the cultural work of this show place foreign cultures in the role of others, but it prevents many American contestants from assimilating into the national culture, particularly African Americans, women, and homosexuals. Chip and Kim were not supposed to win season five, but their late night finish on the second to last leg allowed them to gain information the other two "all-American" groups were not privy to.[13] Nevertheless, the perceptions of Chip and Kim were unfavorable from the standpoint of the white teams. Uchenna and Joyce's victory on season seven only solidifies the negative characterizations of black contestants. Instead of portraying the black participants as winners, the producers showcased their begging for money in Jamaica. With Rob and Amber headed toward an anticlimactic finale, the airlines re-opened the doors to the plane (a regular occurrence for all of us travelers) and allowed Uchenna and Joyce to catch and pass Rob and Amber. Cheating, lying, and luck seem to be the only way black teams can defeat the powerful white couples. Instead, *The Amazing Race* provides the black teams with a homecoming to their native Africa. Filled with emotion, all of the black teams rejoice in the chance to walk on their native soil, even if their lineage traces back to a site tens of thousands of miles away.

By concentrating on the perceptions of race and gender roles displayed on the show, we begin to see the ideal definition of an American. Women and gays are not admired for their physical and emotional abilities. Instead, these two groups are discounted because of their inferiority to young, white males. No female team is strong enough to win the race, and no gay team or gay member of a team can win because of their femininity. The ideal winners of *The Amazing Race* should always be a white couple or two white friends; any other winning couple is an aberration (Reichen and Chip from season four, Chip and Kim from season five, and Uchenna and Joyce from season seven). Ultimately, with its ability to promote hegemonic ideals of America's culture, *The Amazing Race* continues with the long-standing western tradition of assimilating white culture while pirating and rejecting the others. In the end, we learn who the amazing race truly is, white American males.

Works Cited

Allen, Dan. "Amazing Travel Tips." *Advocate* 884 (2003): 32.

Altman, Rick. *Film/Genre*. London: British Film Institute, 1999.

Baker Jr., Houston A. *Black British Cultural Studies: A Reader*. Chicago: Chicago UP, 1996.

Behr, Zachary G. "Around the World in 30 Days." *New York Times* 22 Aug. 2004, Travel 15.

Bhabha, Homi K. "The Other Question: Difference, Discrimination, and the Discourse of Colonialism." *Black British Cultural Studies: A Reader*. Chicago: University of Chicago Press, 1996.

Bianco, Robert. "And the 'Race' Is on—for a Fifth, Fun-Filled Season." *USA Today* 6 July 2004, 1D.

Hall, Stuart. "Minimal Selves." *Black British Cultural Studies: A Reader*. Chicago: University of Chicago Press, 1996.

_____. "New Ethnicities." *Black British Cultural Studies: A Reader*. Chicago: University of Chicago Press, 1996.

Hilmes, Michele. *Radio Voices: American Broadcasting, 1992–1952*. Minneapolis: Minnesota UP, 1997.

Keveney, Bill. "New Travel Realities Add Tension to Amazing Race." *USA Today* 11 March 2002, Life 4.

Rhodes, Joe. "An Audience Finally Catches Up to Amazing Race." *New York Times* 16 Nov. 2004, Arts 1.

Rogin, Michael. *Blackface, White Noise: Jewish Immigrants in the Hollywood Melting Pot*. Berkeley: California UP, 1996.

Said, Edward W. *Orientalism*. New York: Random House, 1978.

Tucker, Lauren and Hemant Shah. "Race and the Transformation of Culture: The Making of the Television Miniseries *Roots*." *Critical Approaches to Television*. Ed. Leah R. Vande Berg, et al. Boston: Houghton Mifflin Co., 1998.

Notes

1. *The Amazing Race*, (season seven) episodes aired March 1 and 8, 2005 respectively.

2. Choosing these four seasons has more to do with their availability than a discrepancy in content from the first three seasons. As of yet, there are no DVDs of the series on sale.

Instead, I have relied on my own tape recordings, which allows me to cite specific descriptions of content and ideas similar to those found on the first three seasons.

3. *The Amazing Race*, (Season 5) episode aired August 31, 2004.

4. Ibid., (Season 4) episode aired July 3, 2003.

5. See Joe Rhodes, "An Audience Finally Catches Up to Amazing Race," *New York Times* 16 Nov. 2004, The Arts p. 1. Co-creator and Executive Producer Bertram Van Munster of *The Amazing Race* (former producer for *COPS*) claimed in the article when talking to leaders in international locations, "I'm not here to criticize your country or your culture. I'm here to bring Americans to learn from you and have a good time."

6. For a good example on turning black cultural diversity into a white-friendly text see Lauren Tucker and Hemant Shah's "Race and the Transformation of Culture: The Making of the Television Miniseries *Roots*," *Critical Approaches to Television*, ed. Leah R. Vande Berg et al. (Boston: Houghton Mifflin Company, 1998) 405–416.

7. *The Amazing Race*, (Season 5) episode aired August 17, 2004.

8. Ibid., episode aired August 24, 2004.

9. Ibid., (Season 6) episodes aired on December 7 and 14, 2004.

10. Ibid., (Season 7) episodes aired on March 29 and April 5, 2005.

11. Ibid., (Season 5) finale episode aired on September 21, 2004.

12. Ibid., (Season 6) episode aired January 4, 2005.

13. By arriving later than the other teams to the hotel, Chip and Kim learned that the flight everyone else was on would be delayed due to fog. By the time the teams learned of the delay the next morning, it was too late to make-up the head start Chip and Kim attained by changing their flight.

Part V
Representation and Power
How Does Reality TV Represent Politics?

14

Games of Sociality and Their Soft Seduction

WESLEY METHAM

Though Gareth Palmer points out that for some in the television industry the term reality television is "so awkward as to have no value" (21), much of his critique of reality television relies on its generic originality. He describes the genre in terms of a development, and a distortion, of documentary's social realism, stating that "such programs illustrate what happens when documentary is loosened from its moorings in public service" (23). Palmer tracks reality television from its beginning in programs such as *COPS, Nannies from Hell,* and *The Secret World of Hidden Cameras.* That is, he locates the origins of reality television in texts prior to *Big Brother,* a show first released by Endemol in 1999. For Palmer, reality television signals a dangerous anti-social realism, a perversion of documentary that attempts to exploit the legitimizing aura of the documentary form to "parade random images of unfortunates behaving badly" (40).

Palmer's account, however, does not recognize that, after *Big Brother,* reality television rapidly developed, and the genre's popularity sky-rocketed, so that this program should be seen as one of the genre's turning points, rather than its end-point. After Dutch company Endemol produced the first series of *Big Brother* in 1999, reality television's popularity skyrocketed, fueling important innovations in the genre. Though reality television's affinities with documentary cannot be dismissed, this paper argues that to conflate these affinities with a generic characterization is to ignore the tradition of reality television that developed after *Big Brother.* It is to ignore at least half of the story, a period when this later tradition of reality TV has undermined its affinities with the documentary tradition. The mature form of reality television has challenged the documentary tradition less through the ethical irresponsibility of its anti-social realism, than through the pervasive, influential integration of games into the genre. This is a genre of games-as-documentaries, and documentaries-as-games, a place in which the ethico-political values of social realism do not have the relevance that Palmer, for example, wants them to.

This paper will use Baudrillard's account of the game, from his book *Seduction*, to interpret the program *Paradise Hotel* (2003), which dramatized some unique ethical problems in playing games whose rituals and rules are designed to exploit the social. *Paradise Hotel*, like many reality television programs since *Big Brother*, introduced the ethics of its game to challenge its characters' relationships with the social. That is, the characters' participation in the program challenged their particular social identities, as well as their general identification with the social as the fabric of community. After developing this argument, the paper also attempts to make a theoretical point, considering the ways in which Baudrillard's account of games resembles and differs from Slavoj Zizek's Lacanian-Marxist interpretation of the use of cyberspace as participation in the symbolic order.

To Treat Sociality as a Game

Often *Big Brother* is named as the first important reality television program. Andrejevic understands *Big Brother* as the genre's "ideal type," arguing that this program "most rigorously adhered to the promise of portraying unedited access to the mundane daily routine of its cast members" (117). In locating *Big Brother* at the zenith of reality TV, Andrejevic employs a definition of the genre that is close to Palmer's notion of the distorted development of the documentary tradition of social realism. For Andrejevic, the proper characteristics of reality television involve the transparent, ubiquitous pervasiveness of mass mediating technologies, bringing mundane, quotidian content to its audience. Here the genre is defined in terms of the reproduction of the social, the bits of the everyday that perpetuate themselves within the text: chatter about friendship, sex, and family creates social bonds in the textual household, and connects the program's audience to the members of the simulated society. Under such a definition, the genre reaches its proper place in the mass mediation of the content of the social for a consuming and participating society.

Andrejevic's and Palmer's emphasis on the importance of a type of social realism to reality television represents an important dimension of the reality television genre. *Big Brother*'s own discourse, as well as public discourse produced about it, understood it as a social experiment, facilitated by technologies of mass-mediation and mass participation. Series of the show around the world utilize hundreds of cameras within the household's confines to capture the smallest details of the society's development, and though the regular programming is heavily edited, audiences are able to watch live streaming on the Internet. In this sense, *Big Brother* emphasizes the audience's role as observers and critics of their micro-society, and the pervasiveness of mass observation and participation.

However, though Andrejevic's account of *Big Brother*'s place in the genre is useful, like Palmer he ignores that, by imposing game-like structures on its characters, *Big Brother* broke with earlier nascent versions of reality TV. Only through these omissions can Andrejevic understand *Big Brother* as the genre's zenith, rather than as a watershed in its history. *Big Brother* utilized game-like structures including small tasks and competitions within each series, the process of evicting housemates one by one from the program, and the cash prize for the last remaining member of the society. The game-like impositions are directed by an omnipotent figure named Big Brother, who is not really a tyrant, but only a television producer or an actor, yet at the same time he directs the housemates as he pleases, putting them under considerable psychological pressure by imposing harsh impositions on them, and arbitrarily abusing his authority. Nonetheless, though *Big Brother* did introduce games into its social realism, these games were subservient to the emphasis on the text's ability to facilitate mass observation and participation.

In 2000, CBS produced the first series of *Survivor*. This was an important moment in the genre both because *Survivor* was the first major American contribution to reality television, and because it overturned *Big Brother*'s emphasis on mass observation and participation. Whereas *Big Brother* emphasizes a claim to realistic representation of the social-as-it-is, that is the act of making transparent the banal content of everyday life, in *Survivor* there is no such pretense. Rather, *Survivor* exploits its self-consciousness as a game, with a large cash prize at its end, through a series of smaller games, which individuals and teams must win in order to move toward the final prize. For the duration of the game, the teams live in camps on an island, and the text exploits the simultaneity of the formation of the society and its political alliances. The politics of *Survivor*'s societies is so intense that the players know that before the game begins they must develop some strategy for negotiating it. Whereas in *Big Brother* the game is subservient to the social-as-it-is, in *Survivor* the social is riddled with the game. Both texts combine games and social realism, allowing each to bleed into the other, though they do so in different ways, emphasizing different sides of the equation. The generic significance of reality television is this hybrid experimentation.

Paradise Hotel was produced by the American FOX network, was 16 weeks longs, and ran from June to September, 2003. It puts 18 young adults (9 men and 9 women) in an isolated luxurious mansion, which is pervaded with television cameras. Each week one guest at the hotel is voted out through a process designed to ensure the program's slogan: "hook up or get out." The voting process is organized so that each week guys and girls swap roles, in gendered groups, as the voters and the potential evictees. So, every second week all of the female guests at The Hotel individually choose which guy they want to room with for the coming week. The following week the men take this role. The numbers are arranged so that each week one of the potential evictees is not chosen. He or she must immediately leave *Paradise Hotel*.

At the same time, during the weeks in between voting, the guests are immersed in a unique social world. Because the voting system is based on choosing someone of the opposite sex to room with, the hotel guests often swap partners. There are cameras in every bedroom. Also, as part of their luxurious stay in what the official website describes as "the most exclusive luxury resort ever," the guests also participate in extravagant games and activities. In the beginning it is said that the winner, the last guest at the hotel, will be awarded a mystery prize, which at the conclusion is revealed to be $500,000.

Among reality TV fans, the narrative and structure of *Paradise Hotel* are regarded as exceptionally long and complicated. I will choose a few moments and relationships from the program in order to develop my thesis. The first drama that I am interested in involves a conflict between two groups that form in the Hotel. The largest group involved is constituted by 14 of the 18 guests. For want of a better term, I refer to these contestants as "the ethical group." This group is characterized by commitment to social values, the most important of which are fun and friendship. The character Amy is the most prominent, and the most ideologically committed, among this majority. She continually professes her desire to "keep *Paradise Hotel* real," and discusses with other members of the ethical group their belief that "it is always the good people that leave" the Hotel. This group of 14 wants to treat their stay at *Paradise Hotel* as an opportunity to enjoy the most exclusive luxury resort ever built, to use the opportunity to have fun and make friends. In a way, these participants do not want to recognize the presence of the rules of the game. Or rather, they do not articulate their participation in the game, but make their social identity the most recognizable feature of their characters.

In conflict with this ethical group of 14 is a smaller group of 4. In about the fifth week of the show, an alliance is formed between these guests, an alliance constituted by two couples: Keith and Tara, and Dave and Charla. Because Keith and Tara are models, within the Hotel this gang of four conspirators came to be known as "Team Barbie," so I will use that term. If the ethical majority of participants are concerned with upholding the values of fun and friendship at the expense of the game, the members of Team Barbie are anything but. This distinction is established early in the program, when the ethical majority continues to vote for housemates based on friendships and relationships, while, from the tenth episode, Keith, Dave and Charla conspire to use their combined voting power to vote off whoever they want to, that is whoever will promote their collective success in the game. In the eleventh episode, they strengthen their alliance, explicitly contractualizing it, while the other participants in the Hotel continue to concentrate on having fun, using the Hotel's luxurious facilities to the best of their disposal. In secret, this alliance of four is able to broker power so that by the show's last episodes all of the other 14 characters have been evicted from *Paradise Hotel*, and the prize money is divided among these four players.

This group of four conspirators capitalizes on the unwillingness of the other 14 characters to participate in, and exploit, the rules of the game. That is, *Paradise Hotel* explores whether social reality can and should be treated as though it were a game. Catharine Lumpy emphasizes the social permeability of *Big Brother*, arguing that it allows its audience, particularly teenage girls, to negotiate the social problems they encounter on a daily basis. However, the increasingly dominant pattern of reality television is to expose these social problems to the framework of games, creating a permeable boundary between text and game, reality and fiction, persona and personality. *Paradise Hotel* explores the social-psychological implications of the choice of the game, the actions and feelings of those who choose to participate in the game, versus those who do not. In this sense the show self-reflexively exploits some of reality television's generic characteristics, and occupies a distinct place in the genre.

The philosophy of games makes an important appearance in Jean Baudrillard's text *Seduction*. Here Baudrillard uses the unique discursive characteristics of games to develop a post-anarchist philosophy. That is, he conceptualizes what is outside of the Law, in terms of the Lacanian Law of the Symbolic. In Lacan, the means of primal repression and the paternal metaphor allow the mediation of language to be imposed on desire, an instance of the Symbolic of the domain of Law. Baudrillard shares this conception of Law, so that for him the politics of the Symbolic order is always-already enmeshed in the Law: "Ordinarily we live within the realm of the Law, even when fantasizing its abolition ... the discourse of law and interdiction determines the inverse discourse of transgression and liberation" (*Seduction* 131).

However, argues Baudrillard, though the Symbolic and the Law are complicit, this is why a path must be found out of the Symbolic. The regime that best describes this reversion of the symbolic is the regime of the game:

"it is not the absence of the law that is opposed to the law, but the Rule" (*Seduction* 131). The game acquires this post-anarchistic status because it is not of the symbolic order; its rules are "arbitrary and ungrounded, because they have no referents" (136). Whereas the Law is determined by a direct relation between a signifier and signified, or between a social principle and its realization in the social, rules do not have such a relationship with the social. They rely only on participation in a cycle of rituals, and so they are immanent, arbitrary, and circumscriptive (134). In the simplistic sense of being codes that are designed to be followed, rules may resemble laws, but when compared with their differences this similarity is inconsequential:

> The Rule plays on an immanent sequence of arbitrary signs, while the Law is based on a transcendent sequence of necessary signs. The one concerns cycles, the recurrence of conventional procedures, while the other is an instance based in an irreversible continuity. The one involves obligations, the other constraints and prohibitions. Because the Law establishes a line, it can and must be transgressed. By contrast, it makes no sense to "transgress" a game's rules; within a cycle's recurrence, there is no line one can jump (instead, one simply leaves the game) [*Seduction* 131–132].

Baudrillard's conception of games is part his assertion of "the political destiny of *Seduction*." For Baudrillard, seduction is unique in that it is the most important game. In establishing some of the basic premises of his theory of seduction, he is interested in "the most banal games of seduction," meaning inter-personal games of seduction between two participants, in a type of courting ritual: "I shy away from you, it is not you who will give me pleasure, it is I who will make you play, and thereby rob you of your pleasure" (*Seduction* 22). However, though these games might take place in a sexualized context, "one cannot assume that sexual strategies alone are involved." Rather, in this context seduction alludes to sexuality at the same time as seduction hides it, effacing the sovereignty of sex, and so displacing the goal toward which it originally alluded to: "There is above all a strategy of displacement ... that implies a distortion of sex's truth. To play is not to take pleasure" (22).

As long as such a game of seduction is maintained, it continually displaces the sexual pleasure that it alludes to, thus turning the signs of sexuality away from their meaning. That is, the signs of sexuality are made to appear without meaning, giving appearance sovereignty over meaning. Just as Giorgio Agamben's politics of the qualanque identity set the task of returning "appearance itself to appearance," of causing appearance itself to appear (*Means* 93), so is Baudrillard's seduction the movement toward "the sacred horizon of appearances." But this strategy of the appearance of the sign entails the disappearance of its meaning. For Baudrillard this is the sense in which seduction is political, since "the only way the Other can exist" is "on the basis of one's own calculated disappearance (according to the rules of the game of disappearance" (*Art* 1). Seduction is the game of the disappearance of identity, what Agamben would call the movement toward whatever identity. Seduction makes the signs of identity signs without connections to the meaning of identity, and so it plays with the order of identity, precisely in order to transform identity into a game.

In Baudrillard, to cultivate the sovereignty of appearances that is proper to the game of seduction is to "die as reality and reconstitute oneself as illusion. It is to be taken in by one's own illusion and move in an enchanted world" (*Seduction* 69). In reality television, this challenge to the real status of social identity is important. In *Big Brother* this challenge is nascient, as is the role of the game in that text. Andrejevic notes that in chat rooms attached to *Big Brother*, fans often debate this question of who is "playing the game," versus who is being real. However, he writes, "the defenders of authenticity" in these debates found a way of reconciling authenticity with the game by arguing that "the best way to win — hence, the most effective strategy — was not to be strategic: to be 'real'" (Andrejevic 125).

By contrast, the four finalists of *Paradise Hotel* are those four who choose participation in the game over their participation in the Hotel's society, suggesting that in this text no such reconciliation of the social and the game can be made. Rather, *Paradise Hotel* exploits a contrast between characters who remain committed to their social identity, and thus alienate themselves from the game, versus characters who subject their social identities to the game, and are thus alienated from the social. In *Paradise Hotel* the truth of social identity has little value. Rather, identity only has value insofar as it can be put to use in the game. Insofar as seduction is the game of illusion, and games of illusion are seductive, such a challenge to social identity mimics Baudrillard's contention that "the social is without seduction," that the social is "the degree zero of seduction" (*Seduction* 155).

Anti-Social Ethics

From early moments of *Paradise Hotel*, before the establishment of the alliance between "Team Barbie" that split the guests at the Hotel into two, the guests' ethical code emerges. Charla's actions during the show's early episodes allow the larger group at the Hotel to establish its identity according to a code of sociality. In these early episodes, immediately after Charla's introduction to the Hotel, her behavior is the topic of conversation that most occupies the other guests at the Hotel. Charla distinguishes herself from the other characters by withdrawing herself from the Hotel's social activities. When she is among the other guests, she almost always sits quietly as the others speak, without making clear what is on her mind. While Charla sits in her room, alone, seemingly doing nothing, the other characters use the Hotel for its proper purpose, living a luxurious life and partying. For example, in episode thirteen the houseguests play a "whipped cream game," where one guest puts cream on another's body and then licks it off, which prompts Charla to go to her room, saying to the cameras that she "has no desire to leave her room anymore." Again in episode fifteen, after one of the men jumps naked into the Hotel pool, some of the girls take turns kissing him, while Charla stands back and describes the incident as "immature." This refusal of the Hotel's sociality quickly provokes the society's interpretation of Charla's anti-social behavior as snobbish. By the sixth episode Charla is widely named as someone to be sent home, precisely because she is "quiet and boring," an ethico-political attitude that persists until almost the very end of the series.

Thus Charla's character is, in the most direct sense, anti-social. From a Baudrillardrian point of view, however, this anti-sociality is seductive. At one moment Charla attempts to include herself; at the next she withdraws without reason, playing games with her society. This lack of social reason provokes a mixture of resentment and fascination from the rest, so that, though Charla is alienated from the social, at the same time she is the center of social discourse. She provokes and challenges the principled content of the Hotel's society, in particular its Law of fun. This is Law in the Levi-Straussian sense, the sense that is picked up by Lacan as the set of universal principles which make social existence possible, the structures that govern all forms of social exchange (Evans 98). *Paradise Hotel*'s Law says that "anything goes," that the guests should feel free, liberated from the norms of work and money. This is a pluralistic ethic that the society polices, since without it the social fabric would be invaded by the threat of the game. Sometimes Charla plays within that Law; sometimes she plays with it.

Paradise Hotel and the social games of reality television extend the discourse of the political, but this is not simply a contribution to the identity politics of popular culture. Rather, the politics of social games challenge the poles on which political-philosophy is based, the poles of the social and the legal, and of the law and its transgression. In *Paradise Hotel* the Law is not opposed to the social. Rather the Law is the social, as the social is the Law. In *Paradise Hotel*, there is no confrontation between the law and its transgression. Rather, in *Paradise Hotel* as in Baudrillard, there is only confrontation between the rules of the game and the law. With regard to *Paradise Hotel*, it is not enough to argue the show's outcome depicts the entrenchment of egoism, and the ultimate victory of self-interest in the face of communal values such as friendship. Rather, this text dramatizes a problem that is similar to that posed by Baudrillard, the problem of the social, and its complicity with governance and the Law. The text poses different values, oppositional to the social, and perhaps superior to them:

> Generally speaking, "rituality" is, as a form, superior to "sociality." The latter is only a recent, and not very seductive form of organization and exchange, one invented by humans for humans.... By contrast, rituality succeeds in maintaining—not by laws, but by rules and their infinite play of analogies—a form of cyclical order and universal exchange of which the Law and the social are quite incapable [Baudrillard, *Seduction* 90].

Dave and Charla

Because Keith and Tara are both models, they are understood within the game as a somewhat homogenous pairing, two vapid Barbie dolls who are naturally suited to one another. By contrast, Dave and Charla are quite different people, and their relationship is loaded with more drama than any of the other relationships that developed in the Hotel. *Paradise Hotel* devotes more time to their relationship, and to these two characters, than any of the others, and their relationship is the subject of the show's climax.

The other characters at *Paradise Hotel* regard Dave as the most analytically savvy contestant. At each moment when Team Barbie decides whom to evict, and at the end of the show when the politicking becomes frantic, Dave almost always makes the most complex contributions to their planning. In fact, Dave is almost obsessed with the game. Dave is the most intellectually able to negotiate the game of *Paradise Hotel* in terms of the rules. He is purely and simply involved in the game's complexity, and he seems to take a certain pleasure in negotiating this analytical production of the society, in predicting who would choose whom at the voting ceremony, dependent on the various permutations of friendships and allegiances.

Charla, however, is the show's big winner, in that of all of the people in the show, she comes away with the most money. While Keith and Tara eventually win $125 000 each, Charla wins $250 000. But the circumstances in which Charla's character wins the game are important to her meaning in the text. From the beginning of their alliance, Charla relies on Dave's analytic acumen to get her through the game. Dave is better at articulating their position in the game, and predicting the various scenarios that emerge. But from the first moments after Dave is introduced into the Hotel, he becomes infatuated with Charla. In the third episode, Dave announces to Charla that he likes her, and from this moment on, Dave seems to be continually trying to seek out Charla's feelings. Dave's feelings and Charla's lack of reciprocation are persistent themes of gossip among the other characters. Until the very end of the show, Charla continually tells Dave that she considers him to be her best friend, and that she is closer to him than she is to anyone else on the show. In spite of this, Charla kisses five of the other men at the Hotel, while Dave waits patiently in the background. Nonetheless, throughout the game Charla maintains an emotional connection with Dave that contributes to the maintenance of their allegiance in the game.

Though Dave and Charla are not united romantically, like Keith and Tara they are a couple in the strategic play of the game. They most often align with each other in the voting ceremony, and they share a room for the majority of the series. However, this contractual allegiance is undermined in the final episode, the program's climax, and the end of the game. In this episode, circumstances and the rules of the game produce a situation in which Charla and Keith are each awarded $250,000. They must individually decide whether they will share that money with their respective partners. After deliberation, Keith decides to give half of his money to Tara. However, Charla decides not to share her money with Dave.

Throughout the game, alongside the pact of allegiance between Charla and Dave, there is an uneasy conjunction with Charla's seduction of him, and Dave's seduction by her. At the ultimate moment, when the game reaches its climax and the winner is decided, Charla breaks this contract, making herself the game's winner, and Dave the final loser. In his reliance on this contract he might even have lost more than the other, ethical members of the society because, while they lose their stake in the society and the game *Paradise Hotel*, he loses this as well as the feelings he invested in Charla. Though before this moment Dave is starkly opposed to the ethical members of the *Paradise Hotel*, he is now the object of his own investment in the ethical code of romance, and so is the object of a different but just as powerful ethical failure. When Charla tells Dave that she will not share any of her prize with him, the climax of Dave and Charla's relationship also comes to be the show's final drama. In that, Charla's ultimate rejection of Dave, his ultimate degradation, is also the show's ultimate moment. Her seduction of him, his seduction by her, the transformation of his emotional investment into a game, the seduction of that investment that ultimately destroys it, is the ultimate lesson in the social game.

From the beginning of the program to its end, Charla wields significant influence over Dave. In the beginning of the show, as Charla pursues other men while Dave enjoys only a domestic existence with her, he resembles the old tragi-comic figure of the cuckold. However, after the conspiracy of the powerbrokers is revealed, there is gossip that Charla merely finds his affections useful in the context of the game. At this point Charla stops kissing everyone but him and concentrates more on the game, and Dave's status as the cuckold momentarily ends. However, his humiliation does not reach its climax until the final episode, in which she chooses the game's prize at the sacrifice of Dave's affections for her. In the initial part of the show, Dave is cuckolded by other, better-looking guys. The final climactic scene asks the question of whether Dave can be cuckolded by the game itself.

The failure of Dave's power within the game is the failure of his analysis of it, a failure to master the public realm of *Paradise Hotel,* as well as the private realm of Charla's love. This emerges from the show as a mystery, a question that transcends moral judgment of Charla's betrayal. This mystery revolves around the fact that Dave is better at the game than Charla, in that he can better conceptualize the society's relations of power, and how the alliance should act within those relations. But, as Baudrillard says, analysis is "the least seductive of discourses," since it is what "breaks the appearance and play of the manifest discourse and, by taking up with the latent discourse, delivers the real meaning" (*Seduction* 53–54). Dave's analytical participation in the game takes him to its final stage, but he cannot close the deal. Charla's seductive strategy immediately surpasses his analytical one.

Reality Television's Obscene Seduction

Baudrillard's figure of seduction figures throughout his writing, and is important to his theory of contemporary mass culture. For example, in *Forget Foucault,* he establishes the basic opposition between seduction and obscenity, an opposition that has a complex relation to his cultural writing. For Baudrillard the "natural condition" of "our whole culture" is obscenity. Here obscenity is defined by the compulsion to reveal, to make known, the inability to leave a space for what is unsaid:

> To produce is to force what belongs to another order (that of secrecy and *Seduction*) to materialize. Seduction is that which is everywhere and always opposed to *production*; seduction withdraws something from the visible order and so runs counter to production, whose project is to set everything up in clear view, whether it be an object, a number, or a concept [*Seduction* 21].

Similarly, in *The Ecstasy of Communication,* Baudrillard describes modern obscenity in terms of "a pornography of information and communication, a pornography of circuits and networks, of functions and objects in their legibility, availability, regulation, forced signification" (22). Here the machinery of modern communication provokes its audience's participation in the social, establishing an obscene cultural order, an order of the compulsive production of social identity. However, in his other works, Baudrillard seems to use seduction, otherwise the opposite figure of obscene productivity, to describe contemporary culture. He says our cultural order is one of a "cold seduction." In *Seduction*, Baudrillard argues that the very same networks that facilitate the obscene production of social identity are also the bearers of "the 'narcissistic' spell of electronic and information systems, the cold attraction of the terminals and mediums that we have become, surrounded as we are by consoles, isolated and seduced by their manipulation" (162). In other words, for Baudrillard the modern cultural era is one in which seduction and obscenity are bound together in precisely the same networks. The seduction of the technological objects of communication is contaminated by the obscenity of the social work to which they must be put. The result is an era of obscene seduction, a seduction of low intensity, diluted by our obscene compulsion for meaning.

The history of reality television as a genre can be a metaphor for Baudrillard's theory of contemporary mass culture's obscene seduction. For example, if *Big Brother*'s dominant characteristic is the pervasion of the technologies of mass representation, and the connection of the simulated with real sociality, in Baudrillardrian terms this would be defined as a paradigmatic instance of obscenity. The utilization of the technologies of mass communication to reproduce social identity is part of our "pornography" of information and communication. The audience voting, the website discussion, and the use of normal people as the objects of celebrity-like representation are a pervasion of the obscene ecstasy of communication. Since for Baudrillard the social is one of the least seductive forms of organization, *Big Brother*'s attempt to construct and exploit a simulated micro-society is itself obscene. Also, for Baudrillard, power itself is the "figure of anti-seduction *par excellence*" (*Seduction* 45), and so the mantra of the Australian *Big Brother*, "Remember, you have the power," is indicative of *Big Brother* as a paradigmatic object of obscene sociality.

However, this account contradicts the earlier analysis that reality television problematizes the social through its subjection to the game. For Baudrillard, the game is allied with seduction; it is the means to thinking seduction's political destiny. Equally, as I have argued, the pattern of reality television is increasingly to give the game more sovereignty over the representation of the social, so that the participants' stay in the surveilled environment comes to rely on their participation in, and negotiation of, the game. For example, in *Paradise Hotel*, the rules of the game precede the act of mass-mediated representation, and have a certain degree of determinacy over the act of representation. The symbolic order is no longer the capacity to represent, but rather it is that which allows such capacity to exist, that which keeps subjects within the space of representation. Like *Big Brother*, *Paradise Hotel* takes up the social and exposes it to a game, though the latter does so with greater intensity than the former.

Though the break between *Big Brother* and those other American reality programs that intensify the use of the game illustrates the generic characteristics of reality television as the combination of obscenity and the game, this is an artificial cleavage. The elements of the social and the game are at work in all reality television programs. In reality television the faces of the social and of the game continually shift places, the social is undermined through the game, but the social re-emerges. Though the genre undermines the social, it also cannot exist without the social. Such vacillation, such tight binding of the social and the game, is analogous to Baudrillard's account of modern culture as the binding of obscenity and seduction, producing a cold, diluted seduction. Though for Baudrillard the social is one of the least seductive forms of organization, at the same time "even the most anti-seductive figures can become figures of seduction ... These figures need only move beyond the truth into a reversible configuration, a configuration that is also that of their death" (*Seduction* 45). Reality television's subjection of the social to the game is an example of one such movement beyond the social claim to truth, into the configuration of the social that within the scope of the game threatens the social with death.

The Rules of the Game and the Symbolic Order

That for Baudrillard, Lacan represents the revenge of psychoanalysis' foreclosure upon seduction, and that Slavoj Zizek is often recognised as the most successful contemporary interpreter of Lacan, indicate that Zizek's cultural studies will have relevance to the present discussion. Generally for Baudrillard, psychoanalysis aligns itself with "the side of interpretation," entailing the abolition of seduction "in order to put into place a machinery of interpretation, and of sexual repression, that offer all the characteristics of objectivity and coherence" (*Seduction* 57). Zizek himself provides at least an implicit critique of Baudrillard, since his work is directed at carving out the difference between his own position, and the position that he characterizes as "postmodernist," with which Baudrillard if often associated. This distinction comes from both sides of Zizek's Marxist-Lacanian juxtaposition: at once he attempts to separate Lacan from the rest of "poststructuralist philosophy," and Zizek's Marxism lends him to an equally persistent, and well-known, association of "postmodernism" with neo-liberalism. However, in spite of these differences, I argue that the Baudrillardrian figure of the game and the Lacanian symbolic order can usefully inform each other, and that such an uneasy synthesis can be used to develop some of the problems that I have alluded to.

Zizek has used the Lacanian symbolic order to develop a theory of other textual forms, in particular the consumption, and the ideological subtext, of cyberspace. In both *The Plague of Fantasies* and his essay "Is It Possible to Traverse the Fantasy in Cyberspace?," Zizek contrasts his Lacanian position with what he terms postmodernist cultural studies orthodoxy. This orthodoxy argues that cyberspace allows users to adopt roles that they cannot normally live, in particular the enactment of fantasies that cannot normally be performed outside of the virtual space. For postmodernism, this allows cyberspace to be a "liberating" domain, because it "delivers me from the vestiges of biological constraints and elevates my capacity to construct freely my Self, to let myself go in a multitude of shifting identities" (Zizek, "Is It" 113). Reformulating his ideology critique in psychoanalytic terms, Zizek understands such postmodernist interpretation as "perverse."

Zizek's Lacanian alternative does not attribute radically new epistemological possibilities to cyberspace, but rather is inclined to interpret the experience of cyberspace in terms of persistent psychic structures. This being said, Zizek does recognize certain new problems offered by cyberspace. He is particularly interested in cyberspace as a place in which fantasies can be performed without the normal consequences of such performance, without their actually becoming real. In cyberspace the subject can take on different social identities, effectively playing with, and undermining, the reality of his actual social identity. In experiencing cyberspace, effectively the subject navigates the symbolic order, which is the basis of social identity:

> What is this middle-mediating level, this third domain interposing itself between "real life" and "mere imagination," this domain in which we are not directly dealing with reality, but not with "mere words" either (since our words do not have real effects), if not *the symbolic order itself?* [Zizek, *Plague* 140].

Zizek argues that cyberspace subjects social identity to participation in an order that dissociates the content of social identity from its grounding in the real subject, thus undermining the real status of such identity. This is analogous to a Baudrillardian interpretation of reality television, where participation in social games tends to transform social identity into a conceit, blurring the line between persona and personality. By analogy, a Zizekian interpretation of the rules of the game would label them, like cyberspace, as the material of the symbolic order. That is, a Zizekian critique of games, and of reality television's social games, would recognize no difference between participation in the technological network of cyberspace and participation in the game.

While experience of cyberspace can be described in Lacanian terms as the experience of the symbolic order itself, from a Baudrillardrian point of view, this alliance between such a massive network of communication and the Symbolic is also why cyberspace would warrant the label of a network of obscenity. For Baudrillard, the Symbolic Law is opposed by the game, and by the game of seduction in particular. For this reason the fundamental fantasy cannot be traversed in cyberspace. The subject might be able to use cyberspace to momentarily perform an effacement of his actual social identity, but because he does this through the adoption of another social identity, he does it only through further participation in the social. Thus he ultimately remains caught in the obscene search for social identity, in the pornography of communication networks, and the accompanying Symbolic Law that it embodies.

However, a similar critique can be made of reality television. In that reality television is caught in a vacillation between the social-as-it-is and the social as a game, in Baudrillardrian terms it expresses an obscene seduction. Just as in cyberspace the effacement of actual social identity is only possible through further participation in the social, the social games of reality television are only possible because they take up social identity and subject them to a game. Just as the experience of cyberspace that Zizek interprets provides no space outside of the social or the Symbolic to escape to, in reality television no space can be provided for any game that comes after the text. For Baudrillard, such an inability to escape from this hyper-textual seduction is indicative of the obscene seduction of our time, of the obscene seduction of the technological networks of mass communication.

Here the possibility of representing the obscene seduction of the symbolic order reaches an end-point. Baudrillard argues that in Lacanianism there is a "vengeance of seduction," but one which is contaminated by psychoanalysis, because in it seduction "always occurs within the terms of the Law (of the symbolic)" (*Seduction* 58). In Lacanianism there is no outside of the Law, no place to which the subject can escape, no possible traversing of the fundamental fantasy. Rather, just as Zizek cannot come to any firm conclusion that direct experience of the symbolic order, as in the case of cyberspace, produces any lasting effects in the attempt to traverse the fantasy, Baudrillard's account of Lacanianism argues that there is always-already tension between the particular manifestation of the symbolic and the direct experience of the symbolic itself. This direct experience is as close as the subject can come to the experience of the symbolic. In Baudrillard's terms, in the era of obscene seduction the tension between the particular experiences of the symbolic and the symbolic order itself become intimately bound; reality television is one example of this binding. In such an era Lacanianism is particularly amenable to cultural studies, but it relies for such interpretation on the object of obscene seduction that it professes to traverse.

Works Cited

Agamben, Giorgio. *The Coming Community*. Trans. Michael Hardt. Minneapolis: University of Minnesota Press. 1993.

_____. *Means Without Ends: Notes on Politics*. Trans. Cesare Casarino. Minneapolis: University of Minnesota Press: 2000.

Andrejevic, Mark. *Reality TV: The Work of Being Watched*. Oxford: Rowan and Littlefield, 2004.

Baudrillard, Jean. *The Art of Disappearance*. Brisbane: Institute of Modern Art, 1994.

_____. *The Ecstasy of Communication*. New York: Semiotext(e). 1987.

_____. *Forget Foucault*. 1977. Semiotext(e). New York: Columbia UP, 1987.

_____. *Seduction*. (1979). New World Perspectives edition. New York: St. Martin's Press, 1990.

Bowles, Kate. "Representation," *The Media and Communications in Australia*. Crows Nest, NSW: Allen and Unwin, 2002.

Evans, Dylan. *An Introductory Dictionary of Lacanian Psychoanalysis*. New York: Routledge, 1996.

Lumby, Catharine. "Feminism's Big Sister Misses the Appeal of *Big Brother*." Jan. 2005. <onlineopinion.com.au>

Palmer, Gareth. *Discipline and Liberty : Television and Governance*. Manchester: Manchester UP, 2003.

Zizek, Slavoj. *Did Somebody Say Totalitarianism?*. London: Verso, 2001.

_____. "Is it Possible to Traverse the Fantasy in Cyberspace?" *The Zizek Reader*. Ed. Elizabeth Wright and Edmund Wright. Oxford: Blackwell, 1999.

_____. *The Plague of Fantasies*. London: Verso. 1997.

15

Democracy at Work? The Lessons of Donald Trump and The Apprentice

Elizabeth Michelle Franko

"It's Not Personal, It's Just Business"

In the popular TV series *The Apprentice* (NBC), ideas about a particular American corporate identity are played out and reified for the television viewing public. *The Apprentice* and its omnipresent icon, Donald Trump, teach viewers about the workplace and their own place within corporations, the economy, and the larger contemporary social system, reinforcing an exacting identity for workers. There are winners and losers in *The Apprentice* workplace, and the show vigorously disciplines deviants, creating its own set of norms that actively reflect societal standards. The illustrious Donald Trump takes center stage as CEO, mentor and icon, leading the contestants and the viewers through a hyper-real, dog-eat-dog vision of high-stakes business. With the corporate workplace as a backdrop, *The Apprentice* and Trump actively instruct both viewers and players about success, business, and corporate life. The show makes manifest certain dominant ideologies around work and the employee, departing from a more idealized version of worker as a citizen-participant in the workplace.

Different logics intersect on *The Apprentice*, blending the glitzy world of Trump's celebrity life with all the mundane dramatics of reality pseudostardom. Contestants actively compete for a job running one of Trump's companies, and the show is based on a winner-takes-all gamesmanship. Episodes track the contestants as they perform job-related tasks, and the candidate deemed least successful each week is fired. *The Apprentice* supposedly represents a televised and dramatized version of the culture of advanced managerial capitalism. The show revolves around a boardroom scene, in which contestants judge and are judged upon their ability to uphold the ethos of the Trump corporation. Trump himself acts, without any irony, as the semi-autocratic ruler and the ultimate CEO. In seasons two and three, the show interfaces with a major corporate partner each week, and the contestants battle it out to create a new toy for Mattel, or a new bottle for Pepsi soda. The intersection of "real" corporate America with the artificial world of the game serves as product placement, offering a chance for each company to secure advertising for its brand. Moreover, the brand of Trump, his life, his businesses, and his wife, colors every show — *The Apprentice* is thus a type of ongoing commercial for the Trump name and lifestyle. Baudrillard, in his writings on American television, tells us that in the media sphere, "all current forms of activity tend toward advertising and most exhaust themselves therein" (87), and we see that dynamic each week on *The Apprentice*.

The *Apprentice* is structured as a race between the best and brightest business leaders for the coveted role of Donald Trump's apprentice. The show's contestants compete for a real job with an absolute lack of irony. Although *The Apprentice* might seem to be only an exaggeration and a trope of the work-world, tryouts for the show are systematically packed with well-educated and successful hopefuls. The fantasy that Trump promotes, with endless hyperbole, is actually a conventional one. He says that the winner will have "the dream job of a lifetime," that Trump Tower is "one of the greatest buildings in the world," that his apartment is "the nicest apartment in New York," which he shows to "very few people — Presidents, kings"; and that his golf course is "the best golf course in New York State" (Franklin). Despite the endless exaggerations, the job offered up on *The Apprentice* is real, and the contestants appear to demonstrate a sincere desire for the prize.

While the series supposedly documents the world of high-stakes capitalism, the show itself is big business. In its first season, *The Apprentice* was rated the number one new show in the United States, bringing in an estimated 20.7 to 40.1 million viewers each week.[1] NBC named *The Apprentice* the number one new series of the season, as well as the number one new show in five years. Clearly, the show is wildly popular. The broad appeal of the series demands that we ask what the popular impact of the program might be. I believe *The Apprentice* is a critical artifact in the study of workers and the state of the corporate workplace. By using *The Apprentice* as a sort of symbolic corporation, we can begin to ask questions about what the nature of the contemporary working world might be and how individual workers might feel about their own role as both employees and citizens.

The world of the contestants, Trump and 737 Fifth Avenue,[2] is supposedly very much a high-stakes reflection of corporate America, and the show self-consciously represents itself as a teaching tool and a model for training future executives. The American Management Association, the world's largest membership-based training organization, has partnered with *The Apprentice* and sponsors topical "tips" posted each week on *The Apprentice* website in response to the show, tips such as "How to be a Leader." Moreover, Trump gives explicit lessons each show — he looks into the camera, and addresses the audience, while syllogisms such as "Winning Is Everything" flash on screen. He attempts to indoctrinate both the viewers and the candidates themselves into the singular logic of the business world. Perhaps the most salient message of *The Apprentice* is "It's Not Personal, It's Just Business," a mantra repeated frequently and explicitly on the show. In fact, this text flashes across the screen during the show's introduction. The logic of "It's Not Personal, It's Just Business" permeates every interaction on *The Apprentice*. While a seeming cliché, on closer analysis "It's Not Personal" implies a separation in individuals between public and private life. The workplace is different from personal life. As depicted on *The Apprentice*, the workplace is also a sphere outside of personal morality. Alliances formed on a personal level — friendships, even romantic bonds — are subject to assault and betrayal in the boardroom. "It's Not Personal, It's Just Business" asserts an independent logic for the work world, a sort of winner-takes-all model. The personal and interpersonal are subordinate to the demands of business, and in the world of Trump, business is about ultimate victory and unbridled individualism.

I believe that the show serves as both a reflection and a representation (if exaggerated) of the imagined state of contemporary business in America. When Trump looks into the camera each week and elucidates his lessons, he is teaching us about success in corporate America. The show teaches us about who we are as workers. By analyzing *The Apprentice*, we can focus our scholarly lens on the contemporary status of the worker in the world of advanced capitalism. How does an aspiring businessperson, like the job candidates/contestants on the show, achieve wealth, fame and power? *The Apprentice* literally asks candidates to model themselves after the trope of Trump, and as we viewers are constantly reminded, there is only one winner on *The Apprentice*.

The Apprentice as a Highly Centralized Dictatorship

If *The Apprentice* is a microcosm of the contemporary work world, what does this workplace teach us about the status of work and workers in American society? The corporation itself can serve as a model for how society functions. The workplace is a sphere of daily and engaged involvement for the bulk of contemporary citizens. Americans are spending more time at work, and in many ways, the workplace has become our most salient social sphere. At work, people meet other people, negotiate identities, interact with their communities and participate in creating contemporary social conditions. Business institutions are made up of workers who lead public lives within the context of the workplace. As argued by Stan Deetz in his 1992 book *Democracy in an Age of Corporate Colonization*, we engage with our local community through our work identities and actions. Instead of checking the work persona at the door of the public sphere, work and public bleed into one another continuously.[3] If people spend the majority of their time at work, then this is often the most significant social configuration in contemporary culture.

The workplace serves to structure much of the daily lives of individual citizens. It aligns people with common causes, creates spatial and temporal formulas for everyday life, and supports employees in their pursuit of material necessities. What other institutional location do people visit daily, while having fundamental knowledge about its functioning and a vested stake in participation? The workplace acts as a sphere of practical engagement, where employees are heavily vested in both process and product. Thus, the workplace might serve as a model for how the rest of society should and does function. Carole Pateman, in her book *Participation and Democratic Theory*, tells us that "an individual's (politically relevant) attitudes will depend to a large extent on the authority structure of his work environment" (53). If a workplace reinforces hierarchical and authoritarian ways of being, then for employees, that structure will map itself onto the larger social world. The workplace tells us who we are and how we should act as social beings within the larger society. As industry grows and we see mega-conglomeration ever increasing the power of the corporation, the ethos of the workplace is fast becoming the dominant discourse of contemporary society. Because "the structure of authority at the workplace is probably the most significant and salient structure of that kind with which the average man finds himself in daily contact" (49), in many ways, the state of the workplace is an active reflection of the state of society.

The working environment of *The Apprentice* manifests a grim vision of work, characterized by an authoritarian boss, a ruthless brand of managerial capitalism, and a nasty race amongst fellow employees for a singular prize. There is only one road to success in the world of *The Apprentice*, and we viewers are actively indoctrinated with the logic and lessons of Trump. Analyzing the work-world of *The Apprentice* helps us to interrogate and understand the ever-growing dominant discourse of the corporate workplace in U.S. society. As the work sphere becomes the ultimate way of being, significant television shows like *The Apprentice* give us a unique chance to understand and evaluate the dynamics of the working world and the role we workers might play in the high-stakes game of business.

"There Are No Rules in Trump's Boardroom"

Each episode of *The Apprentice* culminates in a trip to the boardroom. The contestants from the week's losing team are seated on one side of the table, faced by Trump's two stern looking deputies— George and Caroline. After a pause, and once everyone is seated at attention, Trump enters from a secret back door. Teams and team members are variously asked to explain their failure. Trump moderates the conversation, interjecting, interrupting and limiting the discussion. After a brief deliberation, the biggest loser, often the one ousted by his or her teammates, is fired by Trump. Trump holds all the cards and represents himself as the supreme authority on the candidates and on all business relations. In fact, candidates often comment that "there are no rules in Trump's boardroom," using this slogan as another mantra. However, there are rules, and they originate from Trump and only can be broken by him. He is the sole innovator and the ultimate autocrat.

In the boardroom, the candidates are put in the position of vilifying, bickering and backstabbing, as each contestant battles to save him or herself against the onslaught of Trump's condemnation. In what now characterizes the stereotypical reality TV format, the show's contestants are molded into archetypical figures— the sexy girl, the bitch, the southern boy, the outcast, etc. This typecasting, first made explicit on MTV's *The Real World*, acts here to "substitute the signs of the real for the real" (Baudrillard 2). We viewers understand that there might be a real and complex person behind the TV simulation, but the individuals work best when we treat them as clichés. While the contestants compete in teams, and there is a great deal of talk about teamwork and team building, ultimately, each candidate stands alone. In the boardroom, teams are encouraged to bicker and splinter, and best friends in the suite are rarely loyal in the boardroom. This brash individualism reminiscent of *Survivor*[4] also reflects and reifies the logic of advanced capitalism, where "each individual commodity fights for itself, cannot acknowledge the others and aspires to impose its presence everywhere as though it were alone" (Debord 43). The contestants, made tropes, are commodities themselves— and only one can win the job. The contestants frequently say, "We are not here to make friends," and in the boardroom Trump mocks romantic and friendship bonds. Nothing should stand in the way of personal achievement. Remember, in the world of *The Apprentice*, "It's not personal, it's just business."

However, the candidates do need one another because tasks are won and lost as teams. Each week, teams are variously formed and headed by a rotating project manager. The show depicts the foibles of the team and its team members, and the losing team is criticized for its lack of harmony, consensus or leadership. This interplay between teamsmanship and the brash individualism of the boardroom pits gamesmanship against consensus building. Contestants must show that they are team players and band together to win each round of the game, while also fracturing and castigating those very teammates in the boardroom. *The Apprentice* gives us a view of the work world as a tense and uncertain place, where one minute you are bonded with your team and sharing in its success, and the next you are vilified and attacked for your lack of individual leadership.

Because *The Apprentice* is a reality TV show, based on the competitive format of shows like *Survivor*, the things that ultimately count are the logistics of the game and the logic of winning. Trump himself unselfconsciously validates that motto, and frequently declares that "Winning Is Everything." Trump proclaims himself to be the ultimate champion of New York business world. Each show is colored by his large and self-supported cult of identity, culminating in trips to his penthouse, views of his helicopter, and visits with his stunning, super-model wife. Trump advocates a garish preference for his name and image and goes to great lengths to color the show with his various products. On one episode, contestants were asked to sell crates of bottled water emblazoned with his name and image. Trump also advocates a conspicuous consumption, which knows no limits, from his all-gilt apartment to his fleet of cars and jets. Trump shares in the profits from *The Apprentice* itself and has, by his own assertion, made a fortune from the television series. In many ways, Trump is an icon for a certain sort of unbridled capitalism and individual aplomb. However, what is most fascinating is his complete lack of irony as he declares his wife, his apartment, his building, his hotel — the best in the world. "Trump has been in our faces for more than twenty years now, so we shouldn't be surprised by his self-aggrandizement-but occasionally it reaches a truly stupefying level: In one episode, the camera cuts from the Statue of Liberty to a stretch limo in motion" (Franklin). Trump was recently married to the Slovenian model Melania Knauss, and his wedding was described as "lavish," "ornate," and "the wedding to top all weddings."[5]

The Apprentice is at all times personal and biographical, and the show revolves around the figure of Trump, a.k.a. The Donald, marking the absolute irony of the "It's not personal, It's just business" assertion. Franklin notes,

> Although Trump is, to many people, the personification of New York, "*The Apprentice*" seems located nowhere except in the participants' egos. You never

hear any of them express the least bit of curiosity about anyone or anything around them. No one wonders about anything. No one ever asks a question-except Donald Trump, who, one has to admit, breathes life into the show [Franklin].

Trump is the central character; he is he hero; he is the ultimate captain of industry. "A deal-maker without a peer" ("Apprentice Official"), Trump becomes a sort of Horatio Alger for our times.

On *The Apprentice*, Trump serves as teacher, mentor and hero—dishing out sound bites of advice in a direct and explicit manner. Each week, as he doles out some trinket of advice, a slogan flashes across the screen. These tid-bits, such as "Play Golf" or "Make Decisions Quickly" are reminiscent of the over-simplistic mantras of Successories[6] posters. Trump also vigorously asserts the model of the business world as a game. Trump has created and markets a board game based on the *The Apprentice*, where players act as mini-real estate moguls. In fact, the gamesmanship is so explicit that it borders on absolute farce. The glue holding *The Apprentice* together, however, is Trump's very seriousness. You get the feeling that this is how he views the world, and this is an accurate description of his life's motto and mission. Trump advocates an almost wildly irresponsible individualism, where one man is the center of the universe, where one leader decides who lives and who is fired, and where one individual is the sole bearer of wisdom. Trump is the show. He is the ultimate autocrat.

Guy Debord tells us that "the individual who in the service of the spectacle is placed in stardom's spotlight is in fact the opposite of an individual, and is clearly the enemy of the individual" (39), and Trump manifests this sinister dominance. All eyes must focus on Trump, and each candidate must actively strive to be as much like him as possible. There is no room for difference or counter-individualism. There can be only one ego, and that is Trump's ego. The more successful contestants on the show have explicitly modeled themselves after Trump, hanging on his every word and attempting to think like him. The TV screen is not big enough for two, and Trump must serve as the ideological center. He is the ultimate individual, to the detriment of all others. If, following Pateman and her work on democratic intervention, the model of authority at the workplace is the most substantial and relevant structure in the lives of everyday citizens, then the structure of the workplace is the most determinate system of relations for contemporary man. If that structure is based upon a centralized and forceful autocracy, then the world contemporary workers live in is a dictatorship. Despite the patriotic claims of Trump and his constant photo opportunities with the American flag, the world of Trump is far from democratic. The America of Trump is not a liberal democratic state. The American Dream represented by Trump is a mini-monarchy, ruled from a gilded chair and vesting Trump with the supreme authority.

"Do You Think a Leader Really Takes a Vote?"

The world of *The Apprentice* is regulated by the iron fist of Trump and his catch phrase, "You're Fired!" His decisions often seem arbitrary and capricious, but are based upon a set of unwritten rules known only by Trump, rules that demand success and victory in every interaction. We are explicitly reminded that there can be only one apprentice. We are also aware that there can be only one Trump. The two victors of *The Apprentice* in its first two seasons were young, attractive, white men with entrepreneurial backgrounds. They both attribute their success to discovering the logic of Trump and playing by these rules.

Kelly, the victor in Season Two, is a clean-cut and hard-edged former military man. He credits his victory[7] to a conscious attempt to avoid the boardroom, and in fact, to avoid Trump. Kelly actively strategized his victory by avoiding the only forum for deliberation with Trump, the boardroom. Kelly also prioritized his individual victory over critical, if contentious, engagement with the group. Both Kelly and Bill (Season One's winner), laid low and avoided conflict, while steering clear of trips to the boardroom. It seems that avoiding deliberation, then, is the key to success on *The Apprentice*. Trump does not like to share his stage, and cutting a wide circle around him and his boardroom engenders success. Be like Trump, but do not be Trump.

Although the drama of *The Apprentice* revolves around "discussions" in the boardroom, Trump actively denounces open debate. Several contestants have lost their footing and been fired for over-speaking or talking out of turn. Trump controls all dialogue and decides when enough is enough. He has slammed candidates more than once for free speaking and sternly advises each contestant to "keep your opinion to yourself" (*The Apprentice*, November 2, 2004). Those who break the rules or act outside of the norms, as defined by Trump himself, are eliminated. He determines what innovation is and what is just wrong. The final opinion always comes from Trump. When he declares, "You're Fired," you must leave the boardroom immediately, wheel your suitcase to the street and take a cab to the airport. Upon "You're Fired," you become a non-entity.

In one of Trump's weekly lessons on leadership, he discusses the need for leaders to be both bold and exceptionally decisive. In this segment, he shamelessly asks: "Do you think a leader really takes a vote?" (*The Appren-*

tice, April 21, 2005), throwing this question in our face as a ridiculous rhetorical assumption. Far from deliberation among peers to reach a common end, leadership for Trump is singular. Trump has stated that a leader must at some point shun the advice of others and make decisions based solely on his own individual "gut." In fact, Trump states, "I have rarely seen a leader who is able to lead by consensus. A leader will sometimes go against everybody. That's what a leader is" (April 21, 2005). The assumption that a leader acts alone contradicts the very premise of democratic governance, which is based in shared sovereignty. The idea that a leader must work against his peers and colleagues is a direct confrontation with the liberal, democratic model of consensus building. In classical democratic theory, a decision can only be called legitimate if all affected parties are represented in the decision-making process.[8] However, in the world of Trump, legitimacy stems from a single, autocratic source. Because *The Apprentice* explicitly models itself as a training tool for future business executives, we have to assume that in the world of the capitalist elite, there is no significant power sharing. Trump shows us that businessmen act alone, making decisions based on their own, often unspoken codes. The two winners of *The Apprentice* based their own victory on avoiding conversation, deliberation and confrontation. Their strategy mirrored Trump, and they avoided collaboration in a singular grab for power. The world of *The Apprentice* is based around an extreme individualism, where everyone is a master of his (or her) own destiny, to the detriment of all others.

Trump frequently describes the tasks themselves—from selling candy bars to constructing ad campaigns— as military operations. On a particular dog-washing task, a contestant lost the team cell-phone. Trump chided him, asking "what if this were a military operation... ?" (*The Apprentice*, October 21, 2004). Contestants and Trump often talk about the tasks as critical missions, in which the teams must be honed for precision and speed. Following a military model, *The Apprentice* also privileges deference to authority, and a ceding of personal independence for the sake of the mission. This contradicts the raging individualism advocated by Trump's definition of a singular leader. However, in the world of Trump, there is room for both the leader and the follower, and the manager must demand submission from his subordinates. The winner of *The Apprentice* must be a leader, able to command and control his peers and direct activity with a high-level of bureaucratic precision. The business world is a war, and we must gather our troops for the continuous battle against all others. For Trump, the corporation must be a well-oiled machine, ordered by a singular executive willing to "Lead with Authority."

In another dictum from the wisdom of Trump, he tells us viewers that "Winning is Everything," while footage of Trump running with the

Olympic torch flashes by on screen. This might be the show's most explicit lesson. In the world of *The Apprentice*, there are enemies and opponents, and only one victor. Your co-workers are not friends or fellow citizens, but competitors who must be eliminated. If *The Apprentice* is our symbolic workplace, then the work world is a war-zone. The world of Trump forces us to question our identity as both workers and citizens. Is the world divided into winners and losers, with each of us pitted against every other?

Winning the Game

Stan Deetz tells us that "the workplace … produces people as well as information, goods and services" (199). The structure of your workplace is arguably the most significant and salient configuration in your life. Your work identity might always trump your citizen identity. We spend our lives at work, and the state of the workplace is the state of our society. Moreover, when *The Apprentice* tells us that "It's Not Personal, It's Just Business," we understand that the work-world exists outside of personal moral values and norms. Trump tells us not to bring friendship, compassion or emotion to work. He also tells us to check our so-called democratic values at the door. Remember, a leader does not take a vote, and in order to win in the game of business, we must act singularly and against our peers and colleagues.

Because there can be only one apprentice, the contestants are forced to market themselves, positioning themselves as products to be bought by Trump. The logic of reality TV demands archetypes and tropes, and the contestants all too readily become stereotypes like the "hottie," the "bitch," the "self-made man," etc. As the contestants discover the rules of executive capitalism, they also learn to sell themselves to both Trump and the TV viewing public. What is for sale on *The Apprentice* is the contestants' identities, and they seem willing to throw themselves into the free market as products for consumption. Many *Apprentice* contestants have gone on to commercial or modeling contracts, and they all seem to understand the potential of the show as a vehicle for mini-stardom.

Nancy Franklin, in her review of *The Apprentice* in *New Yorker* magazine, makes the case that the world of Trump is nothing but a vast array of smoke and mirrors. "The New York he is showing his protégés is a city of jets, helicopters, limos, and polished marble. They're being treated to what they think is the best of everything — given a prettily wrapped gift that, when opened, turns out to have nothing in it" (Franklin). We are reminded of Jean Baudrillard's assertion that "everywhere we live in a universe strangely similar to the original" (11). This universe might be similar, but it is frighteningly hollow — locked in the shallow logic of television. Moreover, if the work-world of Trump is similar to the workplace of contemporary corporate America, we face a frighteningly authoritarian vision of U.S. business practices. There is no room for difference or deliberation. Personal interests are checked at the door. Winning is everything, and the logic of capital overtakes all other virtues. As Karl Marx tells us, capital will always seek more capital and compound itself without end (see Marx, *Capital*). In this ever-increasing consolidation of money and power, there is no space for citizens' rights, democratic participation or patient consensus building.

Because the workplace serves a major function in contemporary American society, and as time spent at work expands, the work identity becomes more and more dominant for every American. Deetz traces the development of corporate colonization in the lifeworld and proclaims "the greater the work identity, the less the development of community ties and solidarity" (27). Thus, the workplace is the dominant sphere for identity formation in the United States. The values of the workplace have become the most salient principles for each individual.

The Apprentice is, above all, a television program. It is rooted in the rules of the reality TV format, and its plotlines and story substance are based around mass appeal and spectacular showmanship. However, I believe *The Apprentice* teaches us about work and reflects what may already be corporate standards. Baudrillard describes an overwhelming "dissolution of TV in life, dissolution of life in TV" (30), referring to the consistent imposition of television into every sphere of life. *The Apprentice* pierces the so-called executive business world, and shows us one way to succeed in business. "In form as in content the spectacle serves as total justification for the contradictions and aims of the existing system. It further ensures the permanent presence of that justification" (Debord 13). Trump teaches us about the logic of advanced managerial capitalism. Moreover, *The Apprentice* panders to capital. The single-minded pursuit of success and wealth accumulation is never questioned. Individual acquisitiveness and market capitalism are the silent center of *The Apprentice* universe. Ralph Miliband, in his essay "The State in Capitalist Society," describes "the effort business makes to persuade society not merely to accept the policies it advocates but also the ethos, the goals and the values which are its own, the economic system of which it forms the central part, the 'way of life' which is at the core of its being" (190). The basic notions of market economics are not up for debate. Wealth accumulation is good, and corporate profiteering is the ultimate end of extreme individualism. *The Apprentice* functions to validate corporate business, vast hoarding, and single-minded individual victory. What *The Apprentice* teaches us is how to live like Trump — as a mogul in a gilded tower focused on self-interest, and solitary victory in the game of life.

Works Cited

"*The Apprentice* Official Website." 19 Oct. 2005. <www.nbc.com/The_Apprentice/>
"Episode 7." *The Apprentice*. NBC. Season 2. October 21, 2004.
"Episode 9." *The Apprentice*. NBC. Season 2. November 2, 2004.
"Episode 13." *The Apprentice*. NBC. Season 3. April 21, 2005.
Baudrillard, Jean. *Simulacra and Simulation*. Trans. Shelia Faria-Glaser. Ann Arbor: Michigan UP, 1994.
Debord, Guy. *The Society of the Spectacle*. Trans. Donald Nicholson-Smith. New York: Zone Books, 1995.
Deetz, Stan. *Democracy in an Age of Corporate Colonization*. Albany: State University Press of New York, 1992.
Franklin, Nancy. "American Idol." *NewYorker.com*. 09 Feb. 2004. 16 Feb 2004. <http://www.newyorker.com/television>
Marx, Karl. *Capital*. Reprint Edition. New York: Penguin Classics, 1992.
Miliband, Ralph. *The State in Capitalist Society: An Analysis of the Western System of Power*. 2nd ed. New York: Basic Books, 1978.
Pateman, Carole. *Participation and Democratic Theory*. Cambridge: Cambridge UP, 1970.

Notes

1. See the official website for *The Apprentice*, http://www.nbc.com/The_Apprentice/
2. The address of Trump Tower.
3. For a more thorough explanation of the complex interplay between the workplace and the public sphere, please see my work on "The Workplace as Public Sphere?" Available by request, *frankoe@colorado.edu*.
4. In fact, Mark Burnett created both *The Apprentice* and *Survivor*.
5. http://insider.tv.yahoo.com/celeb/insdr20050122t164000001738/
6. For examples of Successories products, see the official Successories Website, located at https://www.successories.com/index.cfm/fuseaction/home.home/successories_country/USA/home.cfm
7. Kelly, Season Two winner, stated in Washington Post (http://www.washingtonpost.com-/wp-dyn/content/article/2005/01/24/AR2005040701160.html), that the key to his success was understanding and following the rules of the game.
8. See the discussion of this issue by Iris Marion Young in her volume *Inclusion and Democracy*. New York: Oxford UP, 2000.

16

Watching Yourself, Watching Others: Popular Representations of Panoptic Surveillance in Reality TV Programs*

Daniel Trottier

Preamble: Situating Reality Television within Surveillance Studies

In a figurative sense, at least, morality and immorality meet at the public scaffold, and it is during this meeting that the line between them is drawn [Erikson 12].

As both a topic of media studies and a genre of televised programming, reality TV has generated a considerable amount of attention in recent years from audience members and academics alike. Although the reasons for this genre's success are manifold, two in particular are of immediate interest. First, reality TV operates through a claim of authenticity that serves to distinguish it from earlier forms of broadcasting. This authenticity can be seen as operating on many layers of both the production and the reception of reality programs. In "The Kinder, Gentler Gaze of Big Brother," cultural theorist Mark Andrejevic suggests two of the more apparent qualities of such shows that speak to their purported authenticity: the employment of non-actors and the unscripted nature of these shows (259). Although many reality programs routinely showcase celebrities such as

*I am indebted to Dr. Bart Simon as well as D'ette Bourchier, who have provided invaluable feedback throughout the multiple drafts of this endeavour.

Ozzy Osbourne in *The Osbournes* and Jessica Simpson in *Newlyweds*, the fact that these shows concentrate on the daily routine of these entertainers leads us to believe that we are watching authentic, if mundane, footage. Similarly, although certain elements of a program — such as the food rationing and mandatory evictions on *Big Brother*—can be understood as a form of engineering to guarantee dramatic behavior, the behavior itself is purportedly authentic.

The second relevant determinant of reality TV's recent success is its alleged ability to transcend barriers separating private and public spheres. Indeed, one of the main criticisms against the genre is the claim that it cultivates a form of voyeuristic consumption among audiences. In the case of *Big Brother*, one of the genre's most long-standing and world-renowned programs, subjects are enclosed in a fully monitored communal dwelling. Here, audience members are accorded full access to the subject, who is not equipped with a backstage to escape the public gaze. As such, surveillance emerges as one of the predominant themes when discussing reality programming. This form of broadcast media is characterized by purporting to offer the audience a privileged viewpoint, transcending previously impermeable barriers. Hence, the *Big Brother* website offers viewers around-the-clock access to all of the enclosure's cameras. There is little doubt as to who plays the role of big brother in the program. Already, one is able to draw parallels between the role of the viewer and that of a security guard who, through the use of a closed-circuit television (CCTV herein) network, monitors a pre-determined area for suspicious behavior. Indeed, in the case of crime-based reality programs such as *COPS*, the viewer is given partial access to such surveillance apparatuses (Prosise and Johnson 73). Relying solely on the contents of these programs, one would arguably foster an understanding of surveillance as being an invaluable (or at least entertaining) component of social relations.

Based on the previous considerations, the goal of this paper will be to examine the manner in which reality TV legitimizes contemporary surveillance practices. The particular manner in which these practices are portrayed will be understood as a form of discursive engagement whereby real-life surveillance is both necessary and ultimately beneficial for the viewer. In order to attain a clearer understanding of the relations between surveillance and mass media, we will consider Michel Foucault's work on panopticism alongside Thomas Mathiesen's recent appraisal of this work. An understanding of surveillance and the media will emerge in which these two processes are regarded as operating in tandem with one another. In order to demonstrate the manner in which surveillance and mass media operate in tandem, I will explore crime-based forms of reality programming using earlier academic material. Here, it will be shown that these programs operate as a broadcasting of surveillance practices, engaging audiences and encouraging them to understand themselves as dependent upon the expertise of law enforcement officers. Moving beyond crime-based reality programming, I will consider contemporary forms of makeover themed reality broadcasting insofar as they engage the audience to submit to panoptic forms of consumer surveillance. Employing Erving Goffman's approach regarding the use of expertise in total institutions, I will argue that these programs engage the viewer to rely upon the knowledge derived from experts of consumer behavior (fashion, cosmetics, etc....), a state of dependency that necessitates an active engagement with panoptic forms of consumer surveillance. *Queer Eye for the Straight Guy* will be examined as case study, as it serves as an exemplar of this sub-genre of reality programming.

Panopticism and Synopticism: Reconciling Mass Media and Surveillance

Michel Foucault's seminal work *Discipline and Punish* offers a description of panopticism that serves as an invaluable starting point for our understanding of surveillance practices and mass media. Based on a form of prison architecture originally designed by Jeremy Bentham, Foucault describes a scenario whereby inmates are located around the periphery of a central guard tower (200). Guards operating from the tower have visual access to all inmates at once, and the inmates in turn are never sure when they are actually under watch. As a result, inmates come to behave as though they are permanently and continuously under the watch of the guard tower, internalizing its gaze and acting as their own guards. Foucault's work is particularly helpful for articulating the manner in which institutions discursively engage individuals as subjects who are dependant upon their expertise. The presence of authoritative figures such as guards enables inmates to come to understand themselves as subject to a particular regime of the self, an idea that resonates with Erving Goffman's description of the staff's role within total institutions (83).

In addressing what he recognized as shortcomings in Michel Foucault's work on panopticism, Thomas Mathiesen wanted to emphasize the role of the mass media as a counterpart of modern surveillance. Acknowledging Foucault's assertion that panoptic surveillance enables the few to oversee the many, Mathiesen added the notion that through the rise of synoptic apparatuses like the mass media, "the many have been enabled to see the few — to see the VIPs, the reporters, the stars, almost a new class in the public sphere" (219). In other words, modern day forms of surveillance are no less dependent on the spectacle than they were prior to modernity.

In order to drive home the interdependent relationship between the panopticon and synopticon with regards to social control functions, Mathiesen draws three parallels between them. First, both have undergone acceleration from the 1800s onwards (219). That is to say, panoptic techno-social innovations ranging from the modern prison to closed-circuit television infrastructures arose in conjunction with synoptic mass-media counterparts such as the mass press and satellite television. Secondly, Mathiesen contends that panoptic and synoptic models "go back far beyond the 1700s, and that they have historical roots in central social and political institutions" (222). Third, the development of both models is said to have occurred through a symbiotic relationship, a fusion of systems (223). Mathiesen characterizes panoptic and synoptic development in the 20th century as a result of joint technology, the site of the aforementioned fusion. This is probably Mathiesen's most significant contribution to the understanding of panoptic relations. As apparatuses of information management, surveillance structures can be understood as operating through both panoptic systems where the many are rendered visible to the few as well as synoptic systems where the few are visible to the many. In order to illustrate this, we can consider George Orwell's dystopian novel *1984*, where the ever-present telescreen serves to both monitor subjects as well as provide them with knowledge regarding proper conduct (4).

Mathiesen expands on his notion of synopticism in order to speak to its purpose as a control function. Teasing panopticism and synopticism apart from one another with regards to their respective manners of targeting the many, it is purported that the former has a bearing on the target's behavior, whereas the latter digs deeper by targeting one's consciousness (229–30). To clarify the first statement, Mathiesen cites his experiences in the United States under McCarthyism. In response to the threat presented by fierce anti-communist surveillance, "[c]ommunists remained communists, but they became cautious, secretive and partly silent" (230). In other words, those who become cognizant of panoptic apparatuses become habituated to this sort of relation through the performance of a set of behaviors.

On the other hand, synopticism is said to operate through the mass media in order to shape the subject's consciousness. For Mathiesen, this serves as an answer to what is perceived as the Foucauldian desire of "the creation of human beings who control themselves through self-control" (230). Understood in this manner, synopticism is reminiscent of the Frankfurt school's hypodermic understanding of media effects, whereby the mass media is understood as being capable to inject knowledge into receptive audience members (Morley 88–89). From this distinction, the duality that operates in systems of control becomes more apparent: a hegemonic discourse is broadcast through synopticism, whereas panopticism is utilized to ensure that this discourse is implemented and acted upon. Thus, for Mathiesen, the spectacle has not given way to panoptic surveillance, but rather has developed alongside it.

At this juncture, it is beneficial to expand upon several of Mathiesen's arguments. First, panoptic and synoptic systems are portrayed in Mathiesen's *The Viewer Society* as oppositional in their directional flows, a notion that might incite the reader to understand synopticism as an opportunity for many to see the few as the many themselves are seen by the few. It would appear necessary to clarify that, while synoptic knowledge is understood as disseminating from the few, the content being disseminated might have the many as its focal point. In other words, it would be incorrect to suppose that synopticism allows the many to access the few in the same manner that panopticism renders the many accessible to the few. Whereas Mathiesen formulates synopticism as a configuration where the many are able to see the elite few, both surveillance and media studies might benefit from regarding it as the elite few broadcasting knowledge to the many.

To obtain a clearer understanding of the greater implications of synopticism within surveillance studies, I wish to draw upon some of Bill Brown's findings during the filming of one of the Surveillance Camera Player's walking tours of New York (Schienke and Brown). During this walking tour, two kinds of CCTV cameras were pointed out that appeared to serve different functions. The first camera, by virtue of its atypical appearance, was meant to not be perceived as one. On the other hand, the second device merely resembled a camera, yet was incapable of recording or transmitting any footage. We find an important distinction between the different synoptic relations that these devices establish between the many and the few. Hidden cameras are built in a manner which prevents the betrayal of their presence. The many that fall under the gaze of a hidden camera are intended to remain unaware of the fact that they are being filmed. Conversely, the decoy camera only serves to convey to the many the knowledge that they are being surveyed. Analogous to the decoy camera, we can consider the example of the fake patrol car. Strategically located on a quiescent stretch of highway, the inoperable junker is meant to simulate the presence of a highway patrol officer, much like the manner in which the inoperable decoy camera is meant to feign the presence of a surveillance infrastructure (Bogard 25).

These cameras each implicate different relationships between synopticism and control functions. In the case of the hidden camera, it could be argued that no information is being disseminated synoptically from the few to the many; the device allows for a unidirectional flow of information from the many to the few. In this regard, it would qualify as a purely panoptic apparatus. On the other hand, the decoy camera serves the unidirectional

flow of information from the few to the many and by extension would qualify as a purely synoptic apparatus. Although these examples represent two
extremes, as such they illustrate the synoptic functions that many seemingly
panoptic devices may (or may feign to) perform. Thus, for Mathiesen control is derived not only from panoptic flows of information, but synoptic
ones as well. Although the two types of cameras would appear to signify
instances of either panoptic or synoptic relations, it would appear as though
most types of surveillance apparatuses encapsulate both relations.

In spite of critical appraisals that claimed his work lacked the recognition of mass media and other synoptic control functions (Mathiesen 219),
Foucault would appear to speak to the panoptic-synoptic duality in his discussion of carceral institutions where "[t]raining was accompanied by permanent observation" (294). Thus, it is possible to gleam elements of
synoptic flows of knowledge within an institution that has typically been
understood as the poster-child of panopticism. In this example, one gains
an understanding of the manner in which knowledge is synoptically transmitted to inmates, whose internalization of this knowledge was subse-
quently monitored through panoptic devices. The co-presence of synoptic
and panoptic features can even be found in the guard tower, which has formerly been illustrative of purely panoptic relations. Although the use of
blinders along with the manipulation of light sources obfuscate the presence or absence of a guard, thus preventing the transmission of this information from the few to the many inmates, the mere presence of the tower
itself can be understood as synoptically broadcasting the possibility of being
monitored, to say the very least. In *Arresting Images*, Aaron Doyle notes:

> The Panopticon, like the camera in the corner of the convenience store, doesn't
> just watch the public; perhaps more importantly, it communicates to them. But
> it communicates much more than simply that one is being watched. As tech-
> nologies of surveillance pervade our society, so too do the cultural implications
> of surveillance (Staples 1997): that crime is everywhere; that others among us are
> not to be trusted, especially those who are visibly different; that technology rather
> than community is our safeguard [153–154].

Here, the security camera is seen to possess synoptic properties by virtue
of its ability to communicate a nuanced relationship which implicates the
few (the owners of the store, law enforcement agents who might refer to
recorded footage) as well as the many (anybody within its field of vision).

One of the consequences of the events of 9/11 for panoptic and synoptic structures has been the (re)production of recorded footage surrounding these events. Images surrounding these events are collected through
panoptic structures and transmitted through synoptic ones. Hier elaborates
on this point in his discussion of synopticism:

[R]epeated exposure to the fantastic spectacle served to invite a global audience to consume the hybrid image of fascination and repulsion whilst those same images served as, and remain, the central discursive resource oriented towards consolidating panoptical aspirations through the intensification of information gathering, data sharing and risk management techniques [405].

Panoptic and synoptic functions could thus be understood as coexisting not only within technological fusions, but from within forms of media as well. The very same footage of suspected terrorists recorded by airport surveillance mechanisms and intensely scrutinized by panoptically structured security organizations can simultaneously exist as a synoptic broadcasting projected onto a seemingly limitless amount of television screens.

What emerges from our theoretical consideration is an articulation of contemporary surveillance practices as operating through synoptic relations of knowledge transmission, where expertise is exercised to induce proper conduct in its subjects. In the following pages, I wish to explore the manner in which the mass media facilitates the panoptic features of control apparatuses. In particular, reality TV will be understood as a synoptic vessel for criminal-judicial and consumer control functions. To begin, I will argue that reality TV enables the synoptic broadcasting of panoptic operations, drawing upon research on earlier forms of crime-based reality TV programming. What will be worth noting here is how selective editing in these shows serves to publicize as well as legitimize specific panoptic surveillance practices. Subsequent strains of reality TV programming, such as *Queer Eye for the Straight Guy*, will also be examined in order to highlight the manner in which they can be understood as synoptically facilitating confessional statements from audience members. It will be argued that through the process of "self-identification and self-understanding" (Boyne 301), these programs may persuade audience members to be identified and assessed by panoptic apparatuses. In other words, I will verify the extent to which these shows portray being on the grid — regardless of your actual coordinates — as the only safe/legitimate option for audience members.

COPS *and Other Crime-based Reality Programs:* Big Brother's *Older Brother?*

Several years prior to the purportedly unscripted and unmistakably Machiavellian co-habitation reality shows *Survivor* and *Big Brother*, programs like *COPS* and *America's Dumbest Criminals* were making big waves among media theorists. These two latter programs were the prototypes of a genre that can be regarded as a precursor to post-1999 reality TV. These shows offered the spectator a previously inaccessible (and therefore highly privileged) glimpse of law enforcement operations. Following Mathiesen's model, crime-based reality television (CRTV herein) appears to utilize synoptic channels of information to legitimize and promote the use of panoptic means of surveillance. Scholarly material on this subgenre supports the proposition that this legitimization occurs in two distinct ways. First, CRTV can be understood as a simulated projection of democratic access to panoptic apparatuses. Heavily edited footage of surveillance-bound control functions presented using an anecdotal production style serves to implicate to audience member in a (symbolic, at the very least) participatory manner. Secondly, CRTV legitimates panoptic forms of law enforcement by presenting the latter as a necessary apparatus. This is seen to occur through the aforementioned editing process, resulting in a discrepancy between the law enforcement apparatus as it appears synoptically on CRTV programs and how it operates panoptically in actual practice. For Bogard, innovations in the realm of televised programming serve "[t]o eliminate the distraction of the technology itself by making its images more and more real, more real than real" (60).

Prior to CRTV programs, the police, as Doyle and Ericson lucidly suggest, maintained a public (read synoptic) image through the mass media relative to other crimino-justice branches such as the penal system (158; Biressi and Nunn 2). Expanding upon Mathiesen's framework of synoptic control functions, much of the literature on CRTV supports the notion that these programs serve to legitimize panoptic elements of law enforcement. This would appear to signify a renegotiation of a hegemonic discourse that is more celebratory of the panoptic control functions inherent in police work. One of the manners in which this appears to be accomplished is by rendering a select portion of panoptically collected information accessible through synoptic avenues. At the very least, this serves to blur the boundary between panopticism and synopticism, not unlike a prison guard who keeps a publicly accessible diary of his observations.

Particular editing techniques inherent to CRTV programs mold panoptically-collected information into anecdotal events conceptualized through a binary distinction between the protagonist/narrator (in the case of *COPS*, the two are indistinguishable) and the antagonist. In addition to reducing crimino-justice discourse into carefully selected and generalizable anecdotes, it likens panoptic events to a narrative text not unlike those of fictional crime dramas, a determinant of popular success/transmission. However, unlike its fictional predecessors, CRTV purports to offer access to previously forbidden spaces (Goffman's backstage) through panoptic apparatuses (Palmer 157). Although the voyeuristic implications of audience participation are worth psychologizing, Biressi and Nunn push this concept a step further, saying, "The vicarious pleasures of witnessing crime, disaster and other life-threatening occurrences are sanctioned by the moral discourses of criminal justice, the address to the responsible citizen and overt support for the emergency services" (4). In other words, the synoptic transmission of a voyeuristically desirable product of panoptic operations is mediated by shaping this information into a carefully edited discursive text. The boundary between panoptic information and synoptic knowledge would appear to blur at this juncture.

Congruent with Mathiesen's understanding of synoptic flows as shaping mass consciousness, one of the apparent functions of CRTV is to implicate the audience member (the many) in the panoptic apparatus, in effect, to situate them on the crimino-justice grid. One of the more visible manners through which this is accomplished is direct invitation from the narrators of many CRTV programs to volunteer information that might serve to capture fugitive antagonists. For instance, *America's Most Wanted* invites audience members to get involved by disclosing pertinent information via the show's hotline (by 1994, the show averaged 3000 calls per episode) (Donovan 125). This feature is not unique to *America's Most Wanted*; similar shows across Europe incorporate this interactive function (Brants 175). By disclosing information through such hotlines, audience members are encouraged to behave according to their position on the grid. In effect, this confession is indicative of the audience's internalization of a simulated self-as-victim. Related to this point, it is worth noting that many police academy students have reported that shows such as *COPS* and *America's Most Wanted* prompted them to enlist (Doyle, Aaron 60). Undoubtedly, this could be considered as one of the most definitive manners of gridding one's self in congruence with hegemonic crimino-justice discourse.

Through synoptic broadcasting, CRTV provides audience members with discursive knowledge in regards to their position in the crimino-justice grid. Prosise and Johnson contend that the anecdotal format of such programs offer audience members "equipment for living" (74). Put otherwise, synoptically disseminated texts enable audience members to develop responses to situational cues and ambiguities in real life, a claim that resonates with Mathiesen's consciousness-shaping properties of synopticism. With regards to crime and law enforcement in particular, the lack of direct experience that characterizes many audience members serves to reinforce the influence of CRTV programs. As a result, these programs could be understood as synoptically legitimizing panoptic control apparatuses through the particular context in which these apparatuses are presented.

CRTV programs such as *COPS* present the law enforcement apparatus through a narrative that emphasizes the "clear moral distinction" which demarcates criminals from ordinary citizens (Prosise and Johnson 80). For instance, shows like *America's Most Wanted* and *Unsolved Mysteries* have been noted to present the criminal/victim distinction much in the same manner as the criminal/officer distinction; that is, by personalizing through the context of the latter's experience. As Cavender notes, "Family and friends personalize them, hosts speak as if they know them, and the camera dramatizes crimes from the victim's point of view" (82). Arguably, the viewer is encouraged to identify with the plight of the victim. In this context, the audience member becomes implicated as a potential victim of the criminalized other. According to Biressi and Nunn, "it is the collective victimage of viewers, that posits them as citizens in the battle against crime" (10). By gridding the viewer as a (potential) victim of criminal behavior, CRTV programming by extension seeks to instill a sense of dependency upon panoptic control apparatuses. Coupled with the binary treatment of individual actors, police officers are understood as "provid[ing] a thin line between the 'criminal insanity' and ordinary law abiding citizens" (Prosise and Johnson 82).

From this it would appear that CRTV programs provide viewers with a context in which law-enforcement practice can be understood. Crime and other forms of deviance are reduced to instances of individual pathology that necessitate the intervention of morally and technically infallible officers (Prosise and Johnson 78). In this regard, critical approaches to police work are obviated, with the exception of when said criticisms prescribe increased monitoring and discipline by agents of social control. In the case of racial profiling, law-enforcement practice is treated at the anecdotal level. The selective broadcasting of successful police work not only misrepresents the effectiveness of such practices, but also sends out the message that those who happen to fall under the crimino-justice gaze are, by definition, guilty.

It would appear reasonable at this juncture to rearticulate the manner in which CRTV implicates the viewer into the panoptic crimino-legal grid. As a result of the narrative that many of these programs employ (Doyle, Aaron 54; Donovan 126–127), members of the audience are invited to engage in an oppositional stance against criminal behavior, as manifested by antagonistically-cast individuals cast in the crimino-justice gaze. Although viewers themselves can thus be understood as being gridded as dependant upon the panoptic branches of this control apparatus, there is very little that is said about them beyond this statement. Bearing this in mind, a more comprehensive understanding of the synoptic properties of reality television might be obtained by examining a more recent strain of this kind of programming.

Self-Help through Surrender and Surveillance: The Case of Queer Eye

More recently, audiences have been inundated with a heavy dose of makeover themed reality programs, where potentially any aspect of an individual's sense of self can be deemed unfit and in need of intervention. One of the more recent programs to enjoy the spotlight of the mainstream press is *Queer Eye for the Straight Guy*. In what could be considered the intersection of self-help literature and voyeuristic entertainment, each episode of *Queer Eye* consists of an intervention between five acclaimed experts of various socio-consumer domains (Grooming, Food and Wine, Fashion, Interior Design and the ambiguously denoted Culture) and a heterosexual male who has been deemed incapable of self-governance in these five domains.

Already, one is able to draw a parallel between this program and its CRTV predecessors: both are structured as exchanges between individuals rather than between social aggregates or institutions. It could be argued that *Queer Eye* operates through a narrative consisting of the collective knowledge base of the five experts. It is possible to consider how this narrative serves to frame the show, as both the opening and closing scenes in each episode consist of an assessment by way of verbal exchange between the experts. In considering the manner in which *Queer Eye* synoptically reaches audience members, it will be possible to establish that the show, not unlike *COPS*, serves to convey the desirability of being panoptically visible. What distinguishes *Queer Eye* from earlier reality programming is its emphasis on market-based consumer surveillance. In this particular context, optimal self-expression is portrayed as resulting from maintaining a certain visibility in the eyes of knowledge-imparting experts. Furthermore, this focus on consumption habits pertains to Andrejevic's qualification of reality TV as "the surveillance of the rhythm of day-to-day life" ("Kinder" 260). In other words, by approaching surveillance at the level of the mundane, *Queer Eye* portrays the monitoring of everyday events as ultimately beneficial for the subject. Employing Goffman's work on expertise within total institutions, a further look at *Queer Eye* will serve to uncover how the show's narrative celebrates this panoptic relationship.

By examining the basic plot structure common to every episode, it will be possible to produce a general framework of *Queer Eye*'s construction of consumer-based control functions. As was stated earlier, the opening scene consists of a verbal exchange between the five experts based on information provided in form of a preliminary report. Prior to any physical encounter, the five experts are already negotiating an identity-label for the subject. For instance, on the basis of photographs provided by one subject, his sense of style was dubbed "cowboy gone bad" ("He's a Little Bit Country"). It is also during this assessment stage that the five experts determine the episode's mission. Simply put, the mission (which is clearly articulated both verbally and in writing at the bottom of the screen) consists of an event upon which the transformative process is pegged. In the case of the bad cowboy, the mission was a marriage proposal to the subject's girlfriend. Other missions have included hosting dinner parties, exhibiting one's artwork, blind dates and a chance encounter with a rock star. Typically, the subjects enlist themselves, although there have been a few exceptions in which loved ones have applied on behalf of their boyfriends/husbands. Surprisingly, this did not detract from the receptiveness that subjects manifested towards their transformation. This would initially appear to be caused by the subject's identification with their mission, which necessitated panoptic intervention. As the show progresses, it could be argued that the mission ends up taking a back seat to the panoptic relationship itself, as the subject grows habituated to his five-man inspection team. Already, one is able to draw parallels to Goffman's total institutions, where curative functions were treated as contingent upon establishing particular relationships between inmates and experts (generally through a mortification of the self) (14).

(A) THE INSPECTION

[H]e may be confronted by high-ranking staff arguing that his past has been a failure, that the cause of this has been within himself, that his attitude to life is wrong, and that if he wants to be a person he will have to change his way of dealing with people and his conceptions of himself. Often the moral value of these verbal assaults will be brought home to him by requiring him to practice taking this psychiatric view of himself in arranged confessional periods, whether in private sessions or group psychotherapy [Goffman 150].

Upon arriving at the subject's residence, the team of experts swarms the subject and his living environment in a manner that evokes imagery of some governmental task force (it is no wonder their vehicle of choice is an ominous-looking black SUV with tinted windows). The first encounter between the experts and the subject is always characterized by a five-point inspection of the latter's living conditions. By virtue of the team members' respective areas of expertise, a multi-dimensional inspection of the subject's consumption habits is etched. Everything from the medicine cabinet to dirty laundry is publicly exposed, inspected and generally ridiculed. What is of particular interest in this process is the fact that the subject appears to lose access to any functional backstage, as his entire domicile — the most intimate of private spheres— has become subject to the panoptic gaze. Furthermore, with little exception, this process would appear to be voluntary and met with very little resistance on the part of the subject. As a *Globe and Mail* column recently noted, "it's all so nice and loving [...] He's not a victim.

He's genuinely grateful" (Doyle, John R2). The voluntary nature of this inspection remains congruent — though markedly atypical — with Goffman's framework, as he was even able to conceive of subjects entering total institutions willingly (131). In other words, even the most radically transformative process might be willfully initiated by the target of said transformations.

As a simulation of consumer surveillance, it is apparent that *Queer Eye* accords little room for resistance against the confession-like process of information disclosure that accompanies the transformation. Through the broadcasting of this one-on-one — or rather five-on-one — interaction between the consumer experts and the subject, the viewer is invited to consider this voluntary disclosure of consumer habits as a therapeutic process. As a result, the audience is invited to consider user benefits of surveillance, while other uses of such infrastructures are obviated. For instance, what is not addressed in this narrative is the potential aggregation of this consumer information. As Andrejevic notes, "Corporations can exploit information precisely because they can aggregate it — because the information gains in value when it is placed within a larger information environment that individuals cannot access" ("Kinder" 258). Thus, *Queer Eye* synoptically transmits a portrayal of panoptic data collection as benefiting members of the audience rather than the corporate bodies that retain ownership of such databases.

(B) THE MAKEOVER

If the psychiatric faction is to impress upon him its views about his personal make-up, then they must be able to show in detail how their version of his past and their version of his character hold up much better than his own.... The patient must "insightfully" come to take, or affect to take, the hospital's view of himself [Goffman 154–155].

Through a face-to-face assessment, the five experts are understood as having collected a sufficient amount of information about the subject in order to re-work him. Great effort is undertaken to allude to the fact that the subject's new image is a product of the information he discloses — in effect, his old self — rather than from an external standard of proper consumerism. According to Carson Kressley (the fashion expert), the *Queer Eye* philosophy is "you — only better" (qtd. in Hanafy F4). Based on the biographic information provided during the opening sequence as well as the experts' assessment from their encounter with the subject, a series of stores and product labels are introduced as being in conjunction with the subject's consumer tastes and habits. One of the aspects of this segment of *Queer Eye* that is of particular interest is that upon their first encounter, the experts already claim to possess a better understanding of the subject's self-expressive style than the subject himself. In Goffman's work on total institutions, the process of reworking the patient was greatly accelerated when they came to share the same knowledge base as the professional care-takers (154).

The particular context in which *Queer Eye* presents new self-knowledge into the subject also sheds light on how this process appears to occur so effortlessly. As this transformation largely takes place by way of consumer products (the other half of the equation being the actual — and proper — consumption of said products), the subject is bombarded with up to $10,000 worth of renovations, furniture and fashionable apparel (Devin and Siges-mund 50). Coupled with the prototypical life-altering event whose success-ful completion is predicated on a successful transformation, gridding one's self appears to be dramatized as a lottery that the subject wins when he needs it the most. Coined by many popular critics as the kindest incarnation of the reality-makeover subgenre (Ryan R2; Doyle, John R2), *Queer Eye* appears to portray the consumer grid from its most flattering angle

(C) THE RELEASE

> Often he leaves under the supervision and jurisdiction of his next-of-relation or of a specially selected and specially watchful employer. If he misbehaves while under their auspices, they can quickly obtain his readmission.... These discharge procedures, then, provide a built-in lesson in overtly taking a role without the usual covert commitments [Goffman 168].

Immediately following the transformation of the subject, he is deemed capable of self-governance without the experts' assistance. The experts, now relieved of their interventionist duties, monitor the subject's performance by proxy. From the vantage point of a series of cameras that follow the sub-ject throughout his living quarters and anywhere else he should happen to go, they are able to asses the extent to which the subject's new self-image has been internalized. As they prepare for their first public performance, subjects are seen consuming newly acquired products. Generally, these scenes will repeat actions subjects have already performed in front of the camera, this time in the absence of any (immediately) intervening expert. For instance, one episode featured the subject being instructed on how to prepare a frozen fruit-based beverage. While being monitored by proxy, he attempted to recreate the same drink, only to use the wrong ingredients ("Help the Hard-Rocking Host"). While his punishment consisted of dis-approval verbalized by the food and wine expert, the possibility of a fol-low-up re-evaluation looms in the background (one full episode has already been dedicated to such encounters). On the heels of the intensely scruti-nized preparatory phase, the actual social event, while still monitored, almost comes off as an afterthought. This would appear to be in line with the reasoning that only the right kind of consumption habits could save the subject. Although this post-transformation evaluation marks the end of the episode, the implication is that the newly gridded subject will be expected to maintain his new consumer identity. This would appear to be why the products bound to the subject's new self-image are purported to reflect not only their tastes, but their budgets as well (Gordon and Sigesmund 50).

Thus, *Queer Eye* could be understood as a synoptic broadcasting of a particular relationship between subjects and a panoptic consumer apparatus. In this program, subjects are seen disclosing information relating to their consumption habits in a confession-like manner through the dissolution of any functional backstage. Voluntarily, dirty laundry, medicine cabinets and moldy refrigerator contents are placed in front of the cameras. Upon the disclosure of this information, the consumer apparatus is able to feed back knowledge to the subject about his self-image. In this light, panoptic forms of consumer surveillance are celebrated for purportedly allowing self-expression in a manner that the subject would be unable to accomplish by himself. In other words, consumer monitoring is portrayed as a crucial process by which the few are capable of answering the demands of the many. This form of marketplace surveillance pertains directly to Andrejevic's discussion of mass customization, which "claim[s] that surveillance works to the advantage of consumers by allowing producers to more closely meet their wants and needs" ("Kinder" 256). The narrative style inherent to *Queer Eye* would appear to represent the periodic attainment of this claim. With each episode, a new subject is introduced to the consumer grid. As a simulation of panoptic relations between consumers and corporations, then, *Queer Eye* synoptically presents being situated on the grid as a necessary step towards self-governance.

Discussion

Through an examination of both academic materials on popular culture as well as popular culture itself, this paper has served to highlight the specific manner in which reality TV programming synoptically legitimizes panoptic forms of surveillance by portraying the latter as both necessary and desirable. Starting with a discussion of the nuances between panopticism and synopticism as well as the simultaneous functioning of the two as parallel control operations, this paper moved onto specific forms of reality-based broadcasting to assess their portrayal of surveillance. By and large, these programs treated panoptic forms of surveillance as concurrent with the interests of the viewer, who was either in danger of becoming victimized by violent and irrational criminals (as in the case of CRTV programs), or by their own inability to maintain an adequate public image (as in the case of *Queer Eye*). Through the exercise of expert-positions, programs such as *COPS* and *Queer Eye for the Straight Guy* discursively engage viewers to come to understand themselves as benefiting from otherwise questionable surveillance practices associated with law-enforcement practice and consumer monitoring, respectively.

However, a fully comprehensive understanding of the synoptic control functions of reality TV would necessitate the expansion of a number of issues that were not fully addressed in this paper. First, it is crucial to consider the role that the audience plays as active interpreters of mass media. Although programs such as *Queer Eye* have been shown to influence the consumption habits of audience members (Florian 38), a greater emphasis on the cultural context in which such programs are viewed would undoubtedly enrich the synoptic model of information transmission. While an audience-centered approach to reality TV does not deny the existence of a preferred reading of these programs, its main emphasis is on the viewer's construction of meaning, and how the latter might deviate from the former. Stuart Hall's work on negotiated and oppositional audience-positions would provide necessary insight regarding how local conditions might influence viewers (137–138). Similarly, we can consider Ien Ang's work on the fictional drama *Dallas* and the interpretations of Dutch audience members. Through her research Ang was able to demonstrate the diverging interpretations of a single cultural text, suggesting that audience members might consume television programs in a manner that was not intended by the show's creators (11). Other studies, such as Fuller's work on *The Cosby Show*, have focused on cross-national differences, thus implying that cultural context might radically alter how an audience watches a program (110).

In the case of crime-based reality programs, an audience member's particular cultural context might result in a diametrically opposed reading of controversial police practices. For instance, audience members who have themselves been targeted by measures such as racial profiling might interpret a show such as *COPS* as a testament to everything wrong with current police practices, a far cry from the intentions of the officer-narrator. What is more, even a dominant (Morley 88) reading of reality programs can result in a misuse of synoptically transmitted knowledge. In his discussion of agency within panoptic structures, Simon lucidly suggests that by obtaining knowledge about proper behavior "one is also more able to feign conformity" (8). In the case of CRTV, programs like *COPS* could conceivably be interpreted by audience members as disseminating knowledge about feigning innocence in front of surveillance cameras and other components of panoptic infrastructures.

Finally, it should be noted that, when discussing both CRTV programs and *Queer Eye*, the panoptic apparatuses which they were said to legitimize (the crimino-justice grid and the consumer grid, respectively) were deliberately treated as separate institutions. Although this might be read as an endorsement of a post-panoptic, de-centralized conception of surveillance (Boyne 299), the intention was simply to withhold the claim that both types of reality programming legitimized the same, central, panoptic apparatus. In order to address this issue, subsequent research ought to address how reality television as a whole shapes audience member's comfort with surveillance in general, as opposed to particular forms of surveillance that relate to specific programs or types of programs. Intersecting this consideration with the subject of audience interpretation, a potentially fruitful area of research might be how viewers— either studied as individuals or social aggregates—construct different interpretations of surveillance based on the viewing of different reality TV programs.

Works Cited

Andrejevic, Mark. "The Kinder, Gentler Gaze of Big Brother: Reality TV in the Era of Digital Capitalism." *New Media and Society* 4.2 (2002): 251–270.
_____. *Reality TV: The Work of Being Watched.* Lanham, Maryland: Rowman and Littlefield, 2004.
Ang, Ien. *Watching Dallas.* New York: Methuen, 1985.
Biressi, Anita, and Heather Nunn. "Video Justice: Public Anxiety and Private Trauma." Conference Paper. 2004.
Bogard, William. *The Simulation of Surveillance: Hypercontrol in Telematic Societies.* Cambridge: Cambridge University Press, 1996.
Bondebjerg, Ian. "Public Discourse / Private Fascination: Hybridization in 'True-Life-Story' Genres." *Media, Culture and Society* 18.1 (1996): 27–45.
Boyne, Roy. "Post-Panopticism." *Economy and Society* 29.2 (2000): 285–307.
Brants, Chris. "Crime Fighting by Television in the Netherlands." *Entertaining Crime: Television Reality Programs.* Eds. Mark Fishman and Gary Cavender. Hawthorne: Aldine de Gruyter, 1998. 175–191.
Cavender, Gary. "In 'The Shadow of Shadows': Television Reality Crime Programming." *Entertaining Crime: Television Reality Programs.* Eds. Mark Fishman and Gary Cavender. Hawthorne: Aldine de Gruyter, 1998. 79–94.
Cavenderm Gary and Mark Fishman. "Television Reality Crime Programs: Context and History." *Entertaining Crime: Television Reality Programs.* Eds. Mark Fishman and Gary Cavender. Hawthorne: Aldine de Gruyter, 1998. 1–19.
Crawford, Charles. "Race and Pretextual Stops: Noise Enforcement in Midwest City." *Social Pathology* 6.3 (2000): 213–227.
Donovan, Pamela. "Armed With the Power of Television: Reality Crime Programming and the Reconstruction of Law and Order in the United States." *Entertaining Crime: Television Reality Programs.* Eds. Mark Fishman and Gary Cavender. Hawthorne: Aldine de Gruyter, 1998. 117–137.
Doyle, Aaron. *Arresting Images: Crime and Policing in Front of the Television Camera.* Toronto: University of Toronto Press, 2003.
Doyle, Aaron and Richard V. Ericson. "Breaking into Prison: News Sources and Correctional Institutions." *Canadian Journal of Criminology* 38.2 (1996): 155–190.
Doyle, John. "A Fab Debut Far From Makeover Meanness." *The Globe and Mail* 8 Oct. 2003: R2.

Elmer, Greg. "A Diagram of Panoptic Surveillance." *New Media and Society* 5.2 (2003): 231 247.

Erikson, Kai T. *Wayward Puritans: A Study in the Sociology of Deviance.* New-York: John Wiley and Sons, Inc., 1966.

Florian, Ellen. "Queer Eye Makes Over the Economy!" *Fortune* 9 Feb. 2004: 38.

Foucault, Michel. *Discipline and Punish: The Birth of the Prison.* New York: Vintage, 1995.

Fuller, Linda K. *The Cosby Show: Audiences, Impact, and Implications.* Westport: Greenwood Press, 1992.

Goffman, Erving. *Asylums: Essays on the Social Situations of Mental Patients and Other Inmates.* New-York: Anchor Books, 1961.

Gordon, Devin and B.J. Sigesmund. "Queen for a Day: Bravo's 'Queer Eye for the Straight Guy' has Exploded. It's a Makeover Takeover." *Newsweek*, 11 Aug. 2003: 50.

Hanafy, Erin. "Queer Guru Offers Style; Look Like Yourself, Not Somebody Else." *The Windsor Star* 3 Apr. 2004: F4.

Hall, Stuart. "Encoding / Decoding." *Culture, Media, Language: Working Papers in Cultural Studies, 1972–1979.* Eds. Stuart, et al. London: Hutchison, 1980. 128–138.

"Help the Hard-Rocking Host." *Queer Eye for the Straight Guy.* Perf. Kyan Douglas, et al. Bravo. 2 Dec. 2003.

"He's a Little Bit Country." *Queer Eye for the Straight Guy.* Perf. Kyan Douglas, et al. Bravo. 29 Jul. 2003.

Hier, Sean. "Probing the Surveillant Assemblage: on the Dialectics of Surveillance Practices as Processes of Social Control." *Surveillance and Society* 1.3 (2003): 399–411.

Mathiesen, Thomas. "The Viewer Society: Michel Foucault's 'Panopticon' Revisited." *Theoretical Criminology* 1.2 (1997): 215–234.

Morley, David. *Television, Audiences and Cultural Studies.* London: Routledge, 1992.

Orwell, George. *Nineteen Eighty- Four.* London: Penguin Books, 1949.

Palmer, Gareth. *Discipline and Liberty: Television and Governance.* Manchester: Manchester University Press, 2003.

Potter, W. James, et al. "Antisocial Acts in Reality Programming on Television." *Journal of Broadcasting and Electronic Media* 41.1 (1997): 69–89.

Prosise, Theodore O. and Ann Johnson. "Law Enforcement and Crime on Cops and World's Wildest Police Vidoes: Anecdotal Form and the Justification of Racial Profiling." *Western Journal of Communication* 68.1 (2004): 72–91.

Ryan, Andrew. "It's a Man's, Man's, Man's World." *The Globe and Mail*, 14 Aug. 2003: R2.

Schienke, Erich W. and Bill Brown. "Movie of SCP Tour with Bill Brown." *Surveillance and Society* 1.3 (2003) <http://www.surveillance-and-society.org/articles1(3)/SCP.mp4>

Simon, Bart. "The Return of the Panopticon: Supervision, Subjection and the New Surveillance."
Surveillance and Society 3.1 (2005): 1–20.

About the Contributors

Mark Andrejevic is an assistant professor in the Department of Communication Studies at the University of Iowa. He has numerous publications related to reality television, including *Reality TV: The Work of Being Watched* (Rowman and Littlefield, 2003).

Todd M. Callais is in the Ph.D. program in sociology at Ohio State University, where he studies issues of criminality.

Dean Colby is a lecturer in the Program for Writing and Rhetoric at the University of Colorado at Boulder.

Richard E. Crew is the chair of the Communications Department at College Misericordia in Dallas, Pennsylvania. He is a former television production company owner and during the 1980s was the executive producer of an early form of reality television: the nationally syndicated *PM Magazine* and *Evening Magazine* series.

David S. Escoffery has taught theatre history and critical theory at a number of schools, most recently as assistant professor of theatre and head of the MA Program in Theatre at Southwest Missouri State University.

Elizabeth Franko is a Ph.D. candidate in the Department of Communication (Media Studies) at the University of Colorado at Boulder. She studies the contemporary workforce and its representations in popular culture, as well as the imaginative power of the democratic ideal.

Jordan Harvey is a graduate student at Texas Christian University, where he studies popular culture through the lens of post-colonial theory.

Shana Heinricy is a doctoral candidate in communication and culture at Indiana University. Her current research focuses on the intersection of citizenship, the body, and television.

Su Holmes is a lecturer in film and television studies at the University of Kent. She is the author of *British TV and Film Culture in the 1950s: Coming to a TV Near You!* (Intellect, 2005) and co-editor of *Understanding Real-*

ity TV (Routledge, 2004). Her key research interests are British TV history, reality TV, and the subject of celebrity. She has published widely on these topics in journals such as *Screen, Continuum, International Studies of Communication Studies,* and *Television and New Media.*

Elizabeth Johnston is an instructor in the Department of English/Philosophy at the Brighton Campus of Monroe Community College. She received her Ph.D. from West Virginia University and takes an interdisciplinary, cultural studies approach to her study of 18th-century British fiction.

Chris Jordan is an assistant professor in the Department of Theatre, Film Studies, and Dance at St. Cloud State University. Working on film studies in an interdisciplinary way, he has published *Movies and the Reagan Presidency* (Praeger, 2003).

Barry King is an associate professor and head of the School of Communication Studies at the Auckland University of Technology. He studies performance, media culture, the history of stardom, and the globalization of culture.

Wesley Metham is a Ph.D. candidate in cultural studies at the University of Sydney in Australia. His thesis explores post-anarchist interpretations of the public sphere.

Bethany Ogdon is an assistant professor of media studies at Hampshire College. Her areas of study include television history and theory, media culture, and psychoanalysis.

Elizabeth R. Schroeder is a graduate student in the Department of American Studies at St. Louis University, studying representations of race and gender in popular culture. She has presented her work at the Popular Culture Association.

Andrea Schuld-Ergil is a lecturer and interdisciplinary Ph.D. candidate in the departments of Human Ecology and of Sociology at the University of Alberta, where she studies youth identity formation via dress and culture.

Melissa Szozda is a law student at the University of Toledo.

Daniel Trottier is completing an MA in sociology at Concordia University. His thesis deals with the forms of audience participation and viewership that are cultivated through reality television. He also is interested in the connections between reality television and issues of surveillance.

Index